W9-CBF-739

3 3013 00120583 4

WITHDRAWN

DATE DUE

GAYLORD   PRINTED IN U.S.A.

* Volumes with an asterisk following the title are a part of the NCRLL set: Approaches to Language and Literacy Research, edited by JoBeth Allen and Donna Alvermann.

(Continued)

WHAT WAS IT LIKE?

Teaching History and Culture Through Young Adult Literature

LINDA J. RICE

FOREWORD BY ALLEEN PACE NILSEN

Teachers College, Columbia University
New York and London

To my beloved parents, Jan and Charlie Rice, whose examples of faith, creativity, hard work, immense generosity, and genuine goodness have made a difference in the lives of many.

Published by Teachers College Press, 1234 Amsterdam Avenue, New York, NY 10027

Library of Congress Cataloging-in-Publication Data

Rice, Linda J.
    What was it like? : teaching history and culture through young adult literature / Linda J. Rice ; foreword by Alleen Pace Nilsen.
       p. cm. — (Language and literacy series)
    Includes bibliographical references and index.
    ISBN-13: 978-0-8077-4712-4 (cloth)
    ISBN-10: 0-8077-4712-2 (cloth)
    ISBN-13: 978-0-8077-4711-7 (pbk.)
    ISBN-10: 0-8077-4711-4 (pbk.)
      1. United States—History—20th century—Study and teaching. 2. History, Modern—20th century—Study and teaching—United States. 3. Young adult fiction, American—Study and teaching. 4. Historical fiction, American—Study and teaching. 5. Literature and history—Study and teaching—United States. 6. Young adults—Books and reading—United States. 7. Active learning—United States.
    I. Title. II. Language and literacy series (New York, N.Y.)

E741.R53 2006
973.91071—dc22

                                        2006040957

ISBN-13: 978-0-8077-4711-7 (paper)   ISBN-10: 0-8077-4711-4 (paper)
ISBN-13: 978-0-8077-4712-4 (cloth)   ISBN-10: 0-8077-4712-2 (cloth)

Printed on acid-free paper

Manufactured in the United States of America

13 12 11 10 09 08 07 06   8 7 6 5 4 3 2 1

Contents

Foreword

The year that Ken Donelson and I were beginning to write our *Literature for Today's Young Adults* textbook—I remember because of arguing that we had to make room in the car for my typewriter and a box of notes—my husband took a summer job teaching linguistics at Concordia University in Montreal. We moved to Canada for 6 weeks, taking our two youngest children with us. Our daughter was in middle school and our son in high school. On our second Sunday there, we were invited to a cocktail party. It was to be a backyard event and since the hosts knew we were strangers in town and would be uncomfortable leaving our children alone, they graciously told us to bring them along. We dressed in our best finery and were glad we did because people in Montreal were considerably more formal than our friends "back home" in the Arizona desert.

At the party, we didn't pay much attention to our children as we wandered from group to group eagerly trying to make a good impression by matching names with faces and learning the interests of these new acquaintances. We had been there about an hour when our two children sidled up and asked in low tones, "When's it going to start?" We must have looked surprised because our son clarified with, "Aren't we going to do *anything?*"

This was 25 years ago, but I still remember the disappointed look on their faces when they realized that at this party, which they had looked forward to all week and had dressed for in their best clothes, there was nothing to do but "talk."

The memory came flooding back to me as I read Linda Rice's manuscript and was reminded of how important it is for kids to be able to combine actions with talk. Of course we are all hoping for kids to have those "grand conversations" that teachers dream about, but for most kids such conversations are more likely to happen if they have something to hold in their hands and explain, or to stand beside or behind as they make the big move from "show and tell" to what we teachers view as "grand conversations" and they view as "blah, blah, blah."

In some ways, today's lifestyles have brought about a reversal of the functions of school and home. When America was a rural society, children were active at home and were expected to sit quietly at school. Girls were apprentices to their mothers. They tended younger siblings; helped with gathering, preserving, and cooking the family's food; and with mending, washing, and ironing the family's clothing. Boys were apprentices to their fathers. They did the farm chores; helped with planting, weeding, and harvesting; and learned to repair tools and vehicles.

In today's world, families are smaller and few parents have jobs where their children can serve as apprentices. The work that goes along with taking care of a home and family is greatly simplified because of fast-food restaurants and grocery stores filled with prepackaged and partially prepared food, and because of vacuum cleaners, dishwashers, permanent-press clothing, and automatic washers and dryers. It is the unusual parent who encourages or even allows children to "mess up" the house with craft projects, or the driveway or garage with vehicles under construction or in various stages of repair. At home, young people are encouraged to sit quietly and watch television or to play electronic games, and talk on the telephone or surf the web and communicate through chat rooms. This change makes it all the more important that schools provide students with opportunities for active involvement—for chances to cooperate with other students in putting on skits and re-enacting scenes; for learning from each other how to prepare PowerPoint (not "PowerPointless") presentations; for creating scrapbooks and displays, writing scripts, and extending stories through music and poetry.

Another reason for providing ideas and materials for students to work with is that thinking takes time, and while kids' hands and bodies are busy with the activity, their minds are focusing on the story and what it means to them. This is true whether they are posing for pictures on an antique train for Cynthia DeFelice's *Nowhere to Call Home*, writing a news broadcast or giving themselves a "handicap" before playing the piano for Karen Hesse's *Out of the Dust*, designing a semantic map of incidents related to racism against Mexican Americans for Victor Martinez's *Parrot in the Oven* and Pam Munoz Ryan's *Esperanza Rising*, or working in a group to make a display about the internment of Japanese Americans connected to Jeanne Wakatsuki Houston and James D. Houston's *Farewell to Manzanar*.

The important thing is that students are interested and involved, which means that teachers need to have what seems like a never-ending supply of good ideas that truly relate to the literature and encourage higher level thinking. Jim Burke (1999) gave a negative example in *The English Teachers' Companion* of a teacher who kept her students "busy" while they read *The Scarlet Letter* by having each of them knit a letter *A*. It speaks well for Linda Rice and her colleague, Jackie Glasgow, that there are no exercises of this type in their book. It is also to their credit that they have tried out the activities and that we as readers get to see student-made products and to read student responses and writing.

We owe them a big thank-you not only for the specific ideas they suggest but for the reminder to all of us that for most young people, talking is fine, but the party does not really start until they get to *do* something.

Alleen Pace Nilsen
Arizona State University

REFERENCE

Burke, J., & Claggett, M. F. (1999). *The English teachers' companion: A complete guide to classroom, curriculum and the profession.* Portsmouth, NH: Boynton/Cook.

Acknowledgments

I wish to thank the many people who have informed and supported my work in a variety of ways during the 14 years I have been a teacher. First and foremost, I extend loving gratitude to my students who have been so open to exploring active learning strategies with me. Their creativity, resourcefulness, cooperation, diligence, and enthusiasm have been truly uplifting. The pre-service English teachers I've worked with at Ohio University have been especially wonderful—they give me great hope for our nation's future as they commit their professional lives to delivering the promise of education to young people.

The many fine authors whose books are featured in the chapters that follow also have my heartfelt appreciation for giving us so much to talk about. These writers have brought light and life to history and culture; they have found ways to make words touch us, move us, and help us to better understand the world in which we live. Thanks especially to Trudy Krisher whose interest in my work has been very motivational; I look forward to our presenting at conferences together.

Special thanks go to my mentor, colleague, contributing author, and friend, Jacqueline Glasgow. Jackie has been a superb professional role model and helped my life in higher education take flight.

I also extend deep appreciation to one I have developed a very high regard and sincere admiration for, Carol Chambers Collins from Teachers College Press. Carol's gentle critiques, insight, and expertise have provided continual support throughout the publishing process and inspired me to make this book the best that it can be.

Thanks also to Wendy Schwartz whose careful reading of the manuscript brought very helpful suggestions. I extend gratitude to Jessica Balun and Nancy Power at Teachers College Press for their work in publicity and marketing and to my exemplary copy and production editors, Myra Cleary and Lori Tate. Myra and Lori gave me an entirely new vision of what "editing" means, and I am most impressed by their precision, skill, and superior attention to continuity and detail.

I also would like to thank those in my broad professional community who have been such cheerleaders over the years including the OCTELA board, my co-presenters at NCTE, and many notable teachers from my days at Howland High School and Grove City College, especially Judy Jones and Cindy Benton.

Heartfelt thanks go to my very generous friend, Gerri Lux, who flew me to Phoenix so I could have a mini-vacation and uninterrupted work week. The time to focus on my writing, combined with Gerri's fun, hospitable ways, gave me the momentum necessary to finish the draft manuscript.

Enduring gratitude also goes to long-time friend and teaching colleague from Lakeview High School, Catherine Howard. I can always rely on Catherine to offer personal support, a sound perspective, and plenty of encouraging words.

I also would like to thank Carolynn Orr, who helped in a variety of ways from working in my yard to patiently listening to me read aloud what I'd written or talk through a day's progress. Carolynn made a point to celebrate the big steps of the journey with me, and she even learned some history in the process.

I also want to thank my sisters, Susan Colborn and Amy Young, for the interest they showed in rendering early feedback on the project proposal and to other endearing friends who have showered me with love and prayer, in particular Larry and Maureen Coon, Sheila Knudson, and Jeff and Christy Schofield. I am also grateful for the friendship and collegiality of Barbara Grueser and Sam Scott, two people I could always rely on for kindness, listening, and support.

Most of all, thank you to my parents, Jan and Charlie Rice, who have blessed my life beyond measure and always encouraged my effort to make meaningful contributions.

Introduction

*Aristotle observed, "All men by nature desire to learn." It might be added
that some men seem to desire it more than others. And what makes the
difference? In part, the difference is superior teaching. Outstanding teachers
do more than convey knowledge; they also spur the desire to learn.*
—Criswell Freeman (1998)

Identifying the themes, questions, and active learning strategies that link
books with students' lives and interests is the charge of a successful English teacher. This book is written for middle and high school teachers and
college professors who want to engage students with thoughtful and challenging learning experiences that involve important themes and historically based young adult novels. The themes and literature presented in this
book will help students to better understand other cultures, time periods,
conflicts, and even themselves. Research on active learning provides the
theoretical underpinning of this book, and the theory comes to life as examples of student work demonstrate specific active learning strategies in
each chapter. Most of the examples have been created in actual class settings by preservice teachers at Ohio University where I (Linda Rice) and
contributing author, Jacqueline Glasgow, teach Young Adult Literature
and the English methods courses Teaching Language and Composition and
Teaching Literature.

Having spent 10 years teaching middle and high school English, I find
it important to emphasize that while the examples of student work in the
book are by college students, they are not unlike what I came to expect from
my high school students. The point here is not to imply that the college
students have not grown intellectually and deepened their capacity to
analyze literature and express themselves creatively, but rather to make
clear that the active learning strategies that are presented and modeled in
this book are applicable to a wide range of students, and that teachers
should see the strategies as adaptable, expecting less or more depending
on their unique student population. Here, too, while some examples may
be viewed as "representative" of what many students are capable of doing,
others may be presented as "exemplary," thus setting a high standard, but

not making it a requirement that all students will write as well, draw as artfully, act as skillfully, and so forth. My desire is to present active learning strategies and models that are thoughtful, creative, and engaging—strategies that readers of this book will be inspired to try out in their own classroom settings and view as springboards for the kinds of progressive teaching and learning experiences that students so yearn for today.

ORGANIZATION OF THE BOOK

This book is organized in eight chapters. Chapter 1 presents the theory and research of active learning, including general characteristics of active learning and an explanation of the major concepts that are woven into each of the remaining chapters. The major concepts include the Interplay of Thoughtfulness and Reflection; Talking and Listening as Keys to Active Learning; Strategies to Promote Empathy and Understanding; and the Role of Creativity and Collaboration in Active Learning. Chapter 1 concludes with my reflections and rationale for the book's overarching theme: Conflicts in History at Home and Abroad. Chapters 2–8 each focus on a theme linked with an historical era or conflict from the 20th century and one or more historically based young adult novels that illustrate the theme and establish its relevance to students' lives. Parallel elements across each chapter include:

- A concise review of the historical era or conflict
- A brief summary of the featured young adult novel(s)
- Explanations and examples of active learning strategies to foster Thoughtfulness and Reflection, including
    —Socratic Seminars
    —Simulation and Role Play
    —Active Learning Projects involving Creativity, Collaboration, and Peer Teaching
- An Annotated Bibliography of other historically based texts that might be taught using similar strategies.

THEMES AND HISTORICALLY BASED YOUNG ADULT LITERATURE

Whereas Chapter 1 focuses primarily on the theory of active learning, Chapters 2–8 show the theory in action. These chapters center on themes and young adult novels that highlight particular eras and conflicts of the 20th century.

Chapter 2 features three novels set in the Great Depression era (1929–1939): *Nowhere to Call Home* (DeFelice, 2001), *Out of the Dust* (Hesse, 1997), and *A Long Way from Chicago* (Peck, 1998). These novels depict protagonists who lose loved ones, experience homelessness, and overcome economic hardship and physical disability.

Chapter 3 focuses on young adult literature written by Mexican American authors who render their experiences of hunger, hardship, and discrimination as migrant farm workers (1940s–1960s). While exploring *Esperanza Rising* (Ryan, 2000), *Jessie de la Cruz: A Profile of a United Farm Worker* (Soto, 2002), and *Parrot in the Oven: Mi Vida* (Martinez, 1996) in depth, this chapter also includes student work in response to *The Circuit: Stories from the Life of a Migrant Child* (Jimenez, 1997), *Breaking Through* (Jimenez, 2002), and *Buried Onions* (Soto, 1999).

Chapters 4 and 5 represent aspects of World War II (1939–1945). Chapter 4 features Elie Wiesel's memoir *Night* (1960) and Lois Lowry's *Number the Stars* (1989) as texts that examine the lives of children who suffered and survived the Holocaust, thus bearing witness to its horrors. Chapter 5 features *Farewell to Manzanar* (1973), Jeanne Wakatsuki Houston's memoir about life in a Japanese Internment Camp, emphasizing how relocation resulted in the deterioration of family structures and cultural identity.

Chapter 6 features Sook Nyul Choi's *Year of Impossible Goodbyes* (1991), a book that reveals the atrocities and cruelties endured by Koreans throughout the Japanese Occupation of their country from 1910–1945. The novel frames the historical context that precipitated the Korean War, often referred to as the "Forgotten War." As part of this unit, students investigate America's involvement in the Korean War from its beginning in 1950 to its end in 1953.

Chapter 7 features three novels that take place during the Civil Rights Movement of the 1950s and 1960s: *Spite Fences* (Krisher, 1994), *Just Like Martin* (Davis, 1992), and *The Watsons Go to Birmingham–1963* (Curtis, 1995). Each having a protagonist who observes or has firsthand experience as a victim of racial violence, these books prompt readers to consider the power of speeches and nonviolent protest to effect change.

Finally, Chapter 8 features three novels that deal with aspects of the Vietnam Conflict that America was embroiled in from 1959–1975. *Fallen Angels* (Myers, 1988) tells the story of a Harlem teen who envisions going to war in Vietnam as a good alternative when his dream of attending college disintegrates. *Dear America: Letters Home from Vietnam* (Edelman, 1985) is a (nonfiction) collection of letters from soldiers who served in Vietnam, each accompanied by a brief note about what happened to its writer. *Song of the Buffalo Boy* (Garland, 1992) tells the story of the "con lai," or "half breed," children fathered (and abandoned) by American soldiers and born to Vietnamese mothers.

All of the chapters fit under the umbrella theme "Conflicts in History at Home and Abroad." This overarching theme was chosen because of its significance and versatility, reminding us that much of the world's great literature shows readers the importance of helping others in their times of need, the cost of freedom, the heartache of fighting our brothers and sisters, and the injustices we must not repeat. Therefore, even though you currently may not teach the novel(s) featured in a particular chapter, keep in mind that, as the annotated bibliographies accompanying each chapter indicate, the overarching theme and active learning strategies are broad and adaptable to many other works of literature that may already be part of your curriculum.

REFERENCE

Freeman, C. (1998). *The teachers' book of wisdom: A celebration of the joys of teaching.* Nashville: Walnut Grove Press.

CHAPTER 1

Active Learning in Theory and Practice

Active learning shifts the focus from teachers and their delivery of course content to students and their active engagement with the material. Through active learning techniques modeled by the teacher, students shed their traditional role as passive receptors and learn and practice how to apprehend knowledge and skills and use them meaningfully.

—(Wager, 2002, p. 8–1)

Think of a time you had a great experience in a classroom, either as a teacher or a student. What were the qualities that made the experience of learning so memorable? If the experience that comes to mind is you as a teacher, chances are the "experience" was not where you were delivering the lecture of a lifetime, although the feeling we have when we "really know our stuff," and it flows forth with passion and clarity, is certainly very rewarding. If you were a student, the same is probably true. Sure, we've had moments such as those depicted in films like *Dangerous Minds*, *Educating Rita*, or *Dead Poets Society*, where we feel we are sitting at the feet of a master teacher who inspires us with his/her knowledge of poetry and drama. But more often, the memorable moments are not ones where teachers lecture *to* us, but where they interact *with* us or structure learning so that we are integral to the process.

Consider Robin Williams as the beloved Mr. Keating in *Dead Poets Society*. He wanted to make a point about individuality versus conformity, so he took his class to the courtyard and asked four of the students to take a stroll. Within a few seconds, the four students had formed a line and begun marching in cadence as the other students stood and watched them, clapping with the same rhythm. Keating calls off the marching and asks the students to consider the dangers of conformity, of not thinking independently from the crowd. Lest those standing on the sidelines think they would have done differently, Keating asks them to consider why they were clapping.

Poignantly, experientially, through personal engagement and example, these students realized the teacher's point. Asked again to take a stroll, the students wander about, finding their own step—one even walking like a chicken and another opting to stand still. Have you experienced moments like this as a student? Have you created experiences like this as a teacher?

THE CHARACTERISTICS OF ACTIVE LEARNING

The character of Mr. Keating, based on a real teacher, highlights the characteristics of active learning. His innovative teaching methods and ways of structuring learning ensure that students have no choice but to get involved, be active, and reflect personally and analytically about the subject at hand. Active learning fits in the realm of constructivist teaching geared to help students make meaning and develop skills. In their process of making meaning, students "evaluate new information and experiences against their current theories, rules, and notions" (Brooks, 2002, p. 130). In contrast to the direct teaching model that speaks to students as blank slates, the active learning model places students at the center of the learning experience. Active learning means students *participate* in their own education and *do* active things that result in learning (Young, 1994).

Active Learning Fosters Inquiry

As students make connections among ideas and integrate what they know into a network that includes their own experiences, beliefs, and values, they develop deeper understanding through *inquiry* (Brooks, 2002; Browne & Keeley, 1997). Busching and Slesinger (2002) define inquiry not as a specific kind of assignment, but rather a stance brought into operation by the "unsatisfied curiosity" of students that causes them to think differently about the world around them because they "are looking for clues and hints that will provide answers" or deeper understanding (p. 93). Teachers also might envision inquiry as progressive problem solving where students grapple with questions and issues that are multifaceted and lack quick resolutions (Glassman, 2001).

Involving students in active learning processes means going far beyond standardized tests and incorporating music, dramatic performance, simulation, role play, experiences outside the classroom, and a variety of hands-on creative displays of critical thinking and meaning making to ensure student learning. As students pursue deep understanding through inquiry, they will be able to exchange "their poorly examined theories and beliefs to more rigorously examined concepts that are personally meaningful"

(Adams & Hamm, 1994, p. 27). By tapping into students' natural curiosity and individual ways of learning, teachers find multiple points of entry to engage students with subject matter (Davis, Hawley, McMullan, & Spilka, 1997). This challenge is at the heart of active learning: capturing and keeping students' attention so that they draw near to the course content and assimilate it with what they already know. Then, they may either build on that knowledge and alter former beliefs and modes of thinking to see the world anew; understand a problem more deeply; empathize; or even be moved to action, intervening to right a wrong or to educate others about history and/or issues that affect our world.

Active Learning Aids Retention

In essence, active learning shifts the focus of instruction from what teachers teach or deliver to what the students do with the course material (Wager, 2002). To this end, teachers become less focused on their teaching and more focused on their students' learning. This benefits both teachers and students because active learning maximizes students' attention and increases the likelihood that learning is occurring (Stover, Neubert, & Lawlor, 1993). In addition to facilitating retention, active learning also improves critical thinking and interpersonal skills, and increases motivation and the transfer of new information (Center for Teaching and Learning Services, 2003).

THE INTERPLAY OF THOUGHTFULNESS AND REFLECTION IN ACTIVE LEARNING

"Be gone, J. Evans Pritchard, Ph.D.," declares Mr. Keating, asking his students to rip out the introduction to the poetry book they've been given at Welton Academy, the famed fictitious boys' school featured in Dead Poets Society *(Weir, 1989). "Now, my class, you will learn to think for yourselves again. You will learn to savor words and language. No matter what anybody tells you, words and ideas can change the world."*

Meyers and Jones (1993) contend that although teachers tend to "love the life of the mind," few of our classrooms evidence an atmosphere of reflection that encourages students' insight into their personal and academic lives (p. 28). Students who engage in critical reflection through active learning gain the ability to restructure old ways of thinking and move on to new understanding; therefore, opportunities to reflect and grapple with literature, ideas, and interpretation, instead of being handed the answers by a teacher, is paramount to critical thinking, learning to think for oneself, and cultivating thoughtfulness. Adams and Hamm (1994) describe *thoughtfulness* as the "tendency to support a position with carefully examined reasons," thus promoting the tendency "to be reflective, to think problems through, and to have the flexibility to consider original solutions and the curiosity to pose new questions" (pp. 20–21). These qualities of thoughtfulness, linked with critical reflection, advance the learning process by helping students to integrate and appropriate knowledge, information, and skills (Meyers & Jones, 1993).

Newmann's (1990, 1992) research into promoting high-order thinking in high school classrooms identified six key indicators of thoughtfulness. These indicators help teachers to determine whether the learning environment enables students to formulate and utilize new knowledge.

- Teachers give students adequate think time before expecting them to answer questions.
- Curriculum design and delivery emphasize depth over breadth (i.e., sustained examination of a few topics is emphasized over superficial coverage of many).
- Teachers challenge students to explain and support opinions with sound reasoning.
- Coherence and continuity characterize classroom interactions.
- The teacher shows interest in students' ideas, grapples with complex questions, and engages in problem-solving processes rather than just giving answers, thus modeling the characteristics of a thoughtful learner.
- Classroom interaction results in students' generation of original and unconventional ideas.

The interplay of thoughtfulness and reflection is inherent in nearly every active learning strategy students engage in, whether participating in a Socratic Seminar; stepping into a character's shoes and seeing the world from a different point of view; or researching an issue, conflict, or era to gain a broader perspective.

Several chapters in this book also draw on the interplay of thoughtfulness and reflection to introduce a unit or provide background knowledge. For example, Chapter 3 opens with an Anticipation Guide and Semantic Map to help students consider the plight of the migrant farmer and reflect on the impact of racism on Mexican Americans. Chapter 5 begins with two Guided Meditations to help students put themselves in the position of the Japanese citizens who were ordered to relocation centers during World War II.

Chapter 4 presents the T-Chart as a strategy to help students explore the concept of indifference and its relevance to what happened during the

Holocaust. Finally, Chapter 8 opens with an exploration of Vietnamese vocabulary to help students think about and reflect on how Vietnamese culture differs from American culture.

Studies by the U.S. Department of Education (1986) indicate that learning increases when students have opportunities to talk about what they are studying and personalize it, and Meyers and Jones (1993) assert that "learning is truly meaningful *only* when learners have taken knowledge and made it their own" (p. 20). In this way, education is largely about self-development, yet self-development in active learning often involves dialogue and collaboration with others.

TALKING AND LISTENING AS KEYS TO ACTIVE LEARNING

Consider these two statements:

- We often do not know what we think until we try to say it.
- There is value in hearing the responses of others.

Do you agree? What have been your experiences with class discussion, Socratic Seminars, and talking and listening in a collaborative classroom environment to facilitate learning? Meyers and Jones (1993) characterize "talking and listening" as key elements of active learning, and it is no surprise that they do not mean that *teachers talk* and *students listen*, but that the classroom is structured in a way that encourages student voice and sharing, exploration and collaboration. "But is there a real danger to lecturing?" we may inquire. "What's so bad about this time-honored tradition in teaching? Does it really have a negative impact on student learning?" As we weigh these questions, let us think of our experiences not only as teachers, but as students, as well. Then, consider these research findings:

- During lectures, students are not attentive to what is being said 40% of the time (Ohmer, Pollio, & Eison, 1986).
- Students retain 70% of what they hear during the first 10 minutes of a lecture, and only 20% of what they hear in the last 10 minutes (McKeachie, 1986).
- As lectures proceed, students lose their initial interest, and their attention level continues to drop (Verner & Dickinson, 1967).
- Four months after taking an introductory psychology course, students knew only 8% more than a control group who had never taken the course (Rickard, Rogers, Ellis, & Beidleman, 1988).

If we are to take these findings to heart and apply them to our teaching, we know we must foster student involvement. Class discussions and Socratic Seminars are two ways to do just that, in contrast to lectures, which make it easy for students to sit back and absorb very little of what a teacher deems to be of importance. Class discussions and Socratic Seminars create a "spirit of joint adventure where students' questions are encouraged and their viewpoints are valued" (Guthrie & Wigfield, 1997, p. 164). Given opportunities to interact and discuss how they and others think, students become better learners, able to explore topics in depth and recall information (Astington, 1998). Furthermore, class discussions provide an important venue for the exchange of ideas that is vital to the learning process and to participating in a democratic society (Alexopolou & Driver, 1996). Class discussions and Socratic Seminars are effective ways to shift the balance from teacher-centered to student-centered instruction, thus increasing students' engagement and providing forums for learning to be more personal, meaningful, and memorable.

Class Discussion

Class discussions give students a chance to be heard, share ideas, and develop understanding in a collaborative forum. Class discussions can be formal or informal, directed by the teacher or the students, and take all or just part of a class meeting. Typically, formal discussions are prepared in advance by the teacher to engage students in dialogue on predetermined issues. Questions can help students ponder a new topic or investigate a theme, clarify their understanding of what they have read, share ideas and interpretations, negotiate meaning, or take inventory of their beliefs concerning a particular issue.

While typically beginning in a whole-class forum with students directing responses to the teacher and building on what others say, these discussions also might involve students breaking up into small groups to develop the dialogue in more personal ways. Students also might discuss a question in their small groups, then report out to the whole class, thus merging into a larger discussion forum.

Informal discussions don't tend to last as long, but emerge on a more frequent and spontaneous basis. Teachers can draw students into routine informal discussions by simply inviting them to share their thoughts on their current reading or research, something they are puzzled by, what they wrote in response to a journal prompt, and so forth.

Chapters 3 and 8 offer models for formal discussion. Chapter 3 poses questions for discussion after viewing *Escuela*, a documentary film on the education of migrant farm children and in preparation for students' writing of Position Papers. Chapter 8 uses discussion in two places. First, for students to consider the effect embedded Vietnamese words have on their reading of *Song of the Buffalo Boy*, and second, as a lead-in to an active learning project called "The Shoes Tell the Story." The discussion begins as students explore the adage, "Never judge others until you have walked in their shoes," then expands to their own lives and the featured novel.

Informal discussions can be drawn from students' responses to the list of personal/analytical questions for *Farewell to Manzanar* in Chapter 5, to the topic of nonviolence as it relates to *Just Like Martin* in Chapter 7, and to various other themes, shared creative responses, and reflections following role play and simulation exercises modeled throughout this book.

Socratic Seminar

The Socratic Seminar is based on the Greek philosopher Socrates's technique of developing reliable knowledge through the practice and discipline of conversation known as the *dialectic*. In developing this dialectic, the participants in the Socratic Seminar seek to deepen their understanding of complex ideas in a text, rather than memorizing bits of information (Stumpf, 1999). Sample Socratic Seminars appear in Chapter 3 for *Parrot in the Oven: Mi Vida* and in Chapter 6 for *Year of Impossible Goodbyes*. Procedures for preparing and conducting the Socratic Seminar follow.

Opening Questions. The success of the seminar rests on the quality of questions asked, and this is where the teacher/facilitator's role becomes vitally important. Typically, once students have arranged their desks into a circle, the Socratic Seminar begins as the teacher/facilitator poses one to three open-ended statements or questions that any student who read the book could answer. For instance, "*Spite Fences* is really about . . ." or "What character most attracted your attention and why?" The Opening Question(s) is one that every student in the class should respond to, and this can be done easily just by going around the circle. This gives every student a chance to be heard and (hopefully) the confidence to contribute in the remainder of the seminar. The teacher's role at this point in the seminar is to listen, not to critique or clarify.

Core Questions. Once all students have responded to an Opening Question, the bulk of the seminar proceeds as the teacher/facilitator poses, one at a time, three to five Core Questions. A good Core Question is one that encourages students to draw on their knowledge of the text (and even provide evidence from the text), but is not finite in terms of its answer. In other words, an effective Core Question is rooted in the text,

but still open-ended and challenging so as to promote a thoughtful dialogue. While writing a few questions may sound very easy, those who
have facilitated Socratic Seminars will attest that finding questions that
work really takes some practice. A strong Core Question can easily
prompt 15 minutes of student dialogue, but a weak Core Question can
fall flat in less than 2 or 3 minutes. Therefore, teachers employing this
technique for the first time should prepare some extra questions and have
some specific passages of the text ready to support students' initial dialogue and generation of ideas. While the teacher/facilitator *does* need to
prepare Core Questions before the seminar, listening carefully to student
responses to the Opening Question(s) is another way to draw on what
students "see" or value in a literary text, and to form additional questions for the Core set. "How" and "why" questions work particularly well
for the Core set, as do questions that help students evaluate characters'
actions, relationships, and motives. As the seminar develops through the
Core Questions, the teacher/facilitator may intervene to ask follow-up
questions, help participants clarify their positions when arguments become confused, and involve reluctant participants. However, the key to
a successful seminar is letting the line of inquiry "evolve on the spot rather
than being pre-determined by the leader," so too much intervention is
discouraged (Murphy, 2000, p. 1).

Closing Questions. A Socratic Seminar ends with Closing Questions
that are designed to help students personalize or bridge the text with their
own lives or world in some way. For instance, "If you could give advice to
any character in the book, who would it be, what advice would you give,
and why?" or, "Having read this book, do you find yourself to be more
committed or less committed to affirmative action and why?"

A final note about Socratic Seminars: One of the hardest things for students to adjust to when first engaging in a Socratic Seminar is the silence
that fills the air after a question has been posed, before the first student vol-
untarily responds, and between periodic gaps between students responding to one another. Many students are so accustomed to lectures or quick
series of question–answer sessions that they feel awkward in the silences of
classrooms where time is given for serious thinking before speaking. To this
end, it is a good idea to let students know in advance that "there *will be* gaps
of silence, and I [teacher] am not going to rush in and rescue you [students]
when they come. I am comfortable with silence, and will wait, within reason, for one of you to pick up the dialogue and take us forward." Then reit-
erate your awareness that "the silence may feel a bit awkward, but we all
know it's a sign that we're thinking, and thinking is paramount to great ideas
and conversation, so there's no need to feel nervous or embarrassed."

ACTIVE LEARNING STRATEGIES TO PROMOTE
EMPATHY AND UNDERSTANDING

Picture the line of students from *Dead Poets Society* standing in front of the trophy case, peering through the glass, looking at photographs of those who attended Welton Academy before them. Imagine Mr. Keating asking his students to lean in and "hear" what those in the pictures have to say. What were their dreams, their passions, their hopes, desires, hurts, loves, and disappointments? What have they done with their lives? Where are they today, and have they found happiness? As the students ponder faces from the past, Keating delivers his famous carpe diem speech that ends with, "Seize the day, boys; make your lives extraordinary."

Simulation and Role Play

While the "imagining" from *Dead Poets Society* might be characterized as a highly romanticized one that viewers enter into with a sense of eagerness and optimism while considering their own future, it also serves to introduce the concept of simulation or using one's imagination to step into the shoes of another person or perspective. *Simulation* is a kind of "umbrella term" that encapsulates role play (acting a character part), simulation exercises and games (assuming different roles), and even computer models that present students with opportunities to try strategies and see outcomes without danger (Meyers & Jones, 1993). Simulation and role play afford students the opportunity to reach social, artistic, emotional, and academic goals, while making learning more enjoyable and providing opportunities for choice and creativity (Bandura, 1986; Jensen, 1995).

The purpose of simulation and role play as active learning strategies is to help students to come closer to significant issues and themes in historical (and other) literature, such as war, loss, discrimination, and struggle. These strategies fit within the context of dramatic arts and assist students in their development of emotional intelligence by encouraging them to manage feelings, communicate verbally and nonverbally, problem solve, and resolve conflicts (Jensen, 2001). By presenting key concepts in the context of a learning situation, role plays also increase students' understanding and retention of information (Gregory & Chapman, 2002). Simulations can be used in a variety of ways to challenge students, such as: practicing a general skill like interviewing or pantomime; practicing a specific skill such as Rogerian counseling; practicing team skills such as collective bargaining; developing problem-solving skills; engaging in synthesizing skills to deal with a social issue read about in literature; developing basic empathic skills; and developing advanced empathic skills by assuming the opposite side (Meyers & Jones, 1993). In essence, simulation and role play facilitate students' development of literacy skills and confidence, while deepening their sense of empathy and understanding of those who have gone before.

A variety of simulation and role play examples appear throughout this book. For instance, Chapter 2 includes a News Broadcast in which students assume various character roles, participate in interviews, and present commercials reflective of the Great Depression era. Chapter 2 also includes Simulation Learning Centers to help students identify with physical disability and other hardships faced by the protagonists. Simulations for *Out of the Dust* include playing the piano with a handicap and finding one's way home in a dust storm. Chapter 3 depicts role play through two Interactive Writing Strategies, "Unsent Letters" and "Poetry of the Protagonist's Unspoken Thoughts." The chapter also includes "Debate: To Strike or Not to Strike," whereby students examine textual evidence and stage a debate representing sides in favor of and opposing the migrant workers striking for better wages and living conditions.

The simulations in Chapters 4 and 5 are set against the backdrop of World War II. Chapter 4 assigns students roles in a Jewish family living in the midst of Nazi rule in Copenhagen, Denmark. Students work through a scenario whereby they decide whether or not to resist deportation. Chapter 5 offers strategies for simulating life in a Japanese relocation center, including the barracks, bathroom, and mess hall.

In Chapter 7 students use their understanding of characters depicted in the literature of the Civil Rights Movement and their own imaginations to predict how characters would grow and change in their attitudes toward a particular issue, such as nonviolent protest. The culminating role play requires students to assume various character roles, then write and act out a Futuristic Script.

Finally, Chapter 8 includes two strategies for simulation and role play. The Negotiating Survival activity opens with a visualization exercise where students imagine themselves as American soldiers in the jungles of Vietnam. Then, working in groups, students must go through a backpack of 17 items and take only the eight that they negotiate are essential for survival. The second strategy is the Student-Created Simulation/Role Play in which students work in groups to find ways to bring their classmates close to a particular aspect of the text. The student-created example provided in Chapter 8 is a Minefield Simulation, and it includes excerpts from students' reflective papers to show how the experience influenced their learning.

Creative and Personal/Analytical Writing

In addition to using dramatic imaginings to strengthen the connection between books and students, creative writing and personal/analytical writing serve as valuable tools to help students understand underlying concepts, explore and clarify their own thinking, communicate with others, and expand their mental structures and creativity (Kohn, 1999; Meyers & Jones, 1993; Sternberg & Grigorenko, 2000). Writing in a variety of genres, such as journals, newspaper articles, editorials, essays, posters, and short stories, can help students connect literature with their own lives and remember it in detail (Markowitz & Jensen, 1999; Sprenger, 1999).

The goal of active learning as presented here, however, is about more than simple remembering. The concern of this book is to engage students to the point where they deeply consider conflicts and challenges faced in stories by fictitious characters and by real people who record their narratives of hardship and triumph. To this end, each remaining chapter includes several Creative and Personal/Analytical Writing strategies. The range of Creative and Personal/Analytical Writing strategies is designed to help students step into the shoes of another and imagine what that person thought or felt. In considering the perspectives of others, we may grow in understanding, in empathy, in caring—we may even grow in our willingness to take action, stand up and speak out for what is right, and ensure that the horrors of history are not repeated.

Chapter 2 shows how students used photographs from the Great Depression and Dust Bowl of the 1920s and 1930s as entry points to identify with the poverty and despair many people faced. The Found Poem, Recipe Poem, and Villanelle helped students identify with characters and explore themes. This chapter also includes Adding a Scene, a creative writing strategy that requires students to imagine themselves as a protagonist and project into the future.

Chapter 3 includes a Mexican Folk Ballad, Poetry for a Social Issue, Copy Change Song Lyrics, and Double Journal Entry depicting the migrant farmer. Chapter 4 draws on students' responses to film, music, and photographs as ways to keep Holocaust memories alive. Chapter 5 includes various Japanese poetic forms and a range of Personal and Critical/Analytical responses to *Farewell to Manzanar*, including Primary Sources, Reviews, Opinion Essays, Conflicting Opinions, and Critical Analyses.

Chapter 6 includes a writing-rich scrapbook in which students relate personal experiences to *Year of Impossible Goodbyes* and life in Korea during the Japanese Occupation (1910–1945). Chapter 7 includes Speech Writing to reveal multiple perspectives of characters in *Spite Fences*, Grammatical

Music, and Acrostic Poetry to highlight themes in the literature of the Civil Rights Movement.

Finally, Chapter 8 engages students with creative writing strategies that help them trace character transformation and link personal experience with those depicted in the literature of the Vietnam Conflict and its aftermath. Students also imagine themselves as soldiers writing Last Letters from Vietnam and draw on outside sources to create Emotional Word Poems.

THE ROLE OF CREATIVITY AND COLLABORATION IN ACTIVE LEARNING

Opportunities for students to express their creativity, collaborate, and teach one another are integral to active learning. The project method of teaching and learning is a social enterprise where students become aware of individual differences and naturally experiment with Gardner's (1983) multiple intelligences as they work in their areas of strength and find these valued by other class members (Bromley, Irwin-De Vitis, & Modlo, 1995; Young, 1994). According to Dewey (1934), thinking in art precedes improvement in thinking in other curricular areas. "Thinking in art" may involve writing a poem, composing a song, directing a film, acting out a scene, drawing, sculpting, mapping, or a variety of other creative displays. The purpose of these options is to help students express their understanding in alternative formats and simultaneously come to a deeper understanding of literature. Creative projects bring life to learning and facilitate memory by prolonging the experience of reflecting and interacting with a text in a tangible way.

Active Learning Projects

Typically, active learning projects include some kind of creative, artistic visual display. Such displays give students opportunities to showcase what they find to be most important about a theme or work of literature. As in real life, creative, authentic learning experiences can be "inherently messy," but they also involve self-discovery and the merging of the cognitive and affective domains (Daniels & Bizar, 1998, pp. 170–171). When having students create a visual project, teachers should require an accompanying reflective paper in which students discuss what they intended to convey, any symbolism used, what they learned in the process of creating the project, and how the project influenced their understanding of the book/ theme/character under investigation. Sample reflective pieces accompany many of the student-created active learning projects modeled in this book.

This book includes a broad spectrum of active learning projects that give students opportunities to interact with important themes and young adult literature on deep and personal levels that often involve choice. In Chapter 2, the Handbook for Hoboes helps students to reflect on the "language of the street" as they explore vocabulary unique to *Nowhere to Call Home*. Students also pursue various Independent Endeavors (creative projects of their own choosing) such as the Faux Quilt, Photos and Potatoes, and Charcoal Drawings projects in response to *A Long Way from Chicago* and *Out of the Dust*.

The Memory Shoe Box in Chapter 3 is a vehicle for exploring Mexican culture and characters depicted in books by Mexican American writers of young adult literature. In Chapter 4 students imagine themselves living in Germany during the Holocaust and creating Public Awareness Posters to warn their Jewish friends of the Nazi's intentions. Chapter 4 also includes a variety of mapping and action-oriented projects. Students map geographical, relational, and spiritual journeys in order to trace the development of plot and character in the literature of the Holocaust. Students also plan an Empty Bowls Luncheon or join the Kindertransport Association to take action against indifference.

The Hangul Name Journal in Chapter 6 helps students to explore the significance of names in Korean culture. The chapter also includes a Character Portfolio in which students take inventory on what they know about a character from *Year of Impossible Goodbyes* by creating a resume, collage, connection, and poem from that character's perspective.

Chapter 7 features a variety of three-dimensional creations such as Showing the Setting and Plot 3-D Style, Layering the Life of a Character, and Scrapbooking the Story. These projects emphasize what students find to be important in young adult novels about the Civil Rights era. The chapter also incorporates Singing with Symbolism, a project that incorporates music from the 1950s and 1960s. Finally, Chapter 8 features the Thematic Artifact project. Students choose and write about artifacts that convey something significant about Vietnamese culture or the American soldiers serving in Vietnam.

Group Learning

While the active learning projects discussed thus far are those students are most likely to work on individually or in pairs, other active learning projects rely more heavily on collaboration. In contrast to a competitive atmosphere, which "often induces anxiety, fear of failure, and ultimately withdrawal for many students," cooperative learning draws on the unique strengths and abilities of each group member as students work toward a common goal (Adams & Hamm, 1994, p. 42). While team approaches offer students opportunities to achieve more extensive goals than they might achieve individually, they also tap into students' social nature, helping them build social understanding, respect and value one another's differences, and experience the fun of sharing ideas and information (Ilfeld, 1995; Johnson, Maruyama, Johnson, Nelson, & Skon, 1981; Slavin, 1983, 1989). For these reasons, assigning (or letting students choose) groups for collaboration in preparing projects and presentations can be an important part of active learning.

Group learning is embedded in all simulation and role plays that appear in Chapters 2–5, 7, and 8 of this book and can be easily woven into the Korean War Survey, Research, and PowerPoint project in Chapter 6. The Vocabulary Skit in Chapter 2 and the Kabuki Theater production in Chapter 5 place particular emphasis on collaboration, as students must work together to determine what is important about the text and how it might be shared with the rest of the class. While the Vocabulary Skit in Chapter 2 is designed to help students learn words that have particular relevance to the Great Depression era, the strategy may be adapted to any lesson where expanding students' vocabulary is the aim. Similarly, the key strategies in Kabuki Theater are narration and pantomime; therefore, even though it is used to tell the story of *Farewell to Manzanar* in Chapter 5, it, too, can be adapted to other novels.

Peer Teaching

According to the Society for Developmental Education (1995), we learn 90% of what we teach to others. It is no wonder, therefore, that teachers who embrace active learning look for ways to have students share their findings with others. Peer teaching occurs as students present what they have learned in a variety of project endeavors. The articulation that comes with students' presenting their projects and research before their peers, and, in effect, teaching the class, helps students to solidify their knowledge (Stover et al., 1993). Furthermore, as students assume some of the responsibility for finding information and sharing it with the class, the teacher's educational power is multiplied (Kagan, 1986).

Peer teaching can happen in formal and informal ways, before the whole class or in small groups where students "report out" what they have learned. Four chapters of this book include research-based active learning projects that lend themselves to more formal aspects of Peer Teaching. Through the Multigenre Research Project in Chapter 3 students investigate the legacy of Cesar Chavez and the United Farm Workers Union. This chapter also includes a Problem-Based Learning Scenario that focuses on the education of Mexican migrant children. By presenting the written and visual components that make up these two project options, students can teach one another what they learned about crucial aspects related to migrant farmers.

Chapter 5 includes a trifold display of research findings about Japanese Internment Camps, and Chapter 6 features a Korean War Survey, Research, and PowerPoint project. Whether delivering a formal, research-based presentation before the class or sharing informally in small groups, peer teaching is a valuable component of active learning because of its potential to aid students' retention of vital information.

REFLECTIONS ON THE THEME:
CONFLICTS IN HISTORY AT HOME AND ABROAD

For the seeds of literacy to grow, teachers must take themselves seriously as agents of change who arrange classroom environments for cooperation, problem-solving, and engagement. . . . If teachers are energized and really believe in literature-based language instruction, they usually do just fine— even if they have to wait for their school system to catch up.
                        —Adams & Hamm, 1994, pp. 178–179

As a National Board Certified teacher of adolescence and young adulthood English language arts who has taught middle and high school English for 10 years and college courses in teaching methods and young adult literature for 4 years, I have become a strong advocate of active learning and thematic teaching. Structuring curriculum around a theme provides a basis for learning and a focus that facilitates deep exploration of a topic while integrating the language arts strands of reading, writing, speaking, viewing, and listening.

Thematic Teaching

Over the years, I have structured curriculum on numerous thematic tensions, shifts, and questions, such as: Appearance versus Reality, Innocence versus Experience, Conformity versus Individuality, From Helplessness to Resilience, and Am I My Brother's Keeper? These thematic frames have helped me to structure Socratic Seminars, group projects, and teaching presentations for commonly anthologized short stories like Jackson's "The Lottery" and Bierce's "An Occurrence at Owl Creek Bridge," classic novels such as Steinbeck's *Of Mice and Men* and Hawthorne's *The Scarlet Letter*, and young adult books like Cormier's *The Chocolate War* and Cooney's *The*

Face on the Milk Carton. While I have greatly enjoyed teaching all of these works of literature, I am increasingly aware that our students also need insight into our nation's roots, its history, and its conflicts at home and abroad.

Historically Based Literature

The historically based young adult novels featured in this book show us the stories of brave men, women, and children who dared to speak out for justice, make personal sacrifices, and intervene to liberate concentration camps and stop brutal dictators who sought to overtake other nations with force, genocide, murder, and tyranny. These books put a face on history and exemplify the capability of literature to record the past, evoke responses in the present, and envision the future. It is worth noting that while the novels featured in this book were written with the young adult audience in mind, they are by no means simple and unsophisticated. Rather, the trait common to young adult literature that these books share is having young adults as protagonists with significant responsibility and facing serious situations, often without an adult present (Donelson & Nilsen, 2005). The complexity of the problems these young characters face, and the way they deal with emotion, draws even advanced and adult readers into the stories. Compared with the textbook approach to American and world history that I, and probably many readers of this book, experienced, the young adult novels featured in this book will likely teach more. Certainly, these novels provide more depth in terms of vicarious experience, heartfelt emotion, empathy, and deep understanding of the conflicts, some of which had a profound impact on our parents and grandparents.

A Sense of Hope and Purpose

Using active learning strategies in conjunction with historically based young adult novels, it is my hope that we can assist our students in seeing beyond stereotypes and examining the lessons of history with critical minds and compassionate hearts—that we can acknowledge our wrongs, seek restitution where necessary, and forgive where need be. It is also my hope that we will use these stories to give credit where credit is due and honor those who persevered through poverty, war, discrimination, and persecution to give us the many freedoms we enjoy. My hope is that by critically engaging with these texts through the variety of active learning strategies presented in this book, our students will be better informed, make good decisions, and become responsible citizens, willing to intervene where necessary to promote human dignity and fairness.

To some these may sound like lofty aims, but I believe by getting close to others' stories and engaging in the vital work of reflection, we can build a better world instilled with a sense of knowing where we've been, with a sense of empathy and respect for those who have gone before. This addresses a higher reason for studying literature and a higher aim of quality education: helping young people develop civic consciousness, including analytical abilities, groupwork skills, a concern for others, and communicative competence that go far beyond the classroom (Adams & Hamm, 1994). Perhaps Mr. Keating addresses this point most effectively when he asks his students to huddle up so that he may impart to them his sense of why we study literature. Quickly the students draw in around the teacher, who is crouching low as if to let them in on a secret. Keating says to his students:

> We don't read and write poetry because it's cute. We read and write poetry because we are members of the human race. And the human race is filled with passion. And medicine, law, business, engineering, these are noble pursuits and necessary to sustain life. But poetry, beauty, romance, love, these are what we stay alive for.

Keating continues, quoting a passage from Whitman, then closing with this line: "'that the powerful play goes on and you may contribute a verse'— what will your verse be?"

Examining our stance in relation to conflicts in history at home and abroad, we, too, become actors on the stage of life, capable of finding meaning and influencing the future in positive ways. I hope that the literature, themes, and active learning strategies presented in this book assist you in moving your students to better know themselves and positively affect our world. Happy reading!

REFERENCES

Adams, D., & Hamm, M. (1994). *New designs for teaching and learning: Promoting active learning in tomorrow's schools*. San Francisco: Jossey-Bass.

Alexopoulou, E., & Driver, R. (1996). Small-group discussion in physics: Peer interaction modes in pairs and fours. *Journal of Research in Science Teaching*, 33(10), 1099–1114.

Astington, T. (1998). Theory of mind goes to school. *Educational Leadership*, 56(3), 46–48.

Bandura, A. (1986). *Social foundations of thought and action: A social cognitive theory*. Englewood Cliffs, NJ: Prentice-Hall.

Bromley, K., Irwin-De Vitis, L., & Modlo, M. (1995). *Graphic organizers: Visual strategies for active learning*. New York: Scholastic Professional.

Brooks, J. G. (2002). *Schooling for life: Reclaiming the essence of learning.* Alexandria, VA: Association for Supervision and Curriculum Development.

Browne, M. N., & Keeley, S. (1997). *Striving for excellence in college: Tips for active learning.* Upper Saddle River, NJ: Prentice-Hall.

Busching, B., & Slesinger, B. A. (2002). *"It's our world too": Socially responsive learners in middle school language arts.* Urbana, IL: National Council of Teachers of English.

Center for Teaching and Learning Services. (2003). *Active learning.* Minneapolis: Regents of the University of Minnesota.

Daniels, H., & Bizar, M. (1998). *Methods that matter: Six structures for best practice classrooms.* York, ME: Stenhouse.

Davis, M., Hawley, P., McMullan, B., & Spilka, G. (1997). *Design as a catalyst for learning.* Alexandria, VA: Association for Supervision and Curriculum Development.

Dewey, J. (1934). *Art as experience.* New York: Macmillan.

Donelson, K. L., & Nilsen, A. P. (2005). *Literature for today's young adults* (7th ed.). Boston: Pearson Education.

Freeman, C. (1998). *The teachers' book of wisdom: A celebration of the joys of teaching.* Nashville: Walnut Grove Press.

Gardner, H. (1983). *Frames of mind: The theory of multiple intelligences.* New York: Basic Books.

Glassman, M. (2001). Dewey and Vygotsky: Society, experience, and inquiry in educational practice. *Educational Researcher, 30*(4), 3–14.

Gregory, G., & Chapman, C. (2002). *Differentiated instructional strategies: One size doesn't fit all.* Thousand Oaks, CA: Corwin Press.

Guthrie, J. T., & Wigfield, A. (Eds.). (1997). *Reading engagement: Motivating readers through integrated instruction.* Newark, DE: International Reading Association.

Ilfeld, E. M. (1995). *Learning comes to life: An active learning program for teens.* Ypsilanti, MI: High/Scope Press.

Jensen, E. (1995). *Completing the puzzle: The brain-based approach.* Del Mar, CA: Turning Point.

Jensen, E. (2001). *Arts with the brain in mind.* Alexandria, VA: Association for Supervision and Curriculum Development.

Johnson, D. W., Maruyama, G., Johnson, R., Nelson, D., & Skon, L. (1981). Effects of cooperative, competitive, and individualistic goal structures on achievement: A meta analysis. *Psychology Bulletin, 89,* 47–62.

Kagan, D. (1986). Cooperative learning and sociocultural diversity: Implications for practice. In California Office of Bilingual and Bicultural Education, *Beyond language: Social and cultural factors in schooling language minority students* (pp. 98–110). Los Angeles: California State University.

Kohn, A. (1999). *The schools our children deserve: Moving beyond traditional classrooms and tougher standards.* Boston: Houghton Mifflin.

Markowitz, K., & Jensen, E. (1999). *The great memory book.* San Diego, CA: Brain Store.

McKeachie, W. J. (1986). *Teaching tips: A guidebook for the beginning college teacher* (8th ed.). Lexington, MA: Heath.

Meyers, C., & Jones, T. (1993). *Promoting active learning: Strategies for the college classroom*. San Francisco: Jossey-Bass.

Murphy, J. (2000). Professional development: Socratic seminars. *Regions 8 and 11 professional development consortia*. Los Angeles: Los Angeles County Office of Education 6.

Newmann, F. (1990). Qualities of thoughtful social studies classes: An empirical profile. *Journal of Curriculum Studies, 22,* 253–275.

Newmann, F. (Ed.). (1992). *Student engagement and achievement in American secondary schools*. New York: Teachers College Press.

Ohmer, M., Pollio, H. R., & Eison, J. A. (1986). *Making sense of college grades: Why the grading system does not work and what can be done about it*. San Francisco: Jossey-Bass.

Rickard, H., Rogers, R., Ellis, N., & Beidleman, W. (1988). Some retention, but not enough. *Teaching of Psychology, 15,* 151–152.

Slavin, R. (1983). *Cooperative learning*. White Plains, NY: Longman.

Slavin, R. (1989). *School and classroom organization*. Hillsdale, NJ: Erlbaum.

Society for Developmental Education. (1995). *Pyramid of learning*. Petersborough, NH: Author.

Sprenger, M. (1999). *Learning and memory: The brain in action*. Alexandria, VA: Association for Supervision and Curriculum Development.

Sternberg, R. J., & Grigorenko, E. L. (2000). *Teaching for successful intelligence: To increase student learning and achievement*. Arlington Heights, IL: Skylight.

Stover, L. T., Neubert, G. A., & Lawlor, J. C. (1993). *Creating interactive environments in the secondary school*. Washington, DC: National Education Association.

Stumpf, S. E. (1999). *Socrates to Sartre: A history of philosophy* (6th ed.). New York: McGraw-Hill.

U.S. Department of Education. (1986). *What works: Research about teaching and learning*. Washington, DC: Author.

Verner, C., & Dickinson, G. (1967). The lecture: An analysis and review of research. *Adult Education, 17*(2), 85–90.

Wager, W. (2002). *Instruction at FSU: A guide to teaching and learning practices* (4th ed.). Tallahasee: Florida State University.

Weir, P. (Director). (1989). *Dead poets society* [Motion picture]. United States: Touchstone Video.

Young, K. A. (1994). *Constructing buildings, bridges, and minds: Building an integrated curriculum through social studies*. Portsmouth, NH: Heinemann.

Overcoming Economic Hardship and Physical Disability During the Great Depression (1929–1939)

These are days when many are discouraged. In the 93 years of my life, depressions have come and gone. Prosperity has always returned and will again.

—John D. Rockefeller on the Depression in 1933
(Lancaster, 2002, p. 1)

While addressing the severity of poverty, homelessness, and despair that were a part of the Great Depression and the Dust Bowl, *Nowhere to Call Home* (DeFelice, 2001), *A Long Way from Chicago* (Peck, 1998), and *Out of the Dust* (Hesse, 1997) also demonstrate ingenuity, interdependence, resourcefulness, perseverance, and hope as strategies for navigating through life's uncertainties. Through the literary works explored in this chapter, readers will see the human spirit at its most downcast and defeated, and at its most tenacious and triumphant.

A snapshot of the active learning strategies in this chapter appears in Figure 2.1. Collectively, the projects explained and modeled here are designed to help students learn more about the Great Depression and the hardships people faced during that era. By deeply considering the needs of others, readers come to realize how fortunate we are when we have a safe place to live, plenty of food to eat, clean water to drink, and trustworthy people upon whom to rely.

The active learning projects in this unit illuminate dichotomies in setting and character—changes that came about due to the economic hardship of the 1930s. Simulation Learning Centers help students vicariously

Figure 2.1. Active Learning Strategies in Chapter 2.

Featured Young Adult Novels	Active Learning Projects	Creative Writing	Role Play and Simulation
Nowhere to Call Home	• Going on Location with Photography • Handbook for Hoboes • Character Change Illustrations	• Villanelle	
A Long Way from Chicago	• Vocabulary Skit • Faux Quilt • Photos and Potatoes	• Found Poetry • Recipe Poem	
Out of the Dust	• Charcoal Drawings	• Repetition to Emphasize a Point • Adding a Scene to the Book	• News Broadcast • Learning Centers
General, Applicable to Any Historically Based Novel		• Stepping into an Historical Photograph	

experience some of the conflicts, including physical disability, characters face in the novels. An extensive Creative Writing section closes the chapter, offering a progression from simple to complex and balancing structured and open-ended options for composition, each supported by a student example.

PERSONAL/HISTORICAL CONTEXT

Born in 1898 and 1902, respectively, my maternal grandparents Dewey Lowell Bond and Josephine White Bond lived in southern Ohio where they made a living in the orchard business. I grew up hearing stories of what happened on the farm—how my grandmother would hang a chicken on the line and cut off its head, how my mom and her four siblings would nail together apple crates, how grandpa would load up the truck and drive to Columbus to sell apples in the city, and how mom and her three sisters would maneuver to avoid milking the cow that was known for kicking over the milk bucket. Other stories were of "the drifters," people who, during the Great Depression, did not have jobs and would come to the farm or the orchard seeking work, or perhaps just a meal. Grandpa often would hire these helping hands for a few days as they were passing through or during harvest time; when he could not afford to do so, grandma would at least invite the travelers to the table for a meal and offer what she could for them to take on their way. There are also tales of peddlers who would come into the small town selling kitchenware. I treasure these stories, which have given me a perspective on life before all of the "conveniences" we have today—before microwaves, dishwashers, televisions, refrigerated freight carriers, an interstate highway system, and aircraft that make it possible for us to have fresh fruit in- or out-of-season from all parts of America and even the world.

Farmers and the Dust Bowl

In many ways, those who lived on farms during the Great Depression were among the most fortunate, for they had the means of producing food. An exception to this came in the western states where severe droughts and dust storms made planting and harvesting nearly impossible. Again, we can consider how the tragedies of nature, hunger, poverty, and homelessness affect our change and growth as individuals and as a nation. It was in the United States's climb out of the Great Depression and Dust Bowl that we learned to regulate trade volumes in the stock market and institute a federal insurance policy for the money we place in banks. It was from this era that we came to realize the necessity of rotating crops, expanding systems of irrigation, and giving the land time for restoration. It was also during this era that the federal government stepped up its role in an unprecedented manner in order to aid the needy among us. Much of what we think of as the "welfare system" today originated during the 1930s when the federal government sought to provide food, clothing, housing, basic health care, and jobs for those devastated by the fallout from Black Tuesday, the infamous stock market crash on October 29, 1929, in which the Dow lost 23% of its value in a single day ("October," 2003).

The Stock Market Crash

A less-emphasized but exceedingly poignant concept that emerges from an analysis of the Wall Street Crash is the financial interconnectedness of the American people. Even though less than 1% of Americans actually owned stocks when the share prices declined, entrepreneurs lacked the money needed to run their companies. Within a short time, 100,000 American companies were forced to close, leaving many workers unemployed and without a government system of benefits to provide them with even a modest income. Under these circumstances, "the purchasing power of the American people fell dramatically [which] in turn led to even more unemployment" (Simkin, 1997, p. 1). At the depth of the Great Depression in 1933, one in four Americans who wanted to work was unable to find a job (Schenk, 1997). Those who could not find work often took to the road or the rails, and the homeless lived in shantytowns known as "Hoovervilles," as many connected the nation's sore economic state with its president, Herbert Hoover.

The New Deal

With the election of President Franklin D. Roosevelt came a new vision for the nation's recovery. Roosevelt responded to the Great Depression by designing programs that would put Americans back to work. The Civilian Conservation Corps, one of the first emergency agencies, was established in 1933 with a twofold aim: "to reduce unemployment, especially among young men; and to preserve the nation's natural resources" (Herkert, 2004, p. 1). Two years later Roosevelt's New Deal provided additional work relief for millions of unemployed Americans by sending federal money to states for public works programs. In its 8-year history, the Works Progress Administration (WPA) employed more than 8,500,000 different persons on 1,410,000 individual projects, and had spent about $11 billion building 651,087 miles of highways, roads, and streets; and constructing, repairing, or improving 124,031 bridges, 125,110 public buildings, 8,192 parks, and 853 airport landing fields (Johnson, 1966).

Roosevelt's New Deal also introduced the Social Security Act (signed in 1935), which included a federal retirement program for persons over 65 financed by employers and their workers. FDR believed that "federal old-age pensions together with employer-paid unemployment insurance (also part of the Social Security Act) would provide economic security people needed in both good and bad times" (*How Welfare Began*, 1998, p. 4). Whether we find ourselves at a state or national park walking on stairway made of cobblestones, driving over a bridge with a bronze WPA plaque at its base, or wondering about the origins of Social Security, the very program that is in today's spotlight for reform, we can see the impact of the Great Depression. We may come to appreciate thrift and savings; we may gain compassion when we see those whose financial lives have fallen apart, leaving them without work and the means to keep family together. We may understand the necessity—whether by government or the private sector—for people to have a place to turn in times of transition when they are hungry, in need of food, clothing, shelter, and human kindness.

Continued Government Relief

The government programs started in the 1930s aimed to support individuals in times of need, but not replace the will to work by creating a system of dependence. Striking a balance between providing enough—but not too much—has proven to be a complex task. Roosevelt himself seemed to acknowledge this in his State of the Union Address delivered on January 4, 1935. Roosevelt declared, "The time has come for action by the national government" to provide "security against the major hazards and vicissitudes of life." In that same speech, however, FDR recognized the potential danger of too much help arguing that the continuation of government relief programs would not be good for the country.

> The lessons of history, confirmed by the evidence immediately before me, show conclusively that continued dependence upon relief induces a spiritual and moral disintegration fundamentally destructive to the national fiber. To dole out relief in this way is to administer a narcotic, a subtle destroyer of the human spirit. (Roosevelt, 1935, p. 2)

How would the protagonists—Frankie Blue, Grandma Dowdel, and Billie Jo—respond to these ideas? This chapter will offer a variety of ways to delve into the issues of the Great Depression, analyzing not only the facts of the period, but its impact on people's lives.

FEATURED YOUNG ADULT NOVELS

Nowhere to Call Home

Cynthia DeFelice's *Nowhere to Call Home* (2001) tells the story of Frances, a 12-year-old who, after her mother's death, is raised by her wealthy father and his servants. When he loses his fortune in the stock market crash, Frances's father commits suicide; all of his assets are liquidated, leaving nothing for Frances or the house- and groundskeepers, who are Frances's closest "family" and friends. Faced with the option of moving from Philadelphia to Chicago to live with an aunt she does not like, Frances escapes to "ride the rails," for she has heard the family servant, Junius, tell romanticized stories of the freedom that comes from doing so. Frances disguises herself as a boy and befriends another child vagabond who calls himself Stewpot. While the first day of "riding the rails" does indeed hold a sense of adventure, Frances, now known as Frankie Blue for her mournful look, quickly realizes that life on the streets is both hard and dangerous. Perhaps most harrowing is Frankie's education about life on the street for girls. Although Frances herself is "safe" because she has disguised herself as a boy, one day she sees a girl traveling with a group of men who care for her by providing food; however, her hollow, vacant gaze hints at the abuse she suffers. While this portion of the book is not overt and its meaning and significance may be overlooked by younger readers, high school and adult readers certainly will recognize the author's intended inference, thus opening a door for discussion of the issue of rape and other forms of mental and emotional abuse.

Stewpot is an eternal optimist, resourceful, hard-working, and kind. He reiterates throughout the novel the importance of being persistent, believing things will get better, and finding the small beauties of life. Ironically, or perhaps to emphasize the harsh reality of the Great Depression, Stewpot becomes seriously ill and eventually dies in a Hooverville. At this point Frances has, in effect, realized the foolishness of her ways and decides to go to live with her aunt, hoping the aunt will still take her in. In a final note of encouragement, showing how people help those in need, Frances arrives at her aunt's doorstep and finds a cat painted on the walk. As Frances had learned during her months as a homeless traveler with Stewpot, that symbol means a friendly person lives in the house, the kind of person willing to help the drifters.

A Long Way from Chicago

One of the most entertaining characters willing to help the drifters is the sassy, confident, creative Mrs. Dowdel, the grandmother of Joey and Mary Alice in *A Long Way from Chicago* (Peck, 1998). In contrast to Cynthia DeFelice's *Nowhere to Call Home*, Richard Peck's story is predominantly a humorous one. It does not make fun of those who suffer, but rather highlights the tenacity of one woman who lives by the spirit of goodness rather than the rule of law. Grandma Dowdel poaches catfish in a restricted area and catches the law enforcement officials drunk along the river. Her cooking near the railroad tracks draws drifters to the town, but she emphasizes that as long as the food she serves is on her property, others have no reason to try to limit her actions. The novel unfolds through six short stories that weave together many allusions to famous people, including Al Capone, Herbert Hoover, Charles Lindbergh, and Shirley Temple, as well as aspects of daily life in the 1930s such as Prohibition.

Out of the Dust

Karen Hesse's *Out of the Dust* (1997) also offers insight into life in the 1930s, but focuses on the Oklahoma Dust Bowl. While offering many glimpses into the worn-out land starved for rain, the story is also a deeply moving and personal one. The protagonist Billie Jo loves to play the piano and looks forward to the birth of a baby brother. In a tragic accident one day, Billie Jo's father places a pail of kerosene that he thought to be coffee on the stove. The pail bursts into flames, and in an heroic effort, Billie Jo grabs it with her bare hands and rushes to the door to empty the pail so that the house won't catch on fire. As she reaches the doorway and throws out the burning liquid, her pregnant mother happens to be headed inside. Billie Jo suffers terrible burns to her hands, and her mother ends up dying from her burn wounds and child birth. The baby dies a short time later, and Billie Jo's father hardly communicates with his daughter, leaving her to feel alone in her own home and the world. Although at one point Billie Jo runs away, she realizes that will not solve her problems, so she quickly retuns to Oklahoma seeking to integrate herself back into school activities, work at playing the piano again, and care for her father. Louise, the father's new girlfriend, brings some joy to the home and understands that Billie Jo's mom is irreplaceable, and this helps Billie Jo have the room, friendship, and support she needs to heal.

ACTIVE LEARNING PROJECTS

This section includes five project options: Going on Location with Photography, Handbook for Hoboes, Vocabulary Skit, Independent Endeavors, and Character Change Illustrations. Teachers should pick and choose the active learning strategies that will work best with their students, resources, and teaching style. Teachers also should keep in mind that these strategies do not have to be presented in a particular order and that they are adaptable to other historically based novels, such as those cited in the annotated bibliographies at the end of each chapter.

Going on Location with Photography

As a way to represent a novel and/or its historical context, the teacher and students can brainstorm places in their community they can go—camera in hand—to take photographs or video that will allow them to re-enact or portray the events and setting. Due to the clear "out-of-school" nature of this assignment, teachers should either complete this as a class field trip or make it one of several project options from which students can choose. Sending a letter home, explaining the purpose of the assignment to parents/guardians, is also advisable.

In response to *Nowhere to Call Home*, two students in my Young Adult Literature class, Kristina Maurer and Adam Vorobok, "headed down to Nelsonville, OH, to stop at the abandoned trains just inside town" (excerpted from the students' reflective paper). Kristina and Adam dressed up in old clothes and posed as Frankie Blue and Stewpot, the lead characters of DeFelice's book. Some of the students' photographs show scenery; others represent specific parts of the book such as Frances Barrow's cutting her hair to "become" Frankie Blue, Stewpot and Frankie sitting in a boxcar, Frankie playing the harmonica, and the two young hoboes asking for food. Figure 2.2 shows one of the photos from Kristina and Adam's project, which they called, "A Pastoral Record of Stewpot and Frankie Blue's Adventures Across America in *Nowhere to Call Home*." In Adam's reflective paper accompanying his and Kristina's collection of photos, Adam wrote:

> The experience was beyond incredible. We immediately felt an instant connection, not only visually, but spiritually to the book and to the era. Walking through the old weather-beaten trains, jumping on and off cars, even watching a working train roll past added to the feeling we were experiencing.

Figure 2.2. Students Enacting Scenes from *Nowhere to Call Home*. Photo and excerpt from student project by Kristina Maurer and Adam Vorobok.

Handbook for Hoboes

In *Nowhere to Call Home*, protagonist Frances Barrow's transition from a daughter of a wealthy father to Frankie Blue, a homeless vagabond hopping trains and living on the streets, forced her to undertake a completely different lifestyle. Once Frances, disguised as Frankie, discovers the realities of hobo life, the glamour is wiped away, and she begins to realize that her newly proclaimed independent self has tough encounters ahead. Shortly after meeting Stewpot, Frankie began "to realize there was a lot more to tramping than simply sneaking into a boxcar unseen. For one thing, it appeared the hoboes had their own private language, one she needed to learn" (DeFelice, 2001, p. 56).

While reading *Nowhere to Call Home*, students can keep a log of terms and phrases they encounter that apply specifically to the hobo life. Focusing on the character Frankie Blue, a student of mine, Melissa Eaton, made a dictionary that she imagined would assist Frankie on her journey. Melissa accompanied each term with its part of speech and an illustration. Figure 2.3 provides examples from Melissa's picture dictionary, along with a list of terms and phrases.

Melissa's "Handbook" also included a list of "Top 10 Rules for Hoboes to Live by," shown here.

10. If you are a woman, it is much more dangerous to be a hobo. Dress as a man or find a man to travel with who will protect you and is trustworthy.
9. Make your pack as light as possible.
8. Always bargain for the best price at pawn shops.
7. Ask bakeries for any "day old" donuts.
6. Smile and be polite when asking for work. Finding people who have children may make it easier for you if they have sympathy.
5. Avoid cops always!
4. Stick to northern states; there is more available work usually.
3. Never leave your pack unattended.
2. Carry a knife with you at all times.
1. Always have a dream for your future, and you will be happy! Bonus Advice: If you see this [Melissa included a picture of cat]— a nice woman lives there!

Vocabulary Skit

Besides exploring the vocabulary specifically applicable to the hobo life depicted in *Nowhere to Call Home* (DeFelice, 2001), students can familiarize

Figure 2.3. Student-Created Handbook for Hoboes. Definitions and pictures by student Melissa Eaton.

Private Language of Hoboes:

Bull *n.* a railroad cop

Bum *n.* a person who begs, steals for food, and drinks to get drunk

Crumbs *n.* lice, bugs

Flophouse *n.* a mission house where you can work for food and shelter

Frill *n.* a girl

Ghost Story *n.* fake stories hoboes tell of where they were or where they are going

Green *adj.* young

Grub *n.* food

Hobo *n.* a person who hops freight to freight train looking for work

Jungle *n.* a group of shelters made by hoboes

Makin's *n.* cigarettes

Mulligan *n.* a stew of cabbage, potatoes, and chicken

Punk *n.* a kid

Reefer *n.* a refrigerator car

Sand *n.* sugar

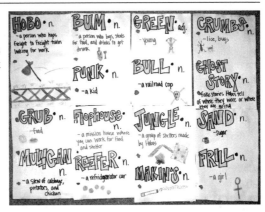

Phrases:

"on the drag"—living the hobo life, hopping train to train

"pounding your ear"—sleeping

"bulls are glimmin'"—railroad cops are patrolling the area

themselves with some of the historical terms and unfamiliar vocabulary from *A Long Way from Chicago* and the Great Depression era in general. To actively engage with vocabulary, students will transform their investigation of terms into a skit to be performed in front of the class. Figure 2.4 includes 30 terms organized in six groups, so each group must investigate five terms. To encourage students to develop a context for each term, the script should be at least a page and a half in length. While watching one another's performances, students should listen for the six words and define them based on context clues. After each skit, the group members can call on volunteers to read the terms and definitions, making sure to correct any misunderstandings.

Independent Endeavors

While as teachers we often assign specific project options, sometimes it is also effective to swing wide the invitation for creativity by requiring

Figure 2.4. Groups for Vocabulary Skits.

Group 1	Group 2
Civil War	Al Capone
Illinois Volunteers	Bugs Moran
U. S. Grant	Prohibition
Grand Army of the Republic	Bootleggers
Rebels	Coolidge
Group 3	Group 4
Black iron range	Orphan Annie
Fatback	Fish trap
Franklin D. Roosevelt	Burgoo
Victrola	Privy
Hoover	Great Depression
Group 5	Group 6
Colonel Charles A. Lindbergh	Grecian draping
Spirit of St. Louis	Shirley Temple
Seersucker suit	Elope
Stocking cap	Cob house
Great War	Stringer

students to pursue an Independent Endeavor, a self-chosen, self-directed project that draws on their interest and conveys something significant about the text. Teachers should ask students to use their imaginations, find something of importance to say about the novel, and create what I like to call, a "really magnificent project." To establish a sense of high expectations, the teacher can tell students that their projects should go far beyond ordinary and indeed "impress." In actuality, not all projects will be particularly original or impressive; however, setting this as an "expectation," then offering some ideas and models—those found in this book, for example—hopefully will raise the bar, challenge students, and result in projects that are thoughtful and well crafted. Additional benefits of this open-ended approach to active learning are that it draws on students' unique abilities and ways of demonstrating understanding and reveals—without teacher influence—what students find to be meaningful and important about the literature. Having presented project assignments and examples in response to *Nowhere to Call Home* earlier in this chapter, examples of Independent Endeavors will come from *A Long Way from Chicago* and *Out of the Dust*.

Faux Quilt. Two of my students, Maureen Montgomery and Amanda Patrick, collaborated to make a "Faux Quilt" (front and back made of cloth with no cotton batting in the middle) representative of the quilts people would have made during the Great Depression when money and resources were limited. The quilt (see Figure 2.5) consists of 12 eight-inch squares.

The first two squares show the book's title and author; the next six represent the book's three main characters, and the final four squares contrast the book's two settings, Chicago and Grandma Dowdel's small town. Each character and setting is accompanied by a quote from the book and a Great Depression era photograph that the students had transferred to fabric. If resources are limited, students can create a mock quilt from paper.

Photos and Potatoes. The next Independent Endeavor, a student project by Kevin Geiger, represents the setting of *A Long Way from Chicago* in an even more imaginative way. Kevin's project, "Photos and Potatoes" (see Figure 2.6) combines a "staple food" of the Great Depression with the

Figure 2.5. Faux Quilt. Student-created project by Maureen Montgomery and Amanda Patrick.

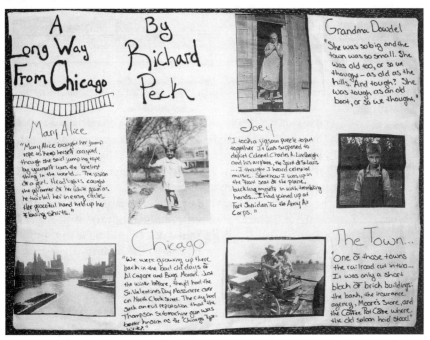

Figure 2.6. Photos and Potatoes. Student-created project and excerpt from accompanying paper by Kevin Geiger.

student's own photos from various hiking trips. Kevin describes his project this way:

> "Photos and Potatoes" is the fictitious town and countryside which Grandma Dowdel inhabits. The juxtaposition of Joey and Mary Alice leaving the big city of Chicago every summer for the country life with Grandma Dowdel during such difficult times for society implies a natural purity, an organic innocence within the "country." Joey and Mary Alice come to stay with their grandmother for reasons beyond their control, but in the end, I don't believe they would have wanted it any other way. For in the country they grow strong, pragmatic, and hopeful.

Charcoal Drawings. The third and final example of an Independent Endeavor for this chapter is a student-created project in response to *Out of the Dust*. As Kevin's "Photos and Potatoes" drew on the student's interest in nature, Robert Berry's charcoal drawings celebrate the student's love of

art. While it should be emphasized that being an "artist" is not a requirement for representing one's understanding of literature in a visual way,
finding ways for artistic students to use their talents in English class is
certainly beneficial. Robert writes, "For my 'really magnificent project'
I've decided to compose four drawings depicting particular scenes . . .
from the novel. I have chosen charcoal as the medium [because] I like
working with it and think it reflects the bleak nature of the narrative."
The drawings focus on Billie Jo, the protagonist of *Out of the Dust*, and
the changing relationships in her family. Figure 2.7 shows one of Robert's
four drawings.

Figure 2.7. Charcoal Drawings. Student drawing by Robert Berry.

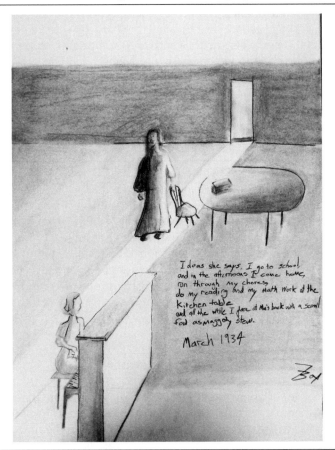

Character Change Illustrations

As was depicted with the Faux Quilt, Photos and Potatoes, and Charcoal Drawings, there are numerous ways to represent dichotomies and juxtapositions of well-defined, realistic literary settings. Similarly, well-developed fictional characters, like real people, are dynamic in nature—they change as a result of the circumstances that befall them, the experiences they embark on, and the relationships they encounter. Some changes are physical and readily visible to others; a striking example of this comes through the protagonist of *Nowhere to Call Home*, Frances Elizabeth Barrow. After her parents' death, Frances chooses life on the street, believing it will hold more adventure and fun than moving in with her aunt. After sneaking out of the house and heading to the railroad yard, Frances cuts her long hair and dons a cap and boy's clothing. Other changes—often more important when analyzing character development—cannot be seen with the eyes, but rather become clear by what the character says, does, and feels. Tuning in to the character's actions and interior thoughts, students engage with the character's life and perspective and subsequently perceive change. To visually represent character change, students will illustrate a character of their choice, as if envisioning two snapshots—before and after some crucial event in the story. Students should accompany their drawing with a collage of words and symbols that support the two snapshots.

A Character Change Illustration by a student in my Young Adult Literature class, Meredith Gray, appears in Figure 2.8. In her drawings, Meredith shows the transformation of Frances Barrow, one of the main characters in *Nowhere to Call Home*, into "Frankie Blue." Meredith's drawing of Frances includes symbols of the character's affluent life of leisure before her dad, distraught from losing his wealth in the stock market crash, committed suicide. While Frances envisioned her life as comfortable, she also longed for adventure. The illustration of Frankie Blue shows Frances's physical transformation, but perhaps even more important, it highlights her changed feelings, after having lived life on the streets. The words, "shame," "discrimination," and "fear" emphasize aspects of the character's change.

ROLE PLAY AND SIMULATION

This chapter offers two options for role play and simulation. The first requires students to tell the story (this could be done in response to any novel) as a News Broadcast, imagining that they are in the time and place represented in the novel and assuming the role of one (or more) of the

Figure 2.8. Character Change Illustrations by student Meredith Gray.

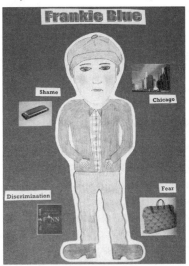

characters. The second challenges students to identify particular conflicts a character(s) faces in the text and to represent these in the form of Learning Centers.

News Broadcast

For this activity, students should divide into groups to role play characters, create commercials relevant to the Great Depression era, and tell the story (of the novel) as a News Broadcast. To get started, each group should appoint one person to be the news anchor, one person to role play a character from the book who will be interviewed in the course of the broadcast, and one person to deliver a public service announcement (PSA) or commercial relevant to the time period. A sample PSA for *Out of the Dust* might be about water conservation, while a sample commercial could be for products advertised in the 1930s such as Ammo washing powder, Anacin, Coca Cola, Coty perfume, Cracker Jacks, the Ford Model A, Goodyear tires, Hershey's chocolate, Morton salt, Penick corn starch, Quaker State oil, or Wrigley's chewing gum.

Turning the novel into a News Broadcast requires students to think carefully about the plot and conflict as they determine what interview questions the anchor will ask the character. One group that presented *Out of the Dust* as a News Broadcast, divided their script into three segments—

morning, noon, and evening news—each bridged with a commercial. An excerpt revealing the interview format appears in Figure 2.9; this was written by one of my students, Katie Higham.

Learning Centers

As a way for students to engage actively and think creatively about vicariously experiencing the challenges faced by the characters in a story, they will work in groups to create Learning Centers that simulate challenges present in their novel. If students have been reading different books in literature circles, each group should create two to four learning centers to represent their assigned book. If students have all been reading the same novel, the teacher should divide the class into groups, assign each group a conflict from the novel, and have group members determine how to make it into a Learning Center. The point here is to avoid duplication. One of my students, Meredith Gray, read *Out of the Dust* as part of a six-member literature circle. Her group (Jennifer Buckley, Katie Higham, Lindsey Soter, Sara Storz, and Diane Weitfle) collaborated to create four Learning Centers that simulate obstacles faced by characters in *Out of the Dust*.

1) Finding one's way home in a dust storm
2) Playing the piano with a handicap
3) Accomplishing an everyday task with a handicap
4) Building under tough circumstances.

On the day that the Learning Centers were to be "experienced" by the class, the group began with a simulation for the whole class: finding one's way home in a dust storm. All students were blindfolded, and the desks were arranged to form a winding path from the door to the far side of the room. As students entered, fans blew on them (resembling the winds of the dust storm), and a CD of winds played. Student Meredith Gray wrote of the group's intended purpose for the simulation:

The storms in the book are violent and leave Billie Jo and her father with injuries . . . it is obviously not our intention to hurt anyone, and therefore we will not carry the simulation out on a grand scale. It is simply designed to [show] how it would feel to be left blinded and vulnerable by the terrible wind and dust during a storm . . . to show the reality of [the] time period when dust storms were an ordinary occurrence.

Figure 2.9. News Broadcast Script by student Katie Higham.

Dusty Evening News

SARA: Welcome to the Dusty Evening News and thank you so much for joining us. I am Sara Storz.

KATIE: And I am Katie Higham. First, we have an update on a story the Dusty News team has been following. Billie Jo Kelby, a member of a family in the Oklahoma Panhandle that has been severely affected by dust storms, was involved in an accident earlier today. Her mother was also burned and died delivering her baby boy. The baby also passed away. In addition Billie Jo's hands were badly burned. Our news team has just discovered that Billie Jo has won third prize at the local talent show for playing the piano.

SARA: Billie Jo is with us now to bring us up to date on what has been happening with her and her father. Billie Jo, it is so nice to have you with us this evening. Please tell us what has been happening.

BILLIE JO: Hi, Katie and Sara. Thank you for having me. As you know I won third prize playing the piano at the talent show at the Palace. The pain in my hands is horrible and in order to prepare for the talent show, "I sit at the school piano and make my hands work. In spite of the pain, in spite of the stiffness and scars. I make my hands play the piano" (127).

KATIE: We are told that you ran away for a few days. Please tell us where you went and what made you decide to return home.

BILLIE JO: As you know there was another terrible dust storm and Pa discovered he had bumps on his face. I was scared. Pa's dad had the same bumps and he died from cancer. I was terrified I was going to lose Pa and then I would be alone in the world. I was so afraid I thought it was better to run away. I took a train halfway across the country and ended up in Arizona. After talking to other runaways, I began to feel sorry for the people they had left at home who would never know if their loved one was dead or alive. At this moment I decided to return home. When I returned from Arizona Pa and I talked for the first time since Ma and the baby died. Pa promised to go to the hospital and get the spots on his face checked out. The doctor said he is going to be just fine. The doctor also gave me some ointment for my hands and they feel so much better.

KATIE: Wow! That is a remarkable story of recovery. We are also told that your father has met someone special. Please tell us about that . . . [script continues for two more pages]

KATIE: This is Katie Higham, signing off for the night. Please join us tomorrow when we will have a special on how to get the Christmas shopping done when you are on a tight budget.

SARA: Everyone's on a tight budget, due to the Depression. Thanks for watching the evening edition of Dusty News. Good night.

For the subsequent three Learning Centers, the group divided into pairs, each facilitating a simulation; the remainder of the class was divided into teams that rotated through the centers, thus making optimal use of class time. Figure 2.10 provides a model of the written format each group turned in to indicate their planning of the Learning Centers; this example was created by one of my students in Young Adult Literature, Meredith Gray.

CREATIVE WRITING

The options for creative writing that follow are presented in the order of difficulty or challenge they offer students. With the exception of the last of the six assignments presented here, which is specific to the poetic form modeled in Karen Hesse's *Out of the Dust*, these assignments are readily adaptable to any novel. These creative writing options also might be taught in progression, as some are designed to show the background of the time

Figure 2.10. Sample Setup for Learning Center. Student-created model by Meredith Gray.

LEARNING CENTER #2: PLAYING THE PIANO WITH A HANDICAP

Supplies:

For this activity you will need large olives and a portable keyboard

Process:

With a volunteer at hand, one person will use any music talent or piano experience to play a simple melody or any course of notes that they desire. After they have completed this, they will then be asked to place a large olive on every other finger of each hand. Then, they will be asked to play the same melody or course of notes with the olives on their fingers. Most likely, the person playing the piano will not yield the same results with the handicap of the olives on their hands.

Purpose/Significance:

The purpose of this activity was to show students how different Billie Jo felt playing the piano before the kerosene accident as compared with after the accident. At one time she felt completely confident in doing this and was proud to share her talent with others. After her accident, she felt a range of emotions such as shame, embarrassment, discouragement, and awkwardness. Because of her painful handicap, her perception of playing the piano was completely changed. Naturally, the addition of olives to one's fingers is not as painful or permanent as burns are, but they still give an insight as to how Billie Jo felt. We hope that in doing this activity, [our classmates] can formulate an idea about how painful it must have been for her to lose a talent, and gain an appreciation for those who face handicaps on a daily basis.

---

period, while others emphasize plot and characterization, poetic repetition, or skills of prediction. Collectively, the examples shared here represent all three novels featured in this chapter.

Found Poetry

Found poetry works well as an introduction to creative writing because it shows students that, in essence, the poetry is already there; all they have to do is find it. In this unit Found Poems become a strategy to help students explore the many historical allusions to people and events from the Great Depression era. To start this creative writing activity, teachers should come up with a list of topics (characters, events, historical figures, etc.) from which students can choose. *A Long Way from Chicago* simply could be divided into the chapter titles or six short stories that constitute the book as a whole; it also could be broken down into the names of the many famous people Richard Peck alludes to in the novel, such as John Dillinger, Henry Ford, Charles Lindbergh, Herbert Hoover, and Franklin Delano Roosevelt. Once the students have a focal point for their Found Poem, they simply go through the text and look for words associated with it. Next, they arrange the words in a fashion that reveals the "poem." Figure 2.11 provides samples of three Found Poems written by two of my students, Amanda Patrick and Maureen Montgomery. Each focuses on a prominent person or aspect of the Great Depression era featured in one of the chapters of Peck's book.

Figure 2.11. Sample Found Poems for Historical Figures. Poems by students Maureen Montgomery and Amanda Patrick.

Charles Lindbergh "The Mouse in the Milk"	*Hard Times* "A One-Woman Crime Wave"	*Shirley Temple* "The Phantom Brakeman"
Shy	Drifters	Curly haired
National hero	Moving on down the track	Child star
Physical daring	Don't feed loafers	Singing and dancing
Pilot	Hollow-eyed men	Age 3
Barnstormer	Hounded out of towns	"Baby Take a Bow"
Airmail pilot	Keep moving	Merchandising cash cow
Nonstop solo flight	Looking for work	"Curly Top"
Across the Atlantic	Shuffling boots	Unspoiled
Spirit of St. Louis	Sometimes a voice	"Bright Eyes"
	To beg for food	Carefully screened friends
	Spooky and sad	"Dimples"
	Slumping figures	Cooperative
	Drifters	"Heidi"
		Outgrown popularity

Recipe Poem

Being such a time of need, the era of the Great Depression and infamous drought and dust storms of the American prairie came with an emphasis on food and hunger. It is no surprise, therefore, that all three novels include related references. While Frankie and Stewpot face hunger and resort to begging for and even stealing food in *Nowhere to Call Home*, Grandma Dowdel feeds the drifters in *A Long Way from Chicago*, and *Out of the Dust* makes mention of over 20 recipes. Playing with the form of the recipe, students are to write a Recipe Poem that reveals something important about a character or theme from the book. Students begin this activity by choosing their favorite character and listing several of the traits and/or things associated with the character. Students should include at least six "ingredients" along with an explanation of what to do with them. Accompanying the recipe (ingredients and instructions), students should offer a brief explanation of why they chose the character or theme, plus a supporting example from the book. One of my students, Molly Sullivan, wrote "Recipe for Trouble" (see Figure 2.12), a Recipe Poem that focuses on Grandma Dowdel, the protagonist of *A Long Way from Chicago*. With this assignment, students also might draw a picture to go with the recipe or even make one of the 20 recipes alluded to in Hesse's *Out of the Dust*.

Figure 2.12. Sample Recipe Poem by student Molly Sullivan.

RECIPE FOR TROUBLE

Ingredients:

One ornery Grandma	Two adventurous grandchildren
People in need of help	Hard times in the neighborhood
Small-town happenings	Big-city spirit
Crazy characters	Strange goings on
One large heart	

Directions:

Place one large heart inside one ornery Grandma and let grow. Place two adventurous grandchildren in the country with one ornery Grandma and let stew. Allow people in need of help to seek out one ornery Grandma and two adventurous grandchildren as needed. Shake up small-town happenings, big-city spirit, hard times in the neighborhood, crazy characters, and strange goings on together and sprinkle over the top. Make sure all is mixed up well and watch the trouble brew!

Stepping into an Historical Photograph

Opening Questions: How would you feel if the bank foreclosed on your farm? If you saw a dust storm approaching? If you had to stand in line at a soup kitchen?

Like the Found Poetry assignment, this creative writing strategy is designed to help students engage with the time period and life stories of people who lived during the Great Depression. Teachers will need to find—or have students find—actual photographs from the 1930s, particularly ones that feature people whose stories can be imagined and told. A search for "photos of the Great Depression" on google.com or askjeeves.com (or a survey of books from the library) will provide an ample number of pictures for this activity. Dorothea Lange (1895–1965) was a particularly well-known photographer who was employed by the U.S. government to document many aspects of daily life during the Great Depression, World War II, and even the Civil Rights Movement of the 1950s and 1960s. Lange's work is powerful in its realism and way of juxtaposing human courage and dignity with backdrops of poverty and despair. Her work is sure to appear in a search for photos of the era, and students will be moved by their profundity.

Once students have selected a photo, they should document its source, then imagine the story the person in the photograph (or who took the photo) would tell. What was the person thinking about? What was he/she feeling? What was it like to live during such a difficult time? In free verse or rhyme, students play with language until a poem emerges. One of my students, Molly Sullivan, wrote a poem in response to Dorothea Lange's well-known photo "Migrant Mother." Molly entitled her poem "Earbobs," which in its entirety is 50 lines long. An excerpt from Molly's poem appears alongside Lange's famous photo in Figure 2.13.

Villanelle

While some students prefer writing free-verse poetry, others find the challenge—or supportive structure—depending on how they look at it, of specialized poetic forms to be more appealing. While there are many specialized poetic forms, such as the rondeau, rondel, sonnet, and sestina, to name just a few, that teachers can offer as options from which students may choose, the villanelle is the focus here. A villanelle consists of 19 lines structured as five tercets (3-line stanzas) and a concluding quatrain (4-line stanza). Each tercet rhymes a-b-a, and the quatrain rhymes a-b-a-a. Beyond this, the villanelle prescribes that line one repeats in lines six and

Figure 2.13. Sample Poetic Response to an Historical Photograph by student Molly Sullivan.

Caption: "Destitute peapickers in California; a 32-year-old
  mother of seven children. February 1936" (commonly known
  as "Migrant Mother")
Date: 1936
Location: Nipomo, California
Credit: Dorothea Lange
Copyright: Public Domain
Available: The Library of Congress Prints & Photographs
  Reading Room *http://www.loc.gov/rr/print/list/128_migm.html*

Earbobs

My Grandmother left me a pair of earbobs—
a reminder of better times.
I take them out of their dainty china box
and hold them in my hands . . .
I don't dare try them on,
afraid their beauty will show the ugly
written all over my face . . .

I imagine a better time—
a time when there is work
and paychecks
and food on the table.
I'll buy myself a smart black dress
and polish my nails to a shiny cherry lacquer
to go out on the town
with a handsome dark haired man . . .

But for now there are only
children
with hungry mouths to feed.
They pull and tug at me.
They keep me up at night,
their pleas for things
(Can't they see I have nothing?)
wringing in my ears.
And I know
that when my time comes,
when this depression is over
and the children are grown,
I will be too old
to have a smart black dress
or dance with a handsome man.
Far too old
to wear such fashionable earbobs.

12 (the ends of stanzas 2 and 4), and line three repeats in lines nine and 15 (the ends of stanzas 3 and 5). The third line also is repeated, but turns into a question, as the last line of the poem. The villanelle has no set metrical pattern, but lines are typically close in syllabic length.

Because of the villanelle's pattern of repetition, this form works particularly well with topics that embed rhythm or persistent questioning. One of my students in a Young Adult Literature class, Adam Vorobok, wrote a villanelle called "1930s Blues" (see Figure 2.14) in response to *Nowhere to Call Home*. In the reflective paper accompanying his poem, Adam explained how he designed each stanza "to increase the tension . . . with the passing hardships the citizens of America faced in the 30s." He also noted the "sense of rhythm and repetition to mimic the sound of a train traveling down the railroad tracks" and his effort to

create a sense of foreboding danger [and paint] some devastating images that became all too real to America. I wanted to show that

Figure 2.14 Sample Villanelle. Poem written by student Adam Vorobok.

1930s Blues

The train wheels play a lazy harmonica tune
Down the great steel beams toward Seattle
Unbeknown to all passengers, tomorrow begins in ruin.

The 'bos sit and wait with knife and spoon,
Dirty faces, dirty mouths, the wind running fingers through unwashed hair,
The train wheels play a lazy harmonica tune.

Business men wake up with 100 dollar smiles, soon
Their faces fall alongside paper stock ticking tape.
Unbeknown to all passengers, tomorrow begins in ruin.

Children don caps, flip rides, sit watching the waning moon.
Home is what they carry, stability they measure in miles,
The train wheels play a lazy harmonica tune.

The water dries up, disappears; the West a sand dune.
Farmers cry, families starve, even the President breathes a sigh.
Unbeknown to all passengers, tomorrow begins in ruin.

The country moans, desperate at midday noon.
The Stock Market crashes and people await their fate,
The train wheels play a lazy harmonica tune.
Unbeknown to all passengers, will tomorrow begin in ruin?

both classes, the working and the rich, were negatively affected by the fall of the stock market and the Dust Bowl which destroyed much of the soil. (excerpted from Adam's paper accompanying the villanelle)

Repetition to Emphasize a Point

Having experimented with a specialized poetic form that offers practice in using repetition, students now venture to compose a poem that utilizes repetition, but in a manner of the students' choosing—free verse or rhymed. Just as Adam Vorobok's example of the villanelle used repetition to emphasize the "harmonica tune" and "ruin" that echoed throughout the main characters' (Frankie and Stewpot) journey in *Nowhere to Call Home*, students working on this creative writing assignment are to determine a point to emphasize and do so with the use of repetition. Two students from my Young Adult Literature class, Courtney Baxter and Sara Roberts, collaborated to compose a poem (see Figure 2.15) that emphasized the impact of the dust storms as experienced by Billie Jo, the main character in *Out of the Dust*. Courtney and Sara reflected on their purpose in writing:

> We felt like [Billie Jo] went through an amazing transformation. . . . Circumstances forced her to grow up extremely fast as opposed to her own choices; this is why each stanza starts with "I can't believe I'm asked." The fire turns her world upside down as she feels that she is somehow responsible for her mother's death and harbors resentment toward her father. We felt like she was trying to make sense of it all and trying to accept her reality. . . . We wanted to illustrate at the end that she did start to heal; that she was willing to look past all that she had lost and realize there was a future. She is a part of the dust.

Adding a Scene

The final creative writing option combines skills of poetry writing and prediction. Using Hesse's *Out of the Dust* as a model for free verse, students are to add a scene to the book. This scene can reveal additional aspects of any part of the text that students imagined or wanted to know more about. One of my students in a Young Adult Literature class, Andrea Hannon, decided to add a kind of epilogue that takes place 4 years after the book's last entry. Andrea's poem "Ending: Fall 1939" (see Figure 2.16) predicts the outcome of the relationship between two characters from *Out of the Dust*, Billie Jo's father and his girlfriend Louise. Andrea explains how her poem

Figure 2.15. Sample Poem with Repetition to Emphasize a Point. Composed collaboratively by students Courtney Baxter and Sara Roberts.

___

In the Dust

I can't believe I'm being asked
To deal with this,
Deal with my father's face
When all I want is to be more like my mom.
Deal with unfulfilled expectations,
When all I want is a little excitement.
Deal with the dust.

I can't believe I'm asked
To understand this,
Understand why I'm being blamed for the fire
When my dad put the kerosene there.
Understand why I couldn't save my mother
When I couldn't imagine my life without her.
Understand the dust.

I can't believe I'm asked
To accept my situation,
Accept that my mother is gone
When I can't play the piano to connect with her.
Accept the deafening silence between my father and I
When we need each other more than anything else.
Accept the dust.

I'm learning to deal with the changes
When I see how much my father needs me.
I'm learning to understand that life goes on
When I play the piano in spite of my pain.
I'm learning to accept my place in this world even
When I am in the dust.

___

parallels the author's (Karen Hesse) writing style and uses the rain to symbolize the decade-long drought coming to an end in the Great Plains.

> Those rainfalls also meant the end of the Depression itself, as the nation entered World War II a few years later, and the once barren fields again fed a nation and the world. . . . In keeping with Hesse's poetic style of writing, my poem's title aims to represent a capstone to her story, which began with "Beginning: August 1920."

Figure 2.16. Adding a Scene to *Out of the Dust*. Poem by student
Andrea Hannon.

Ending: Fall 1939

My father married Louise
three years ago this fall.
She knew how to make cranberry sauce all along,
and asked if we would like her to make some
her first Thanksgiving living under our roof.
It wasn't Ma's recipe.
It was sweeter, thicker.
But it passed my test.

Louise never stepped on the toes of Ma's ghost.
Her baby boy,
born around Christmas time two years ago,
never tried to replace the memory of my brother.
And yet, I grew to love little Roosevelt.
Even though I sometimes pretend he's a pest,
I secretly love it when it crawls over
and pushes the piano peddles at my feet.

At 19 years old, I've grown lanky and long-legged.
A female version of Daddy.
I don't play the piano like Mad Dog sings,
But my hands,
still scarred and stretched,
regained their fever for some red-hot keys.
Arley Wanderdale keeps wonderin'
when I'm gonna kick the dust of these old shoes.

Panhandle A and M, Arley says,
offers more than just music lessons.
These jittery hands could learn to write music.
This restless heart could compose moving pieces.
Someday, I tell him with my best smile.
Someday.
But right now Daddy and Louise need help
Keeping the farm going, and the catfish pond stocked for eager fishermen.

My chance may come sooner than later.
Yesterday, clouds gathered like
a distant herd of cattle on the horizon.
Daddy, Louise and me look out the back window,
and worried whether we should put up blankets.
But as the darkness grew closer, we realized it wasn't dust.
The skies unleashed and
tears streamed down from heaven.

EPILOGUE: OVERCOMING ADVERSITY

In studying the literature of the Great Depression, we learned that good leadership is important in times of distress and that no matter how bad things get, there is always something that can be done to overcome. . . . But mostly, we learned the importance of hope through the character of Billie Jo [from Out of the Dust] *who fought to overcome the death of those whom she loved and the loss of her ability to do what she loved best—play the piano.*
　　　　　—E'lise Flood and Katie Hall, Ohio University students

Rich as they are with realistic hardship, the young adult novels featured in this chapter demonstrate perseverance and the will to overcome adversity—timeless virtues that hopefully will inspire students when they face conflicts. Because we cannot see what tomorrow holds, having a deep reservoir of historical and personal understanding, may be just what helps us in times of need. Whether faced with abject poverty (as Frankie and Stewpot in *Nowhere to Call Home*), being displaced from our home (as Joey and Mary Alice in *A Long Way from Chicago*), or a physical disability and loss of a loved one (as Billie Jo in *Out of the Dust*), the characters in these texts show the will to persevere and overcome. As much as these novels convey the heartless oppressors in society, they also illuminate genuine goodness—people who reach out to provide for the needy and bridge gaps in communication by offering kind words and empathetic ears. These stories depict life as a shared journey, an interplay of relationships that bring us through hard times.

ANNOTATED BIBLIOGRAPHY

Curtis, C. P. (1999). *Bud, not Buddy*. New York: Scholastic.
　　A humorous story about Bud Caldwell, a lively, imaginative, musically talented 10-year-old on the run from his abusive father, foster homes, and the Hoovervilles of Michigan in the 1930s.

Peck, G. (2002). *A year down yonder*. New York: Puffin.
　　Peck's sequel to *A Long Way from Chicago* shows Mary Alice again living with lively Grandma Dowdel in rural Illinois. Embedded with historical references such as the Civilian Conservation Corps and other aspects of the nation's climb out of the Great Depression.

Porter, T. (1997). *Treasures in the dust*. New York: Harper Trophy.
　　Two 11-year-olds who are very different from each other build a friendship and help each other cope in rural Oklahoma during the drought of the Great Depression.

Rylant, C. (1994). *Permanent connections*. New York: Harcourt Brace.
  A collection of 29 short, lyrical poems in response to Walker Evans and James Agee's 1930s-era photographs documenting the lives of impoverished share-croppers.

Stanley, J. (1992). *Children of the dust bowl*. New York: Crown.
  Follows the people driven from Oklahoma to California during the dust storms of the 1930s, with a particular focus on the residents of the Weedpatch Camp, a farm-labor camp built by the federal government.

REFERENCES

DeFelice, C. (2001). *Nowhere to call home*. New York: Harper Trophy.
Herkert, M. B. (2004). *Civilian conservation corps: Protecting Oregon's resources*. Retrieved July 21, 2005, from http:arcweb.sos.state.or.us/50th/ccc/cccintro.html
Hesse, K. (1997). *Out of the dust*. New York: Scholastic.
How welfare began in the United States. (1998). Constitutional Rights Foundation. Retrieved July 21, 2005, from http://www.crf-usa.org/bria/bria14_3.html
Johnson, T. H. (1966). *The Oxford companion to American history*. New York: Oxford University Press.
Lancaster, R. (2002). *Black Tuesday, October 29th 1929 revisited?* Retrieved October 19, 2005, from http://www.gold-eagle.com/editorials_02/lancaster102102.html
October 29, 1929: 'Black Tuesday'. (2003). Retrieved July 21, 2005, from http://www.cnn.com/2003/US/03/10/sprj.80.1929.crash/
Peck, R. (1998). *A long way from Chicago*. New York: Puffin.
Roosevelt, F. D. (1935). State of the Union address.
Schenk, R. (1997). *A case of unemployment*. Retrieved July 21, 2005, from http://ingrimayne.saintjoe.edu/econ/EconomicCatastrophe/Great Depression.html
Simkin, J. (1997). *Wall street crash*. Spartacus Educational. Retrieved July 21, 2005, from http://www.spartacus.schoolnet.co.uk/USAwallstreet .htm

Hunger of Body, Hunger of Heart: Mexican American Young Adult Authors Portray Migrant Farm Experiences (1940s–1960s)

Jacqueline N. Glasgow

It is possible to become discouraged about the injustice we see everywhere. But God did not promise us that the world would be humane and just. He gives us the gift of life and allows us to choose the way we will use our limited time on earth. It is an awesome opportunity.
—Cesar Chavez (Chavez, Jensen, & Hammerback, 2002, p. 167)

In this unit, students will read young adult literature written by Mexican American authors who render their experiences as migrant farmworkers. The novels featured in this chapter include *Esperanza Rising* (Ryan, 2000), *Jessie de la Cruz: A Profile of a United Farm Worker* (Soto, 2002), and *Parrot in the Oven: Mi Vida* (Martinez, 1996). These works of literature contain the recurring themes regarding the injustices of the migrant workers' lives in the areas of education, family life, housing, poverty, labor disputes, immigration, and citizenship during their stay in the United States.

Active learning strategies to engage students in their study of the hunger, hardship, and discrimination faced by the Mexican migrant farmworkers include Socratic Seminar, Debate, Literature Circles, Problem-Based Learning, Interactive Writing Strategies, and Multigenre Research Papers. A summary of the active learning strategies appears in Figure 3.1.

Figure 3.1. Active Learning Strategies in Chapter 3.

Featured Young Adult Novels	Thoughtfulness and Reflection	Role Play	Active Learning Projects	Creative and Analytical Writing
Esperanza Rising	• Exploring Character Development	• Unsent Letters • The Protagonist's Unspoken Thoughts • Debate: To Strike or Not to Strike		
Jessie de la Cruz: A Profile of a United Farm Worker			• Multigenre Research Project	• Copy Change Song Lyrics
Parrot in the Oven: Mi Vida	• Socratic Seminar		• Memory Shoe Box	• Double Journal Entry
General, Applicable to any Novel in the Chapter	• Anticipation Guide • Semantic Mapping		• Problem-Based Learning Scenario • Cinco de Mayo Celebration	• Los Corridos—Mexican Folk Ballad • Poetry for a Social Issue

CULTURAL/HISTORICAL CONTEXT

For hundreds of years, Mexican immigrants have been coming to the United States in order to find work. Recent estimates by the U.S. Department of Labor suggest that approximately 13 million U.S. citizens migrate between states earning their living working in the agricultural industry harvesting crops and working in poultry plants and fisheries. Seventy-seven percent of all farmworkers were born in Mexico. They continue a long tradition of people from Mexico harvesting crops in the southwestern United States, including those who came here through the "Bracero" (Guest Worker) program started in the 1940s to bolster our work force as "soldiers of the fields and railroads" to help the United States win World War II. When the Bracero program ended, Mexicans kept coming and growers continued to recruit them. Today, California agribusiness, which, at $24.5 billion a year, is the state's largest industry, remains dependent on Mexicans (Ferriss & Sandoval, 1997). Yet, migrant workers continue to face innumerable hardships, such as low wages, unacceptable housing, inadequate food, lack of health care, and—most of all—lack of human respect.

The United Farm Workers Union

Almost all the laws and protections farmworkers now have are the fruit of Cesar Chavez's legacy through the United Farm Workers Union. The product of a Depression-era migrant childhood, Chavez was known for having a will as fierce as the growers were rigid. As a child and a young man, he had experienced some of the worst America had to offer to poor minorities. And when he started the movement in the 1960s, farmworkers had very little with which to defend themselves. They didn't have the legal right to organize and vote for collective bargaining. They didn't have the right to have clean drinking water, access to portable toilets, lunch breaks, or short rest breaks during the workday. They were not entitled to the minimum wage or unemployment insurance. Benefits such as health insurance, pensions, and paid vacations were dreams. Housing was horrible, and most migrant kids didn't have a chance of finishing high school—and nobody seemed to care. When he died in 1993, Chavez was continuing a 10-year-old boycott of grapes, which had become more symbolic than practical—a cry of protest against the threat of pesticides, the poisoning of water and workers, and the loss of children who may have died from pesticide-related cancers (Ferriss & Sandoval, 1997).

Working Conditions and Wages

The work ethic exhibited by farmworkers is extraordinary. They often toil 12 to 14 hours a day, 7 days a week, during the harvest season. Hard physical labor, high heat and humidity, dangerous equipment, and pesticide exposure make agriculture one of the most dangerous occupations in the United States. Much farmwork is seasonal and workers cannot earn money in bad weather, while waiting for crops to ripen, when they are sick, or when traveling between jobs. For all this mostly stoop labor, the average hourly wage is $5.94. Some are paid hourly and others earn a piece rate, where a set amount is paid for each filled container. Half of all farmworkers earn less than $7,500 a year and half of all farmworker families earn less than $10,000 a year, far below the 2002 U.S. poverty level of $18,000 for a family of four (Weyer, 2002).

Education

While education is valued, there is only a 50.7% high school graduation rate among migrant teenagers. A nomadic way of life can have particularly far-reaching repercussions for the children of migrant families—some change schools five times in one school year. At least one third of migrant children work on farms to help their families; others may not be hired but are in the fields helping their parents. Often farmworkers attend English language classes at the end of the long workday. Many families have made tremendous sacrifices to see that their children receive an education.

FEATURED YOUNG ADULT NOVELS

Esperanza Rising

Written by Pam Munoz Ryan, *Esperanza Rising* (2000) was inspired by the author's grandmother, Esperanza Ortega. Esperanza is forced by circumstances to leave her privileged life in Mexico and work as a refugee in the fields of California.

Jessie de la Cruz: A Profile of a United Farm Worker

Chicano writer Gary Soto worked in the fields during his high school and college years. Later, he interviewed other farmworkers, focusing on the story of Jessie de la Cruz who, beginning at age 5, worked in the fields with her family. Soto's biography *Jessie de la Cruz: A Profile of a United Farm Worker* (2002) begins in the 1920s and spans 60 years of Jessie's life working the fields of the San Joaquin Valley in California. Through the story of Jessie de la Cruz, the author depicts the daily lives of migrant families and the organization of the United Farm Workers.

Parrot in the Oven: Mi Vida

In Victor Martinez's *Parrot in the Oven: Mi Vida* (1996), readers are introduced to 14-year-old Manny Hernandez. Manny comes from a poor Mexican American family who struggle to make ends meet every day and are living in the projects. One of the reasons the family struggles is because of the father's inability to hold down a job, due primarily to his alcoholism. Because of his ethnicity, Manny faces discrimination at school, in the neighborhood, and in the drugstore. Manny just wants to fit into the crowd and make friends. He is equipment manager for a boxing team and joins one of the project gangs. Getting involved in illegal activities gives him pause for thought.

Additional Texts

While the three novels already mentioned are used most often in this chapter, students also may form literature circles to read other books by Mexican American authors. Specific titles referenced in this chapter that appear in the Annotated Bibliography are: *The Circuit: Stories from the Life of a Migrant Child* (1997) and *Breaking Through* (2002) by Francisco Jimenez, and *Buried Onions* (1999) by Gary Soto.

THE INTERPLAY OF THOUGHTFULNESS AND REFLECTION

Anticipation Guide

To help students engage in the themes and activate prior knowledge for this unit before reading, ask them to respond to the generalizations in the Anticipation Guide that appears in Figure 3.2.

After the students have completed the Anticipation Guide, discuss the topics and encourage students to make personal connections to them. At the end of the unit, refer to this activity and ask students whether as a result of reading the books, they have changed their minds on any of the issues.

Semantic Mapping

A semantic map helps students identify important ideas and shows how these ideas fit together. According to Vacca and Vacca (1999), a semantic map has three basic components: a core question or concept stated as a key word, strands that show subordinate ideas, and supports that clarify the strands and distinguish one strand from another. For this assignment, ask students to create a semantic map for the key term, Racism Against Mexican Americans. For the strands, consider racism at work, home, and school. Begin with what students already know and then, as they read the novel, ask them to find specific quotes from the text to support the strands of their map. This project can be done individually or collaboratively. As students begin their research projects, encourage them to add photos to illustrate racism. See Figure 3.3 for a teacher-created sample of a Semantic Map for Racism.

Figure 3.2. Anticipation Guide for Mexican Migrant Families.

Directions: Read each statement and put a checkmark in the "yes" column if you believe the statement and could support it or put a checkmark in the "no" column if you do not believe it and could not support it.		

Yes	*No*	*Statement*
		1. In a family, members should help one another for the good of the entire family, even at the cost of the individual.
		2. Compulsory education should be enforced in the migrant worker population.
		3. English immersion is the best way for Mexican immigrants to learn the English language.
		4. English language is the primary obstacle that keeps migrant children from making visible, measurable achievement in schools.
		5. Mexican migrant worker parents have the right to keep their children home to work in the fields and to preserve their heritage.
		6. Anyone working in the United States should receive at least the minimum wage.
		7. Migrant students have some of the highest dropout rates in the country.
		8. The government should provide adequate housing for all citizens.
		9. Everyone has the right to work in a healthy environment.
		10. Mexican children should be punished if caught speaking Spanish at school.

Exploring Character Development

Another strategy for helping students to be thoughtful and reflect on their reading is the method of Exploring Character Development. After the students have completed the reading of *Esperanza Rising*, select or ask students to collect memorable quotes from the novel. Collate the quotes and have the students match each quote with the character responsible for it. Students should then pick one or two of the quotes and explain their significance in the story, including:

1. What the quote says about the character's personality/mind-set
2. What it says about the character's role in the novel
3. Why this quote in particular is more important than others in the novel
4. How this quote relates to the general message of the story.

Figure 3.3. Semantic Map for Racism Against Mexican Americans. Teacher-created example by Jacqueline Glasgow.

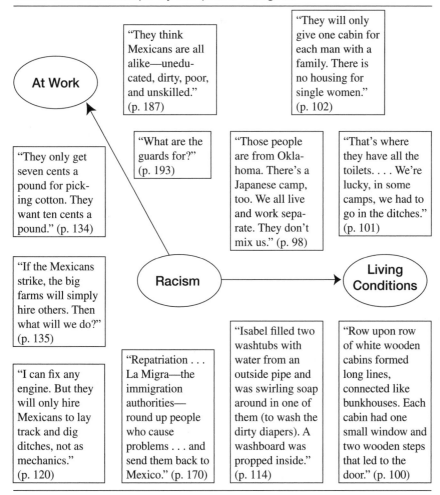

See Figure 3.4 for suggested quotes from *Esperanza Rising* for the Exploring Character Development activity.

SOCRATIC SEMINAR

Socratic questioning is both an innovative and ancient technique that requires students and teachers to assemble in an open forum to

Figure 3.4. Suggested Quotes for Exploring Character Development. From *Esperanza Rising* (2000).

"Did you know that when you lie down on the land, you can feel it breathe? That you can feel its heart beating?" (Father, p. 1)

"Wait a little while and the fruit will fall into your hand." (Father, p. 2)

"Do not be afraid to start over." (Abuelita, p. 15)

"You were right, Esperanza. In Mexico we stand on different sides of the river." (Miguel, p. 37)

"We are like the phoenix, rising again with a new life ahead of us." (Abuelita, p. 50)

"I am poor, but I am rich. I have my children, I have a garden with roses, and I have my faith and the memories of those who have gone before me. What more is there?" (Carmen, p. 76)

"Mama, we are living like horses! How can you sing? How can you be happy? We don't even have a room to call our own." (Esperanza, p. 103)

"La Cenicienta! Cinderella!" (Marta, p. 117)

"I can fix any engine. But they will only hire Mexicans to lay track and dig ditches, not as mechanics." (Miguel, p. 120)

"When you first start in the sheds, the body refuses to bend, but in time, you will get used to the work." (Josefina, p. 121)

"Heulga! Heulga! Strike! Strike!" (Marta and others, p. 133)

"She has Valley Fever. It's a disease of the lungs that is caused by dust spores . . . the dust spores get into the lungs and cause an infection." (Doctor, p. 155)

"Don't worry. I will take care of everything. I will be *la patrona* for the family now." (Esperanza, p. 178)

"Americans see us as one big, brown group who are good for only manual labor." (Miguel, p. 187)

"Immigration! It's a sweep." (Josefina, p. 205)

"Where will it end? Everyone will starve if people work for less and less money." (Josefina, p. 204)

"Is this life really better than being a servant in Mexico?" (Esperanza, p. 222)

---

discuss the comprehension of a work and the important concepts proposed by that work. In ancient Greek times, Socrates raised thoughtful questions without proposing to have all the answers himself. Through discussion and dialogue, he hoped to lead students to discover truth and self-knowledge. Socratic Seminars may have ancient traditions, but they always remain innovative since seminars rely on a modern-day interpretation of a text and connect students to important ideas in light of their current experiences.

Incorporating the seminar strategy into lesson plans is more complex than forming a circle and tossing out questions. Students must prepare for the seminar by identifying significant passages of a novel, journaling to make meaning of the characters and themes, and/or completing a character development project. Teachers must prepare the opening question, core questions, and the closing question in advance of the seminar. Following the seminar, students should be required to complete a post-seminar task that enriches and extends their learning. This could be an essay, multigenre research paper, 'zine, or other multimedia project.

The following seminar is designed as an after-reading activity for *Parrot in the Oven: Mi Vida* by Victor Martinez. Following is a list of questions for teachers' use in facilitating a Socratic Seminar for *Parrot in the Oven: Mi Vida*.

Opening Question

What are the main instances of racism that you see in this book?

Core Questions

1. How are Mexican girls/women portrayed in this novel?
2. How does Manny's race affect his interaction with other characters?
3. How are issues of family and home displayed throughout the book?
4. Why do you think Manny is invited to Dorothy's party?
5. What is the role of gangs in the novel?
6. How do race and identity play into the boxing scenes?
7. What do you think Manny realized at the end?

Closing Question

Do you relate to any of the situations Manny goes through? How? If not, why?

ROLE PLAY THROUGH WRITING AND DEBATE

Interactive Writing Strategy: Unsent Letters

The unsent letter establishes a role-play situation in which students are asked to write letters in response to material being studied. According to Vacca and Vacca (1999), the activity requires the use of imagination and often demands that students engage in interpretive and evaluative thinking. Unsent letters direct students' thinking with particular audiences in mind. For this assignment, students were asked to choose a scene in *Esperanza Rising* that portrayed racism against Mexican Americans. They were to write a letter to the person who was guilty of discrimination. See a student model of an Unsent Letter by Karrie Krouse in Figure 3.5. The letter is from the perspective of Esperanza, whose teacher did not select Isabel for "Queen of the May" in *Esperanza Rising*.

Poetry of the Protagonist's Unspoken Thoughts

This strategy asks students to role play the protagonist's concerns, inner thoughts, longings, musings, feelings, and opinions that reveal the inner workings of the character. Students should choose a passage in the novel and write a poem expressing the protagonist's unspoken thoughts. This activity requires students to fill in the gaps and interpret the character's thoughts and emotions. In one of my classes, Lauren Gura was inspired by the passage where Esperanza was soaking her hands in warm water and no longer recognized them as her own. "Cut and scarred, swollen and stiff, they looked like the hands of a very old man" (Ryan, 2000, p. 180). Lauren wrote her poem in both English and Spanish since certainly Esperanza would be speaking in Spanish. See Figure 3.6 for "Calloused" and "Calloso," sample Poetry of the Protagonist's Unspoken Thoughts.

Figure 3.5. Sample Unsent Letter to a Teacher. Student-written letter by Karrie Krouse.

Dear Teacher,

I am writing in regard to this year's "Queen of the May" competition. It is my understanding that the competition is based upon grades, but historically, no Mexican student has been awarded this honor. I am aware that Isabel currently holds the highest grades in her class, therefore entitling her to this award. Isabel returned home today very disappointed that she was not selected and that another girl had been chosen. I do not understand these unfair practices. What is the point of basing this award on marks if the rightful owner is not the recipient? If promised, hard work deserves to be rewarded, but one lesson this life continues to teach me is that sometimes we do not reap the benefits until later. Isabel's hard work will pay off down the road, even though she remains overlooked at the present. She, too, will reap her harvest.

Sincerely,
Esperanza Ortega

Figure 3.6. Sample Poetry of the Protagonist's Unspoken Thoughts.
Student-written poems by Lauren Gura.

Calloused	Calloso
My hands look like the skin of a pineapple;	Las manos se parecen a la piel de una piña;
calloused, rough, and cracked.	calloso, áspero, y agrietados.
After years of working in the fields	Después que años de trabajar en los campos
I long	yo mucho tiempo
for the soft skin of baby Rosa.	para la piel suave de bebé Rosa.
Slicing vegetable stalks,	Los tallos de la verdura que cortan,
picking fruit,	escogiendo fruta,
and tying grape vines—	y atar vides de uva—
my hands are like a machine.	las manos son una máquina.
They clean the house,	Ellos limpian la casa,
till the land and	hasta la tierra y
feed	alimentan
my family.	mi familia.
These emaciated, coarse fingers	Estos dedos demacrados y toscos
dig	cavan
deep into the earth—	profundo en la tierra—
becoming part of the nourished soil	llegando a ser la parte de la tierra alimentada
although they are not	Aunque ellos no sean
nourished	alimentados
themselves.	a sí mismo.
My hands look like the skin of a pineapple	Las manos se parecen a la piel de una piña

Debate: To Strike or Not to Strike

Divide the class into two groups. One group should look for textual evidence in favor of the migrant workers striking for better wages and living conditions, and the other group should find textual evidence against striking. After all the evidence has been collected from *Esperanza Rising*, each group delegates four classmates to represent them as a debate team. The teams stage a debate in which participants argue the consequences of striking or not striking. Figure 3.7 offers quotes from *Esperanza Rising* that students can use to formulate their debate: To Strike or Not to Strike.

ACTIVE LEARNING PROJECTS

Memory Shoe Box

The Memory Shoe Box is something that 20 years from now the reader may find in the character's house. Ask students to create a Memory Shoe

Figure 3.7. To Strike or Not to Strike. The quotes below are from *Esperanza Rising* (2000).

To Strike	Not to Strike
[Holding up a tiny kitten] "This is what we are! Small, meek animals. And this is how they treat us because we don't speak up. If we don't ask for what is rightfully ours, we well never get it." (132)	"Maybe all the cat wants to do is feed its family. Maybe it doesn't care what all the other cats are doing." (132)
"Were going to strike in two weeks. At the peak of the cotton. For higher wages and better housing!" (132)	"We don't pick cotton on this farm!" (132)
"Senor, does it not bother you that some of your compadres live better than others?" (132)	"That is a chance we cannot take. We just want to work. That's why we came here. Get out of our camp." (133)
"What does it matter? If we all stop working, if all the Mexicans are juntos, together . . . then maybe it will help us all!" (132–133)	"Our camp is a company camp and people who live here don't leave. . . . That is why we came to this country. To work. To take care of our families. To become citizens. We are lucky because our camp is better than most. There are many of us who don't want to get involved in the strike because we can't afford to lose our jobs, and we are accustomed to how things are in our little community." (134)
They get only seven cents a pound for picking cotton. They want ten cents a pound. It seems like such a small price to pay, but in the past, the growers said no. (134)	
"People are coming to the valley to look for work, especially from places like Oklahoma, where there is little work. Little rain, and little hope. If the Mexicans strike, the big farms will simply hire others." (134–135)	"There is talk of striking in the spring when it is time to pick. We are afraid there will be problems. If they refuse to work, they will lose their cabins in the migrant camps. And then where will they live? Or worse, they will all be sent back to Mexico." (171)
"We're going a mile or so up the road to the strikers' farm. We were tossed out of the migrant workers' camp and were told either to go back to work or leave. So we left. We aren't going to work under those disgusting conditions and for those pitiful wages." (192)	"Repatriation . . . La Migra—the immigration authorities—round up people who cause problems and check their papers. If they are not in order, or if they do not happen to have their papers with them, the immigration officials send them back to Mexico." (171)
"There are hundreds of us together at this farm, but thousands around the country and more people join our cause each day. You are new here, but in time, you'll understand what we're trying to change." (192)	"There is also some talk of harming Mexicans who continue to work." (171)
"Do you have food so that I can feed my family? We were thrown out of our camp because I was striking. My family has not eaten in two days. There are too many people coming into the valley who will work for pennies. Yesterday I worked all day and made less than fifty cents and I cannot buy food for one day with that. I was hoping that here, with others who have been through the same . . ." (194)	"My husband says we will not join them. We have too many mouths to feed. And he has told Marta she cannot stay with us. We can't risk being asked to leave the camp or losing our jobs because of our niece." (171–172)
"Everyone will starve if people work for less and less money." (104)	"If so many come and are willing to work for pennies, what will happen to us? But until then, with so many joining the strikes, I might be able to get a job at the railroad." (196)

Box for one of the characters in the book. Students should select at least five items to put in the box and then write up a rationale for why they chose to include them. They also should include a passage or a quote from the book to support the items they selected to put in the box. As a bonus, ask students to decorate the shoe box with representations of the Mexican culture. See Figure 3.8 for a teacher-created model of a Memory Shoe Box for Manny. This strategy was inspired by "Literature Response Guide for *Parrot in the Oven: Mi Vida* by Victor Martinez" on Angie Price's website: http://www.ac.wwu.edu/~bgoebel/response%guides/parrotintheoven.html.

Problem-Based Learning Scenario

Problem-based learning (PBL) is any learning environment in which the problem drives the learning. That is, before students learn some knowledge, they are given a problem. The problem is posed so that the students discover that they need to learn some new knowledge before they can solve

Figure 3.8. Memory Shoe Box for Manny. Teacher-created example by Jacqueline Glasgow; quotes from *Parrot in the Oven: Mi Vida* (Martinez, 1996).

Item for Memory Shoe Box	Quote from the Text
1. Baseball Glove	1. "Baseball had a grip on my fantasies then, and I couldn't shake it loose. There was an outfielder's glove in the window of Duran's Department Store that kept me dreaming downright dangerous outfield catches." (7)
2. Chili Pepper	2. "When we arrived at the chili field, the wind through the window was warm on our shirt sleeves." (9)
3. Bullet from His Father's Gun	3. "He found some bullets inside Mom's dresser drawer, knotted up in one of her old bras." (57)
4. Rifle	4. "He jerked the rifle up to show how high he'd had it up to with my mom and smacked the barrel against his forehead." (57)
5. Boxing Ticket	5. "The boxing tournament was announced in every home room in the school, and on flyers stapled in the hallways." (125)
6. Newspaper Article of Eddie's Purse Stealing	6. "She was stunned. She skidded her heel on the sleek asphalt and plopped down on her butt with a splashy thud. As she did, her purse dropped, and Eddie knelt down quickly to grab it, pushing her leg away." (209)

the problem. According to Fink (2003), "they [students] must learn to make a preliminary analysis, gather information or data, assess the relevance of the new information, propose a solution, and assess the quality of their tentative solution" (p. 21). A PBL scenario allows students to research a real-life problem or issue in depth, identify the different causes of the problem and work together to pose solutions. When students are able to articulate a plan or solution to their particular problem, they are able to write a letter to an editor, a congressperson, or a member of a committee or council already working on solutions to the same problem. Through this process they make real-world connections and take actions that validate their learning experience.

The key to a problem-based activity is an essential question that poses a current relevant issue to be resolved. These questions can be researched on the internet to further students' understanding of the topics as well as the world at large. The questions also encourage cooperative learning among students, teachers, and the community. Students' access to technological resources, ability to communicate via e-mail with professionals in the field, and opportunity to discuss their ideas on a class message board as they collect their data are integral to the PBL tasks described here.

For this unit, the problem relates to the education of Mexican migrant worker children. In Francisco Jimenez's *The Circuit: Stories from the Life of a Migrant Child* and its sequel, *Breaking Through*, the author describes his experiences of both working in the fields and attending school. School meant learning English by immersion because he knew no English. There was no support for Spanish-speaking students. He was made fun of by his classmates because of this and of course had difficulty making friends. Moving from camp to camp and school to school four or five times during the school year to follow the crops also mitigated against learning English and making friends.

As shown in *Escuela* (Weyer, 2002), a film documentary featuring Liliana, a teenager who grew up working in the fields, an entire system of educational support has emerged to facilitate the movement of migrant worker families across the western United States. But bureaucracy does little to shield Liliana and teens like her from the social and educational dislocations of the migrant economy, or the jarring contrasts between the middle-class culture of high school and the stark realities of migrant life. These experiences raise the following questions for class discussion:

- What is the best way to learn a foreign language?
- What is the school's responsibility for educating immigrant children?
- What is bilingual education, and why does it or doesn't it work?

- What is the best plan for educating migrant worker children?
- What can be done about the discrimination children face at school?

When students have had an opportunity for discussion and begun to form a viable solution to the problem, they prepare a position paper, letter to an appropriate authority, or PowerPoint presentation to share with the class. For a student model, see Figure 3.9, Position Paper on Innovative Plan for Educating Migrant Worker Children, created by Karrie Krouse.

Figure 3.9. Sample Position Paper. This student-created Position Paper by Karrie Krouse on an Innovative Plan for Educating Migrant Worker Children.

Children of Mexican Migrants Reap Rich Harvest:
An Education in Plant City, Florida
Teachers move with pupils; only the buildings change

Run by the Sisters of Mercy of the Americas, San Jose School is as mobile as the 50 families that it serves. When fall planting beckons migrant workers to the strawberry and vegetable fields of Florida, San Jose teachers pack up and follow—sometimes breaking camp in Fremont, Ohio, on a Friday and opening in Plant City, Florida, the following Monday morning. The school focuses on the youngest migrant students and their parents, making them partners with the school. It also helps families with health and social services needs. Two other criteria: Families must live within a 20-mile or so school bus ride from the campus, and they must want a Catholic education. The school, launched in 1994, is funded entirely by contributions and grants. Some staff members are nuns. St. Clement Church in Plant City and St. Joseph's in Ohio provide classrooms. The program is the only one of its kind in Florida and possibly the United States, state and federal education officials say.

"It's not the moving. It's not the poverty. It's not the language challenge. It's not the cultural difference," said school founder Sister Gaye Lynn Moorhead, 51, of Rochester, NY. "It is the lack of confidence. It is always being the 'new kid on the block,' always being the outsiders, that hurts."

For the students, only the buildings change. The teachers, classmates, even the school bus they ride stay the same. So do the uniforms, discipline, and high standards. That way, children are never strangers in someone else's school, never behind the other kids, never held up at the starting line. As a result, experts say, while their families toil in the fields, children are reaping a priceless harvest of their own—educational success.

"What San Jose provides is the necessary stability and continuity, which is such a challenge for highly mobile students," said Ann Cranston-Gingras, a professor of special education and migrant-education expert at the University of South Florida. San Jose's students haven't fallen prey to the perils that plague children who move around a lot, Cranston-Gingras said. Instead, those who have graduated on to public schools are doing just as well as their nonmigrant peers.

For more information, go to: *http://www.freep.com/news/nw/mobile21_20000121.htm*

Multigenre Research Project

The focus of the Multigenre Research Project in this section is Cesar Chavez's Legacy: The United Farm Workers Union. Cesar Chavez was the product of a Depression-era migrant childhood who experienced some of the worst discrimination of poor minorities. When he began to organize the farmworkers in the 1960s, Mexican migrant workers had very few civil liberties. They needed adequate housing, pure drinking water, access to toilets, medical benefits, and at least minimum wage to support their families. Chavez succeeded in influencing California's Agricultural Labor Relations Act in 1975, which helped pave the way to dignity for thousands of ethnic-minority workers. The dependence of California agribusiness on Mexican workers is no small matter, considering the staggering array of produce they harvest. According to Ferriss and Sandoval (1997), "California produces almost all the country's artichokes, avocados, apricots, olives, nectarines, prunes, and processed tomatoes; and most of its fresh fruits and vegetables, including broccoli, lettuce, grapes, lemons, strawberries, melons, and peaches" (p. 6). Yet, many workers tack together lean-tos to sleep in at night after a full day of picking. While conditions are much better since Chavez led the revolution, migrant workers still have to fight for health benefits, unemployment insurance, and worker's compensation.

After reading Gary Soto's *Jessie de la Cruz: A Profile of a United Farm Worker*, students created Multigenre Research Projects to extend the meaning of the novel and to learn more about the struggles and redemption of Mexican migrant workers and the farmworkers' movement. As additional nonfiction resources, students should refer to *The Fight in the Fields: Cesar Chavez and the Farmworkers Movement* (Ferris & Sandoval, 1997) and *The Words of Cesar Chavez* (Jensen & Hammerback, 2002); both of these works appear in the Annotated Bibliography at the end of this chapter.

CREATIVE AND PERSONAL/ANALYTICAL WRITING

Los Corridos—Mexican Folk Ballad

The *corrido* is a type of Mexican folk ballad that has been popular in and historically relevant to Mexico since the 1800s. Over time it has become known as *musica de la frontera* (border music) because it is especially popular along both sides of the U.S.–Mexican border. *Los corridos* are stories told in poetic form and sung to simple, basic music, much like English ballads. They are musical narratives about migrant workers and their history. They represent the values, turmoils, and triumphs of various Mexican migrant worker communities. Common themes of corridos range from glorification of folk heroes and revolutionaries, to immigration and natural disasters. Due to a lack of pen and paper, the Mexican migrant workers relied on this oral tradition to tell their stories. Although traditional corridos were always in Spanish, in recent years some have appeared in English as well, or have mixed the two languages. There is some variation in the poetic form, but most corridos have the following structure:

- 36 lines (6 stanzas of 6 lines or 9 stanzas of 4 lines each)
- 7–10 syllables per line (sometimes the lines are repeated)
- Rhyme scheme that varies but most commonly uses an a-b-c-b-d-b form in a six-line stanza or a-b-c-b in a four-line stanza (sometimes couplets are used: a-a-b-b)
- By tradition, the first stanza provides a setting for the story by either giving a specific date or naming a place

For this activity, students will explore historical and cultural matters pertaining to the Mexican migrant worker, and express their findings by writing a corrido. For a student-written model by Anne Doyle, see "From Riches to Rags to an American Dream" in Figure 3.10.

Poetry for a Social Issue

Ask students to select a social issue represented in their novels and write a poem that offers some hope for the situation. While reading *The Circuit: Stories from the Life of a Migrant Child* by Francisco Jimenez, one of my students, Nora Noble, was inspired by the main character's (Francisco) struggle to attend school when he knows very little English. Francisco is often made fun of by classmates because of his poor English and has difficulty making friends. Just when Francisco begins to make friends, his family moves again to another camp. Moving from school to school is hard because he can never finish out the year with his classmates. Many times, Francisco comes close to making a real friend and then has to leave, without being able to explain to his friend why. What my student Nora noticed when reading *The Circuit: Stories from the Life of a Migrant Child* was the high spirits of the children despite the hardship they faced as a result of changing schools often. Nora wrote a poem called "I Made a Friend Today" to explore this issue from Francisco's perspective. Nora's poem in Figure 3.11 is an example of a Poem for a Social Issue in the way it shows sensitivity for the minority status of the Mexican migrant students.

Figure 3.10. Sample Corrido. Student-created example by Anne Doyle.

From Riches to Rags to an American Dream

In the eve of my papa's death
I asked myself, what more?
What will happen to me and Mama?
We could not live here anymore

We had to escape from Tio Luis' wrath
Mama and I had nothing anymore
Except the doll Papa bought for me
We could not live here anymore

We boarded a train
And had to sit with the poor
My regal life a thing of the past
I never did this before

We entered America, torn and scared
With papers as fake as folklore
And bellies as empty as dried wells
I never felt this way before

I entered a life different from my own
My heart was still broken and sore
And I felt so alone
I never felt like this before

Can't change diapers or make them clean
Can't sweep floor
Can't cook, can't even bath myself
I didn't have to do this before

The work is hard, but I can't complain
My Mama works till she is sore
And my hardest task is to watch the babes
I never did this before

My Mama is sick with Valley Fever
And it is ripping me to the core
Because I cannot bear to lose her too
I didn't have to do this before

The Lord sent changes to my life
But gave me something more
He gave me the chance to see real freedom
A thought I never considered before

Figure 3.11. Sample Poem for a Social Issue. Student-composed poem by Nora Noble.

I Made a Friend Today
(told from the perspective of Francisco from *The Circuit: Stories from the Life of a Migrant Child* [Jimenez, 1997])

I am happy, light, a float in the sky
I made a friend today.
I will skip to work and the time will fly by
I made a friend.
The things we will do, I can hardly describe,
I can't describe it—I feel so alive,
All because today I made a friend.
I won't think about tomorrow,
It might bring me down.
Today, things are different and
I have no reason to frown.
Just when I thought I might never again . . .
I made a friend.
You told me it's time again,
but I made a friend!
And of course I knew it—
I knew I'd have to go through it.
Just like every time before,
I just can't pretend I hadn't hoped for more.
A friend to share secrets,
we'd walk to school,
we'd ride bikes in the summer,
and swim to keep cool.
But now we're on our way again,
and reality has hit.
For a while, I thought this friendship
would last . . .
Just a little bit.

Double Journal Entry

The purpose of the Double Journal Entry in this section is to explore gang life in *Parrot in the Oven: Mi Vida*. According to Vacca and Vacca (1999), a Double Journal Entry is a versatile adaptation of the response journal. It allows students to record dual entries that are conceptually related. In doing so, students juxtapose their thoughts and feelings in reaction to the prompts provided by the teacher or passages students select for a particular entry. For this activity, ask students to locate significant passages as they read

Parrot in the Oven: Mi Vida and mark them with sticky notes. Later, ask students to divide sheets of notebook paper in half lengthwise. In the lefthand column of the journal, prompt students to copy the significant quotes or passages from the text and document them with the page number. In the righthand column, the students record their reactions, interpretations, and responses to the text segments they have selected. For a student model of this activity by Michael Vagas, see the Double Journal Entry in response to Manny's gang initiation in Figure 3.12.

When students have completed ten Double Journal Entries, ask them to select the most important quote of the book and write a reflective paper or reflective journal entry on it. This should be a quote that they feel is fundamental to the protagonist's response to bullying. When asked to write a creative piece about the most significant passage in *Parrot in the Oven: Mia Vida*, Michael Vagas wrote a poem that challenges the Manny's of the world to reconsider their choices. For Michael's student model, see Figure 3.13, "Whatcha Gonna Do?"

Copy Change Song Lyrics

The purpose of Copy Change Song Lyrics in this section is to capture the plight of the Mexican migrant worker. Copy Change poetry is a way to

Figure 3.12. Sample Double Journal Entry. The student-written response on the right was written by Michael Vagas.

Passage	*Reaction/Interpretation*
Manny's beating by gang members: "I could smell the acidy stink of the dirt, but strangely enough, there was no fear. Nor could I feel the blows, which felt like instead of me, they were hitting a slab of meat on a table. In my mind I kept saying, Okay, you bastards, go ahead. Go ahead! See where it gets you!" (p. 194)	Coming from Youngstown, Ohio, I unfortunately have very close, personal experiences with gangs. For instance, a best friend of mine was shot and murdered approximately two years ago. After the two young adults confessed to attempting to rob and ultimately murdering my friend, it was discovered that it was most likely related to gang initiation. My friend's life has been taken away and the two young men who killed him have consequently lost their futures as well. Therefore, I think it is extremely important for young adults to fully realize the consequences of being involved in gang activity. Manny may find acceptance and respect from his peers, but he is likely find out that gang activities are dangerous, violent, and illegal.

Figure 3.13. Whatcha Gonna Do? Poem by student Michael Vagas.

Whatcha gonna do?
Goona join, gonna join?
Where ya gonna go? Huh?

Who cares about you boy?
Where you get the love?
Not at home, not at school.

We got the love, we got the drugs.
We do the things that make you feel,
High as a hero, rollin' in the streets.
This is your domain now.

They don't care, they ain't gonna be there,
Who's your family now, boy?
Get with us, you'll be protected,
Stay at home, you'll be neglected.

Whatcha gonna do?
Goona join, gonna join?
Where ya gonna go? Huh?

Say you've got friends, you don't need us.
Work in the fields,
Yeah, you'll be a success.

Go to school, play by the rules.
Or grab a gun and have some fun.
Shoot your way to what you need.
Women, money, fame, and weed.

Education? What's the point?
How you gonna work when you smokin' a joint?

Whatcha gonna do?
Goona join, gonna join?
Where ya gonna go? Huh?

Life. That's what I respect.
A successful job is what I expect.
Family, friends, kids, education.
Jail or hell ain't no vacation.

use the structure of other song writers or poets to create new meanings, new poems for ourselves. In Copy Change poetry, students use the structure of a given song or poem and then substitute new words in place of the existing ones. Ask students to select either a song or a poem that will serve as the form or structure for their Copy Change poetry. Then ask them to use that structure and change the words to create a new poem about a Mexican migrant worker from their reading. A student in my class, Lauren Gura, started with Billy Joel's "We Didn't Start the Fire" and created her own song to express the plight of the Mexican migrant workers in Gary Soto's *Jessie de la Cruz: A Profile of a United Farm Worker*. For Lauren's student model of a Copy Change poem, see Figure 3.14, "We Didn't Start the Picket."

EPILOGUE: A CINCO DE MAYO CELEBRATION

The holiday Cinco de Mayo, The 5th of May, commemorates the victory of the Mexicans over the French army at the Battle of Puebla in 1862. It is primarily a regional holiday celebrated in the Mexican state capital

Figure 3.14. Sample Copy Change Poem. Student-composed poem by Lauren Gura (to the tune of Billy Joel's "We Didn't Start the Fire").

We Didn't Start the Picket

César Chávez, pesticides, employers, suicides,
California, preparation, down in Mexico,
"Barbara Allen," the minstrel stage, Tin Pan Alley, consistent wage,
Grapes of Wrath, immigration, like our value's low,

Employment, Gallo wine, mild climate, lost my mind
Justice, early country, work my fingers to the bone,
Transportation, citrus, baby's got a virus,
Exploitation, discrimination, trouble on the farm,

CHORUS
We didn't start the picket
It was always pending,
Since the team's been suffering.
We didn't start the picket
Well we didn't end it,
But we all should earn it.

Agriculture, child labor, Great Plains, low wage,
Education, disappointment, holes in my socks,
More land, organize, cultivation, harvest,
Conservation, landholders, why are we all mocked?

Dust bowl, "Okies," health care wants to lose me,
Irrigation, Mexican, education, feels like sand,
Lemons, oranges, economic, human rights,
Quality, poverty, farming got a bad name,

CHORUS

city of Puebla and throughout the state of Puebla, but also is celebrated in other parts of the country and in U.S. cities with a significant Mexican population. In honor of this holiday and in celebration of this Mexican Migrant Worker Unit, a Cinco de Mayo party is in order. Students could prepare Mexican food, music, and piñatas as a backdrop for presenting their Multigenre Research Project or displaying their projects at an open house to include other students, teachers, administrators, and parents. This is a great opportunity to celebrate excellent writing and art, while enjoying festivities associated with Mexican history and culture.

ANNOTATED BIBLIOGRAPHY

Ferriss, S., & Sandoval, R. (1997). *The fight in the fields: Cesar Chavez and the farmworkers movement*. New York: Harcourt Brace.
During the Depression, the Chavez family lost their farm in Arizona and moved to California to become migrant workers. As they became victims of racisim, poor through exploitation of their labors, Cesar led a nonviolent revolution by establishing the United Farm Workers Union.

Jensen, R. J., & Hammerback, J. C. (Eds.). (2002). *The words of Cesar Chavez*. College Station: Texas A & M University Press.
Cesar, outraged by the exploitation, racism, and brutality that migrant farmworkers were forced to endure, established the United Farm Workers Union, called "La Cause" by his supporters. His group exposed the injustices through successful grape and lettuce boycotts, which resulted in the first collective bargaining agreements for migrant workers.

Jimenez, F. (1997). *The circuit: Stories from the life of a migrant child*. Albuquerque: University of New Mexico.
Depicts a Mexican family taking the long trip north, then moving from farm to farm searching for the next harvesting job. The child protagonist struggles to be loyal to his family, while longing to pursue an education and a more stable life.

Jimenez, F. (2002). *Breaking through*. Boston: Houghton Mifflin.
With his family, 14-year-old Francisco is caught by immigration officers and forced to leave his California home. Explores prejudice alongside the universal coming of age theme.

Soto, G. (1999). *Buried onions*. New York: Harper Trophy.
Eddie is a Mexican immigrant with a vision to succeed, despite his growing up in a gang-infested neighborhood in Fresno, California.

Steinbeck, J. (1993). *Of mice and men*. New York: Penguin.
The popular classic of friends who work as farm laborers, drifting from job to job in California and longing for a better life. Lennie is mentally disabled

and relies on George for help, while George relies on Lennie for companionship. While not about Mexican migrant farmers per se, the book depicts similar aspects of hard work, discrimination, and the challenge of getting ahead.

REFERENCES

Chavez, C., Jensen, R. J., & Hammerback, J. C. (Eds.). (2002). *The words of Cesar Chavez*. College Station, TX: Texas A & M University Press.

Ferriss, S., & Sandoval, R. (1997). *The fight in the fields: Cesar Chavez and the farmworkers movement*. New York: Harcourt Brace.

Fink, L. D. (2003). *Creating significant learning experiences*. San Francisco: Jossey-Bass.

Martinez, V. (1996). *Parrot in the oven: Mi vida*. New York: Harper Trophy.

Ryan, P. M. (2000). *Esperanza rising*. New York: Scholastic.

Soto, G. (1999). *Buried onions*. New York: Harper Trophy.

Soto, G. (2002). *Jessie de la Cruz: A profile of a united farm worker*. New York: Persea Books.

Vacca, R. T., & Vacca, J. A. (1999). *Content area reading: Literacy and learning across the curriculum* (6th ed.). New York: Longman.

Weyer, H. (Producer/Director). (2002). *Escuela* [Documentary video]. New York: Women Make Movies.

Bearing Witness to the Horror of the Holocaust (1939–1945): Children Who Suffered and Survived

Jacqueline N. Glasgow

I swore never to be silent whenever and wherever human beings endure suffering and humiliation. We must always take sides. Neutrality helps the oppressor, never the victim. Silence encourages the tormentor, never the tormented.

—Elie Wiesel (1986, p. 2)

This unit spotlights incredible stories produced by either personal testimony or fiction based on historical records that render the Holocaust through the eyes of children. Elie Wiesel's memoir *Night* (1960) bears witness to the horrors of life in a concentration camp, including the author's seeing his mother and younger sister sent to the gas chambers and his father's death en route to Buchenwald. Lois Lowry's *Number the Stars* (1989) bears witness to the Danish Resistance Movement and a family's effort to escape when the Germans began arresting and deporting Danish Jews. While reading *Night* and *Number the Stars*, students will grapple with essential questions related to human cruelty, suffering, and sacrifice.

Through the active learning strategies presented in this chapter, students will develop a deeper respect for human decency and a deeper commitment to rejecting indifference to human suffering. Hopefully, they also will be inspired by the spiritual resistance evidenced in the stories of those who actually experienced the Holocaust. Figure 4.1 offers a summary of the active learning strategies in this chapter.

Figure 4.1. Active Learning Strategies in Chapter 4.

Featured Young Adult Novels	Thoughtfulness and Reflection	Simulation and Role Play	Creative Writing	Active Learning Projects
Night	• T-Chart Analyzing Indifference		• Found Poem Poster	• Mapping Journeys: Geographical Relational Spiritual
Number the Stars		• Teacher/ Narrator Speech • Rabbi Speech • Game Board		• Memorial Scrapbook
General, Applicable to Either Novel			• Keeping Holocaust Memories Alive: Responses to Film, Music, Photos, and Possessions	• Public Awareness Poster • Empty Bowls Luncheon • Kinderstransport Association

HISTORICAL CONTEXT

As early as 1919, Hitler wrote that he advocated the "anti-Semitism of reason." His goal was the removal of Jews altogether from German society. The "Jewish Question" remained central to Nazi philosophy throughout the 1920s and 1930s. Hitler compared the Jew to a tuberculosis bacillus that had to be destroyed or that would destroy society. Hitler was obsessed with the Jews, who in his view were the prime destructive influence on the political, cultural, and economic fortunes of Germany. In the view of the Nazi ideologues, the removal of the Jews would allow Germany to realize her full potential and destiny. The program of mass murder of men, women, and children was begun in July and August 1941. The killing squads, roving behind the frontlines of the war, began the mass shootings of Jews in the captured territories and led to the establishment of death camps in which millions of Jews were murdered as part of the "Final Solution."

This sets the context for the literature chosen for this chapter. In Elie Wiesel's memoir, *Night*, he details the horrific experiences he suffered in the work and extermination camps of Buna, Auschwitz, and Buchenwald. Of the 7,000 prisoners found alive when Auschwitz was liberated in 1945, only 600 were under 18 years old. There are therefore precious few firsthand accounts of child survivors of the death camps, and Elie Wiesel's autobiography continues to be the Holocaust book most widely read by high school students.

Hitler intended to arrest all of Denmark's Jews and have them transported to the Theresienstadt concentration camp near Prague. The mass arrest and transport were to take place on October 1, 1943, but Danish government officials were warned of the plan by G. F. Duckwitz, a German maritime shipping expert attached to the German embassy in Copenhagen. Danes quickly set about identifying their Jewish compatriots, hiding them from the Gestapo, and ultimately helping them escape to Sweden. This is the setting for Lois Lowry's award-winning story, *Number the Stars*, which continues to be one of the Holocaust books most widely read by middle school students. Lowry's characters tell the story of dangers and the courage it took to participate in the Danish Resistance.

What is the secret of those who suffered and survived at the hands of such an evil mentality that would have exterminated an entire culture? These stories are filled with horror and unspeakable tragedy, but they are also ones of courage, sacrifice, friendship, and hope that demonstrate the indomitable spirits of these young children who survived the death camps or took part in the Danish Resistance Movement. According to Wiesel,

> Survivors' testimonies are special. They stem from a powerful desire to bear witness. What they say about what was done to Jews by their enemies cannot be said by anyone else. Their personal experience must become part of Holocaust literature. (Lobel, 1998, back cover)

FEATURED YOUNG ADULT NOVELS

Night

Through his book, *Night*, Elie Wiesel (1960) has given us an eyewitness account of the tragic events that occurred in the death camps as he saw his mother and younger sister sent to the gas chambers, and later his father's death while in transport to Buchenwald. He also has given us an analysis of the evil powers that lay behind these unimaginable events in order to expose their motives and question what measures can be taken to prevent a recurrence. Against the backdrop of terror, repression, and racial discrimination that exist in the world, the Nobel Committee awarded Wiesel—a messenger who not only survived, but who came with a message of brotherhood and atonement—the Peace Prize in 1986. In the Presentation Speech, Egil Aarvik, Chairman of the Norwegian Nobel Committee, remarked about Wiesel:

> His aim is to awaken our conscience. Our indifference to evil makes us partners in the crime. That is the reason for his attack on indifference and his insistence on measures aimed at preventing a new holocaust. What are we going to do to prevent it from happening again? Do not forget, do not sink into a new blind indifference, but involve yourselves in truth and justice, in human dignity, freedom and atonement. That is this Peace Prize laureate's message to us. (1986, p. 3)

The purpose of reading Holocaust literature is to awaken students' consciences to the horrors of genocide that took place during the Holocaust. By reading Wiesel's memoir, students will become more aware of this horrific part of World War II.

Number the Stars

Denmark surrendered to Germany in 1940 and overnight the soldiers moved in. The soldiers controlled the newspapers, the transportation systems, the government, schools, and hospitals. In Lois Lowry's *Number the Stars* (1989), the protagonists, Annemarie Johansen and Ellen Rosen, were classmates and best friends living in Nazi-occupied Copenhagen. When the Germans began arresting and deporting Danish Jews, Ellen and her family were threatened. As the danger increased, Annemarie joined her parents and their friends in protecting Ellen's family. In an unforeseen turn of events, the success of the Rosens's escape depended on Annemarie's personal bravery. Despite the unnerving encounter with four Nazi soldiers and their two large dogs, she succeeded in accomplishing her mission. The Rosens escaped safely to Sweden and Annemarie's family continued to support the Danish Resistance.

THOUGHTFULNESS AND REFLECTION

Exploring Indifference

Consider the following quote by Elie Wiesel:

> The opposite of love is not hate, it's indifference.
> The opposite of art is not ugliness, it's indifference.
> The opposite of faith is not heresy, it's indifference.

> And the opposite of life is not death, it's indifference.
> (quoted in Lewis, 2004, p. 1)

What did Wiesel mean by these statements? Such a discussion opens the door for students' exploration of indifference. In order to think of ways to take action against indifference, students first need to explore and understand the concept. Students may benefit from reading and discussing Elie Wiesel's speech, "The Perils of Indifference," given at the White House on April 12, 1999.

In addition, students will benefit by viewing video clips from Ostow's *America and the Holocaust: Deceit and Indifference* (1994). This video paints a troubling picture of the United States during a period beset by anti-Semitism and a government that not only delayed action, but suppressed information and blocked efforts that could have resulted in the rescue of hundreds of thousands of people.

If students have read *Number the Stars*, they are aware of the grave dangers of participating in the Resistance. Peter Neilsen was captured and executed by the Nazis for his Resistance activities. Annemarie's sister Lise, engaged to be married to Peter, was run down by a German military car due to her participation in the Resistance. Annemarie herself risked her life taking the basket to Uncle Henri's boat. Think of the consequences that indifference would have made for the Danish Jews.

Making a T-Chart

After providing a context for the concept of indifference, divide students into small groups and ask them to brainstorm what indifference "sounds like" and "looks like." Students may use dictionaries, thesauruses, and online resources. Then ask students to create a T-Chart Poster with their ideas and examples of modern-day situations such as Kosovo, Rwanda, Darfur, Eritrea, and Ethiopia. See Figure 4.2 for a sample T-Chart for "Indifference" based on Wiesel's *Night* and other famous quotations.

SIMULATION AND ROLE PLAY

This simulation is designed to help students understand the gravity of the decisions Jewish family members made when they heard the Nazi deportation plan. The teacher or student narrator begins the simulation by reading a script, followed by a student volunteer to read the Rabbi's part. Divide the rest of the students into groups of five and ask them to assume one of the following roles in a family: Father (decision maker), Mother (care giver), Son

Figure 4.2. T-Chart for "Indifference." Teacher-created example by Jacqueline Glasgow.

"Indifference" Sounds Like	"Indifference" Looks Like
1. People turned deaf ears and refused to listen: "People refused not only to believe his (Moshe's) stories, but even to listen to them." (Wiesel, *Night*, 1960, p. 4)	1. People live in fear and see persecution against the Jews: "The Jews in Budapest are living in an atmosphere of fear and terror. There are anti-Semitic incidents every day, in the streets, in the trains. The Fascists are attacking Jewish shops and synagogues. The situation is getting very serious." (*Night*, p. 7)
2. Moshe wanted his story and warning to be heard: "I wanted to come back and to warn you. And see how it is, no one will listen." (*Night*, p. 5)	2. People refuse to see the truth and live in denial: "The Germans won't get as far as this. They'll stay in Budapest. There are strategic and political reasons. . . ." (*Night*, p. 7)
3. People heard rumors which they chose to believe: "The Russian army's making gigantic strides forward . . . Hitler won't be able to do us any harm, even if he wants to." (*Night*, p. 6)	3. People see evil and do nothing to prevent it: "All that is necessary for evil to succeed is that good men do nothing." Edmund Burke
4. People gossiped about their incredulous idea: "Was he going to wipe out a whole people? Could he exterminate a population scattered throughout so many countries? So many millions! What methods would he use? And in the middle of the twentieth century!" (*Night*, p. 6)	4. People watch silently and do nothing until it is too late: "First they came for the Jews. I was silent. I was not a Jew. Then they came for the Communists. I was silent. I was not a Communist. Then they came for the trade unionists. I was silent. I was not a trade unionist. Then they came for me. There was no one left to speak for me." Martin Niemoller
5. People chose indifference over listening and believing what they heard: " Indifference is the essence of inhumanity." George Bernard Shaw	

(age 16, somewhat independent), Daughter (age 8, remains silent), Daughter (11-month-old whose crying may give them away). After the Rabbi's speech, provide each family group with a game board that has different choices for students to discuss and make. Conclude by debriefing students using the follow-up questions. This simulation was a collaborative project by students Ashley Feyedelem, Katie Hall, Carrie Verba, and Amy Wilder. The Teacher/Narrator and Rabbi speeches can be read by the teacher or student volunteers to help set up the game board that follows.

Teacher/Narrator Speech

Today you are all Jewish people living in the midst of Nazi rule in Copenhagen, Denmark. Sitting here in the synagogue for weekly worship, you notice that the mood is different than usual. The rabbi and other church officials seem on edge. Although they are outside, you can hear the Nazis' dogs barking as though they are snapping at your heels. [Add sound effects if desired.] The presence of the Nazis looms over your head like a winter fog that simply will not lift.

Rabbi Speech

As you all know, we have been living in some hard times with the Nazis controlling our every move. And despite our prayers that things would get better, I am afraid that they are only getting worse. I have heard from several members of the resistance that the Nazis are about to begin a plan to relocate all Jews. I fear that this war is about to get violent. Each member of this synagogue needs to decide what is best for their own family. The resistance would like each of you to know that they strongly suggest that you all flee this town and seek residence elsewhere. It is no longer safe to meet for worship services. With this mind, Godspeed, my prayers are with each of you.

Game Board: What Will You Do to Resist Deportation?

Provide each family group with a game board that has different choices on it. Each choice will lead to another until the group is left with the family's destiny. See Figure 4.3 for Game Board: What Would You Do to Resist Deportation? Be sure to cover the consequences with paper flaps so that students can't read them before making their choices. Debrief the students' choices by asking each group to respond to the following questions:

1. What happened to your family?
2. Would you stand by your choices or change them?
3. What factors contributed to your decision making?

CREATIVE WRITING

Keeping Holocaust Memories Alive Through Creative Response

It has been said that people of cultures who forget the lessons of history are doomed to repeat it. Elie Wiesel reminds us that we cannot allow

Figure 4.3. Game Board: What Would You Do to Resist Deportation? This game board was created by the following students in a teaching methods class: Ashley Feyedelem, Katie Hall, Carrie Verba, and Amy Wilder.

WHAT WOULD YOU DO TO RESIST DEPORTATION?

Make Your First Choice: Either "Run," "Hide," or "Stay"

(Cover the consequences for each choice with paper flaps that students can lift to read after they make a choice)

Run	Hide	Stay
After running to a relative's house who lives in a safer area, you still feel threatened, would you . . . ?	After gathering supplies for your family, you hide in an annex with four other Jewish families. You hear Nazis say they will be coming back tomorrow to search the building. Would you . . . ?	Your disbelief will cost your family dearly. During one of the massacres, the women and children are shot dead. You are the only one left. Would you . . . ?

Choose to "Keep Running" or "Wait"

Choose to "Wait" or "Run"

Choose to "Run" or "Wait"

Keep Running	Wait	Wait	Run	Run	Wait
Your family has the option to hide in an annex by the shore or risk everything by being transported to Sweden via boat. You know that the Nazis will be present in both situations. Would you . . . ?	Eventually your family is forced from your relative's house. While back in the ghetto, the women in your family are issued a passport by the Japanese government. The men are taken to a factory to work. After years without contact, you find out that your wife died of disease, but you are reunited with both of your daughters. Would you . . . ?	After being helped by the resistance, your family has the choice of trying to swim to freedom or living secretly in the basement of a non-Jewish family. Would you . . . ?	The Nazis unfortunately found the false door and take no mercy on those inside. Your whole family is killed. You have no more choices.	During the chaos, you flee the ghetto and run to the next town. It is left in shambles. You have no way to survive and eventually starve to death.	You are sent to the death camp where you are treated in the worst way, but despite all the horror, you survive.

Choose to "Go on Boat" or "Go to Annex"

Choose to "Swim" or "Hide"

Go on Boat	Go to Annex	Swim	Hide		
It is a long, cold ride. All of your family survives except the baby, who was too small and weak to make the trip.	While you are going out to get food for your family, you are caught. You refuse to give up your family and you are shot. The rest of your family waits safely in the annex until the war is over.	While trying to swim to safety, everyone in your family drowns because the swim is too far and too much for them to bear.	Fortunately, the Nazis are unsuspecting of the family you are staying with and never thoroughly inspect their house. Your entire family survives.		

84

ourselves to forget the fate of those who died. If we do forget, they die doubly, and we become responsible for making their lives—and their deaths—meaningless. "We cannot allow ourselves to be deluded into believing that the unthinkable will not happen. For it has happened once before. History has warned us" (Aarvik, 1986).

Response to Film. To encourage students to contribute to keeping Holocaust memories alive in the minds of people everywhere, first show a video clip from Spielberg's *Survivors of the Holocaust* (1996). This video chronicles the events of the Holocaust as witnessed by those who survived. As survivors relive their stories on camera, many for the first time, those who watch cannot come away without being deeply affected. Creative writing is a therapeutic outlet for strong emotions such as those evoked by Holocaust literature, especially Wiesel's *Night*. Think of ways to publish the students' work so as to include a larger audience beyond the classroom. Invite students to submit pieces for the U.S. Holocaust Memorial Museum May Family National Art and Writing Contest (*For Students*, n.d.) or other Holocaust-related art and writing contests. Invite college students to compete in an ethics essay contest for $10,000 in prizes and the opportunity to meet Elie Wiesel. More details can be found at the Elie Wiesel Foundation for Humanity (2005) website (http://www.eliewieselfoundation.org).

Response to Music. In order to keep Holocaust memories alive, students combined music and creative writing with reading Holocaust literature as part of a Young Adult Literature or a methods course, Teaching Literature. While students were writing, they were listening to the theme song from *Schindler's List* (1993) written by John Williams, with Itzhak Perlman playing violin. This haunting melody inspired their writing. In discussing his poem (see Figure 4.4), student Adam Vorobok says, "There is a binary problem: We must never forget what happened lest we repeat it in the future. It is a horrendous reality that is now over and done with and forgetting makes it easier to survive." He presented both sides: stanzas four and five directly dealing with always remembering, and stanza two with trying to forget.

Response to Photos and Possessions. For this creative writing activity, students selected a photograph from the U.S. Holocaust Memorial Museum website (*Photo Archives*, http://www.ushm.org/research/collections) and then wrote a poem. A student, Shannon Wensyel, chose the photo captioned "A British soldier clearing corpses at Bergen-Belsen." In her poem, "Cradle," Shannon attempted to capture the humanity of the corpses. She tried to return their identities, which were lost through torture and starvation that

Figure 4.4. Remembering the Holocaust Through Poetry. Student-written poem by Adam Vorobok.

Remembering the Holocaust

I wish I had 6 million fingers to count off
the frozen bodies buried beneath stiff bodies
buried beneath bodies still warm. My
grandmother is somewhere under that dirt,
a testament to the Nazis' efficiency. My grandfather
became smoke. So did his brother. The two of them
made it rain down on Auschwitz giving the other Jews
a chance to collect a few drops of water on their
sandpaper tongues.

My heart started this morning in the shower.
I thought poison gas was going to come out
and strangle my last living scream. I rubbed
my arm raw until the very skin broke
and bubbles of blood mixed with soap residue
on the bottom of the tub.
That blasted number remained.

I wish I had 6 million toes to give out to all those
who lost them while marching through the winter storms.
I remember telling my best friend a story in Yiddish
so the Nazi wouldn't understand. I told them
God was waiting for us at the camps and He was going
to invite us to a large dinner. There would be so much food
we would never even want to taste it.
Death greeted us at the door wearing a red armband.

My bookcase is full of titles—*The Pianist, Schindler's List,*
We Are Witnesses, Life Is Beautiful. I couldn't forget if I tried.
But the kid down the street has no idea.
I wish I had 6 million mouths that never stopped telling how it was.

---

rendered their bodies unrecognizable and through their inhumane burial in a mass grave. See Figure 4.5 for a sample poem inspired by a photograph.

Along with responding to a photograph, students were asked to consider what object or possession meant the most to them. When the Jews were deported, they were told they could take only what they could carry. Students were asked, What item would you choose to take that was your most important possession? Then they were asked to write a story about what happened when they were deported with this object. One of my stu-

Figure 4.5. Poem Inspired by a Photograph. This student-written poem by Shannon Wensyel was inspired by a photo* captioned "A British soldier clearing corpses at Bergen-Belsen."

Cradle

The pile of them there,
stacked not neatly, not
filed in rows, not
placed but thrown—dropped
perhaps, to lay as they fell—
like a purse full of trinkets, of do-dads
and whatsits, spilled out
on the counter for easy disposal.

They seem to hold one another.
Benjamin, the man that lived
across from the bakery, reaches
out to grandfather with his
black-licorice fingers, tickles
Papa's torso—skin stretched translucent
over smiling ribs. Aunt Millie's arm
bends, inverted,
to nurse the bludgeoned cheek of
a stranger. The back of a fifteen-year-old
girl arches gracefully over the blackened rubble of
flesh beneath her. Her lips spread slightly, in a whisper. (She
may have been an elegant dancer.)

The pile lives—moves as one
skeleton, uncoordinated
in an off-tempo ballet—as it is lifted
from its bed of dirt and gravel.
The chill metal of the plow cradles them, scoops them
in its mechanical embrace,
rocks them to sleep.

---

*Photo available online at *http://muse.jhu.edu/journals/yale_journal_of_criticism/v014/14.1hirsch_
fig05.html*

dents, Paul Vogelman, chose the violin as his treasured possession. Figure 4.6 includes an excerpt from Paul's short story, "Long Journey."

Found Poem Poster

While there are still people in the world who deny the Holocaust experience, the rest of us celebrated in April 2005 the 60th anniversary of

Figure 4.6. Sample Response to Most Important Possession. Excerpt from student-composed short story by Paul Vogelman.

Long Journey

My violin case banging incessantly against my hip was starting to make me feel an uncomfortable, involuntary twitch in my right leg. How I yearned to be able to sit down, take off my shoes, and stretch for just a minute. I wondered how Anya must have felt. I could feel the sweat building in her hand as I squeezed her tiny fingers comfortingly. He tiny legs could only carry her so far and Jakub could not carry the wagon with both Zayde and Anya on top of it. "We will be coming to a stopping point soon," I whispered to little Anya, "I can feel it." Her big, glossy eyes looked up at me still saturated with hope and the chance that this might all just be a dream or a mistake.

Determined to show Anya strength, I attempted to swing my bundle and violin over to the other side of my back and keep up a decent stride. When doing so, however, I offset my balance greatly and tripped over the end of my violin case sending my bundle and violin case flying. Anya was thrown back a bit as well. My mother turned around to help me but a Nazi soldier quickly advanced on her shouting, "*Schneller, schneller!*" He pointed the end of his rifle at the back of her head and with a maniacal smile blurted out, "Keep up with the rest, woman." My mother, not anxious to die over something so trivial, grabbed little Anya by the hand and started turning to catch up with the others. Just before she turned however, she gave me a look. It was the kind of look that only she could give me. Her glance only lasted a second, but it spoke a thousand words. She gazed into my eyes, past the façade, past the girl I wanted the world to see, and when she found a place deep within my soul her glare told me, "Keep marching and be careful or you will soon join Tata."

I tried jumping to my feet, but the Nazi guard forced me back down with the butt of his gun and screamed loudly, "So, you think you deserve a break while the others have to march? Is that it? Just like you lazy Jews. You all think you deserve more than the others. It's no wonder you people are so inferior and will soon serve the true, master race. Always squabbling amongst yourselves like dogs." The guard threw down a shovel at me and his face contorted into an evil grimace he whispered, "Now, come with me girl, you have sealed your own fate."

---

freedom and release for victims of the death camps. To commemorate these tragic events, ask students to create a Found Poem Poster either individually or as a small-group activity. Ask students to select a short passage in Wiesel's memoir *Night* or Lowry's *Number the Stars* that is particularly poignant and create a Found Poem by organizing words and phrases from the text into a poem. Ask students to go to the Photo Archives Online Catalog of the U.S. Holocaust Memorial Museum (USHMM) to retrieve images to illustrate their Found Poems. Students must document their images to give credit to the USHMM. See Figure 4.7 for an example of a Found Poem Poster entitled "Deportation" taken from Wiesel's *Night*.

Figure 4.7. Sample Found Poem Poster. Teacher-composed poem by Jacqueline Glasgow (based on Wiesel's *Night*, pp. 11–14).

Deportation

Deportation
The Ghetto awoke
Rumors of brick factories
A bag on our backs
Dragging our lives
Get ready for the journey
"All Jews outside! Hurry!"
Police struck with truncheons
And
Rifle butts
Left and right indiscriminately
Old men and women—
Children and invalids
A hot summer sun
Tortured by thirst
"Water, Mummy! Water!"
An open tomb.

Date: 1942–1943
Locale: Warsaw, Poland
Credit: USHMM, courtesy of Zydowski Instytut Historyczny
Copyright: Public Domain

ACTIVE LEARNING PROJECTS

In addition to the Public Awareness Poster and Memorial Scrapbook that open this section, the remaining active learning projects fall into two categories: Mapping Projects and Action-Oriented Projects. The Mapping Projects offer three strategies for tracing character journeys, and the culminating Action-Oriented Projects are designed to mobilize students into taking action against indifference.

Public Awareness Poster

In Wiesel's *Night*, Moshe the Beadle was abducted by the Nazis and forced to dig his own grave, and yet managed to escape the massacre. He came back to his home town, Sighet, bringing the news of what he had seen with his own eyes. The townspeople refused to believe him, taking him for a madman. Whereas Moshe's appeal fell on deaf ears, ask students to consider how they might have alerted the people of the world to the Nazi atrocities and violations of human rights. What were the psychological, emotional, and physical means used by the Nazis to control the Jews?

In Lowry's *Number the Stars,* German soldiers were omnipresent. When the young girls were racing each other along the sidewalk, their carefree play was interrupted by the soldiers, who harshly questioned them and sent them home to study. Germans closed shops, imposed a curfew, and rationed food supplies. They raided homes and threatened arrest. Ask students what kind of public awareness poster they might design to warn their Jewish friends of Nazi intentions?

Ask students to go to the Photo Archives Online Catalog of the U.S. Holocaust Memorial Museum to retrieve images of Nazi atrocities for their posters. Direct them to be sure to document the photo and tailor it to a particular audience—children, adults, Jews, gypsies, Americans, and so forth. Tell them to make sure the poster makes the point of exposing the Nazi atrocities against the Jews.

Memorial Scrapbook

In Lowry's *Number the Stars* (1989), the most poignant relationships had to be with those who sacrificed their lives serving Denmark's Resistance Movement. Lise Johansen and Peter Neilsen, although fictional, represent those courageous and idealistic young people, so many of whom died at the hands of the enemy. Have students make scrapbooks of Lise or Peter to commemorate their courage and bravery. Ask them to include the following:

- Photos like the one of Kim Malthe-Bruun that Lowry mentions in the Afterword of her novel.
- Letters they might have written home to their mothers the night before they were put to death. There is an example of such a letter in the Afterword of Lowry's *Number the Stars.*
- Newspaper articles covering significant moments mentioned in the novel.
- Poetry, elegies, odes, and epitaphs to Lise and/or Peter mentioning specific incidents that distinguished their lives.
- Family photos of the good times before the war.
- A memorial in honor of the bravery and courage of Lise and/or Peter.

Ask students to share their scrapbooks with the class in memory of those who lost their lives serving the Resistance. Reading aloud Innocenti's picture book, *Rose Blanche* (1985), would be an appropriate opening or closing to this activity since the book is about a young German girl who discovers the horrors of a concentration camp.

Mapping Projects

Through Mapping Projects, students will trace geographical, relational, and spiritual journeys of the characters in *Night* and *Number the Stars*.

Mapping the Geographical Journey. For students reading Wiesel's *Night* (1960), provide a map of Hungary in 1938–1945 showing Sighet. Ask them to plot Elie Wiesel's physical journey from Sighet to Buchenwald. For Wiesel and his community, the geographical journey began in 1941 in the Transylvanian village of Sighet, now located in Romania, where he and his family lived peacefully with other Hasidic Jews. In 1944, the Jews were first confined to a ghetto in Sighet before being deported to Birkenau via cattle cars. They spent 3 weeks in Auschwitz before being forced to march to Buna, a work camp where the Wiesels spent the most time. Because the approaching Russians threatened Buna, they were forced to march in the snow to the Gieiwitz camp, where they stayed 3 days before taken once again in cattle cars to Buchenwald. Fifteen-year-old Elie Wiesel was finally liberated on April 11, 1945.

For students reading Lowry's *Number the Stars*, provide a map of Europe that includes Denmark and Sweden. Ask them to think about how geographical factors might have made invasion of Denmark by Germany easier than invasion of other countries. Why did Denmark surrender so early in the war (on April 9, 1940)? Many people are unaware of the heroic 1943 evacuation of nearly 7,000 endangered Jews from Denmark to safety in Sweden during the period of Nazi occupation. Ask students to locate Copenhagen and then identify escape routes for the Jews that the Danes might have utilized, especially ways to get to Sweden.

Mapping Elie's Relationship With His Father. Parent–child relationships are an important part of young people's lives, and Wiesel's chronicle provides a glimpse into human responses in time of great duress. In the small, Hasidic village of Sighet, Wiesel's father was held in high esteem. He was a stoic religious leader, educator, and protector of his family. Wiesel spent a happy childhood. He learned Yiddish from his mother and father, and studied Hebrew in school. Then, with deportment, all of this changed. Young Wiesel first witnessed his father weeping as they moved into the ghetto. He watched his father beaten by a gypsy. Upon arriving at Birkenau, Wiesel lost his mother and sister in the selection process. His father held onto his hand. Wiesel (1960) had one important thought, "not to lose him. Not to be left alone" (p. 27). The bond between father and son held tight throughout many difficult obstacles and crises they had to pass through. It wasn't until the end, when his father fell in the snow in a march, that

Wiesel both argued with him to get up and keep going, and also doubted his own ability to keep him going. In the end, Wiesel had to face what he dreaded most—separation from his father. He was alone.

As students contemplate this father–son relationship, ask them to select a passage or event and write a dialogue that reflects the inner thoughts of each. One of my students, John Eddy, focused his dramatic dialogue on the second-to-last chapter of *Night*. Similar to the book, the consciousness of this dialogue fades in and out like a movie, giving brief, almost fleeting glimpses of their reality. See Figure 4.8 for a sample dramatic dialogue written by John Eddy.

Mapping Wiesel's Spiritual Journey. Familiarize students with religious terms they might not know: Beadle, Hasidic, Cabbala, Talmud, Maimonides, synagogue, kapo, Kaddish, musulman, Passover, Seder, Rosh Hossanah, Yom Kipper, Star of David, and so forth. This might work best by asking students to give brief reports on Jewish religious and cultural customs.

For believers, the Holocaust presents one of the most disturbing theological dilemmas of the 20th century, one that forced Elie Wiesel to reevaluate God in his world. Growing up in a small village in Romania, he lived in a world that revolved around family, religious study, community, and God. Early in his life, long before he was considered mature enough, this very religious young boy wanted to study the mystical books. In an Academy of Achievement interview, Wiesel (1996) said, "I spent most of my time talking to God more than to people. He was my partner, my friend, my teacher, my king, my sovereign, and I was so religious that nothing else mattered" (p. 1). Yet his family community and his innocent faith were destroyed upon deportation of his village in 1944. Imagine his loss of innocence as he watched life become filled with pain, atrocities, and death. It caused his strong faith to waver. When Wiesel witnessed the hanging of a small child, he questioned God's existence and lack of intervention. He failed to understand what he perceived as God's silence in the face of these cruel, inhumane atrocities. He watched his religious friends give up and declare, "It's the end. God is no longer with us" (Wiesel, 1960, p. 73). Wiesel felt terribly alone with his thoughts and beliefs: "In the depths of my heart, I felt a great void" (p. 66). This journey through the death camps profoundly shook, but did not destroy, his faith.

Regardless of our students' personal faith, or lack of it, Wiesel's experiences graphically show the powerful impact of the Holocaust on one person's beliefs. At the end of this discussion on mapping the spiritual journey, students were asked to do stream of consciousness writing that would capture Elie's struggle to believe and their understanding of a particular event in the story. One of my students, Ann Bryson, chose to write her piece,

Figure 4.8. Sample Dramatic Dialogue. Student-composed Dramatic Dialogue by John Eddy.

Father and Son at Buchenwald

"Eliezer . . . Eliezer?"
"Yes, Father."
"I am relieved. I thought you had left me."
"No, I am right here, on the bunk above you."
"That is good."

"Eliezer?"
"Yes, Father."
"Where . . . where is your mother?"
"Mother is . . . out. Somewhere."
"Oh. When will she be home?"

"I need water."
"No, Father. You cannot have water right now."
"Oh son, I am burning inside. Please."
"Water will just make it worse. Would you like some soup?"
"Burning so . . . water . . . mercy."

"What's wrong with the old man?"
"He's my father. He's very ill."
"Well then be a good son and take him outside, for God's sake."
"He can't be moved, he needs to lie and try . . ."
"We don't need this place being any filthier! Take him outside if he cannot take himself!"

"Father . . . Father?"
"Uhhn . . . Eliezer? Nnn . . ."
"Father, here, try to eat this."
"Save the bread for yourself, kid! He's too far gone. Save yourself."
"Father, please."
"Eliezer . . . I am not . . . hungry. Water, though."
"No! You cannot have water."
"Quiet! Make the old man quiet and go to bed."
"Father, please. Here, this bread will be good for you."
"No! No! I am burning! Water, please!"
"Shut up, old man!"
"Try to be calm, Father. Water will only make it worse, but you must eat. You must eat to live, please. Please, live."
"Eliezer, have mercy on me . . . the burning!"
"I told you to shut the old man up!"
"Go back to your bunks and rest, leave him be, he is very ill. No, just leave him be. Please. Please! He is very ill! He is old and weak! No! Go back to your own bed, leave him alone! He is my father! Do not touch him! No!"

"Father . . . Father?"
"Elie . . . ?"
"Father, Mother will be home soon."
"Uhhn . . . guh, good."
"You'll get to see Mother again."

"Elie . . . Eliezer?"
" . . . "
"Water . . . Eliezer?"
" . . . "
"E . . . Eliezer . . ."

which would fit in the last 25 pages of the book, about the time after Elie's father died, but before Elie was liberated. See Figure 4.9 for a sample stream of consciousness that reveals Elie's struggle with guilt.

Action-Oriented Projects

The Action-Oriented Projects in this section offer students strategies to make a difference and take action against indifference as a result of studying young adult literature about the Holocaust. Students can participate in a service learning project through the Empty Bowls Luncheon or join an association such as the Kindertransport Organization, which rescues endangered children.

Empty Bowls Luncheon. The objective of Empty Bowls is to provide support for food banks, soup kitchens, and other organizations that fight hunger. Since hunger was one of the tools used by the Nazis to control the Jews, fighting hunger in the world today could be a valuable experience for our students. The basic idea for Empty Bowls is simple. Participants create ceramic bowls (by making them from scratch or buying cheap bowls and decorating them), then serve a simple meal of soup and bread. Guests choose a bowl to use that day and keep it as a reminder that there are always Empty Bowls in the world (that may or may not actually be used for the soup). In exchange for a meal and a bowl, the guest gives a suggested minimum donation of $10. The meal sponsors supply the soup and bread and choose a hunger-fighting organization to receive the money. The Empty Bowls Project website (http://www.emptybowls.note/EmptyBowlsProject .htm) offers the following vision for this endeavor:

> It is our intent that the Empty Bowls project maintains a high level of integrity; that it is a project of inclusion; that it cuts across social, political, racial, religious, age, and any other perceived boundaries; and that it provides a tool which we can all use in working towards the goal of ending hunger. We ask that some aspect of hunger education be part of your project.

As an alternative, students could be involved in Imagine/Render (*Empty Bowls*, 2002). This organization is dedicated to the Empty Bowls Project, but, in addition, endorses Garden Projects. The Garden Projects contribute produce to emergency food providers. They also endorse Kitchen Gardens. In 1998 they joined with a local chapter of Habitat for Humanity to help families establish household gardens.

Figure 4.9. Sample Stream of Consciousness. Student-written stream of consciousness by Ann Bryson.

Elie Wiesel Struggles with Guilt

Moshe the Beadle says that asking questions is a way of lifting oneself up to God. If this is so, why am I in hell? All I do is question, question, ask, ask. Asking question after question of myself, of my God, of my father, of my people. What am I becoming? My guilt is eating me from the inside and I do not know what I am supposed to do to keep myself from becoming a monster. I do as I am told, I do what I must. I do what I must to survive this place. To be allowed to exit this hell.

Yet I know I am doing wrong. I am becoming evil. I have sold my soul for the price of extending my life a few more days, a few more hours. I have denied my father the last comforts he might have had to avoid a cuff, a blow, a bullet. More than anything else I hate myself for this. More than I hate the SS men who torture me, the Nazis who despise me, the Jews who care nothing for me, the God who has abandoned me, I hate myself. I have become worth less than nothing. I have betrayed my father.

There is still somehow a drive to live left in me. My hatred adds to it rather than diminishes it.

Why is this happening my God, why have you forsaken me?

I feel that if I quit now, if I give up it all will have been for nothing. All the struggles, my father's struggles as well as mine, will have been for naught. If I were to let go, to give up now, what would become of me. I would lie down in the snow somewhere and allow myself to drift to an eternal sleep only to wake up in the hell I have condemned myself to. Some say hell is the absence of God's light. If this is so, I am already dead and imprisoned in hell. No place could be farther from God's light than this.

Father, why did you give up? We had come so far and been through so much together. Father why did you abandon me? You were supposed to be my protector, to guide me, to guard me. You were my parent, the authority of the entire world rested on your shoulders. I stayed when I could have escaped to be with you and you left me at the end. You refused to go on. You died. You left me to go on by myself, despite all the times I stayed with you, to help you and to comfort you. I did my best by you, but you are still gone.

Why is it that we are still here in this place? Why are we, the Jews, so hated, so persecuted? We are sold into slavery yet again, oh Lord, but here the release is death. Why do we not rebel, revolt, rise up against our oppressors? I am just a child; I cannot do what is necessary. Why do we not take our meager lives in our own hands and die free? Some of us still have faith that God will prevail. Fools, God does not exist in this place. We are burdened by a belief that burdens have a purpose: that nothing will happen that is too much for us as a people. We are burdened by a faith in God that is unjustified.

Someday, someday soon, it will end. I will stop caring, stop working to survive. I will lie down and I will be with my family again, and whether it is in heaven or in hell, it will have to be better than this place

---

Kindertransport Association. In 1938, immediately after the November 9th pogrom in the German Reich, the Jews of Britain initiated the unique rescue operation now known as Kindertransport. Within days of the pogrom they obtained permission from the government and, in the 9 months leading up to the war, with aid from Quaker and other non-Jewish refugee organizations, brought 10,000 unaccompanied children from Germany, Austria, Czechoslovakia, and Poland to safety in Britain. Figure 4.10 shows a picture of some of these children.

Most of the children, but not all, were Jews. Most of the parents who had sent them to safety perished in the Holocaust. Most of the children settled in Britain; others re-emigrated to Israel, the Americas, and elsewhere, scattering over the world (Sugar, 2001). *Into the Arms of Strangers: Stories of the Kindertransport* (Harris, 2001) is an Academy Award winner for best documentary feature that captures the stories of the children saved in the Kindertransport. Drucker's memoir, *Kindertransport* (1995), tells the story of one of these children. Students can join this organization as a service project and support its efforts to rescue children whose lives are in danger.

EPILOGUE: NEVER AGAIN

Elie Wiesel's memoir about surviving the Holocaust and Lois Lowry's novel about the Danish Resistance are testaments of the human will, which

Figure 4.10. Jewish Refugee Children, Members of the First Kindertransport from Germany, Arrive in Harwich, England [Photograph #51114].

Date: December 2, 1938
Locale: Harwich, England
Credit: USHMM, courtesy of Instytut Pamieci Narodowej
Copyright: Public Domain

even in the face of the greatest horrors imaginable, survives to bear witness and reject despair. The active learning strategies employed in this chapter assist students in understanding the depth of human suffering that took place in the concentration camps, while also giving light to the way people bonded together to survive when outside forces threatened their very existence. In studying these great works of young adult literature, students learn to reject indifference and do their part in ensuring that such atrocities never happen again. They become bearers of the stories that need to be told. As Elie Wiesel said, "I decided to devote my life to telling the story because I felt that having survived I owe something to the dead. And anyone who does not remember betrays them again" (Panse, 2005, pp. 1–2).

ANNOTATED BIBLIOGRAPHY

Boas, J. (1995). *We are witnesses: Five diaries of teenagers who died in the holocaust.* New York: Scholastic.
Taken from actual diaries, this book depicts five distinct teen voices conveying hope, fear, faith, and skepticism as the Nazis sought to exterminate the Jewish population.

Frank, A. (1967). *The diary of a young girl.* New York: Doubleday.
The beloved classic of a bright, contemplative Jewish teenager who carefully examines love, family, relationships, and the world around her against the backdrop of World War II as her family hides in an annex to avoid capture by the Nazis. Anne died at Bergen-Belsen in 1945.

Holm, A. (2004). *I am David.* San Diego: Harcourt.
David, age 12, has known nothing but life in a prison/work camp. Given the chance to escape, he dodges numerous obstacles and sees the beauty of the human spirit on his journey to Denmark.

Matas, C. (1993). *Daniel's story.* New York: Scholastic.
Camera in hand, Daniel records the atrocities of Nazi Germany from the rise of anti-Semitism, to a ghetto, then to a death camp.

Matas, C. (1996). *After the war.* New York: Simon & Schuster.
An important book to show that anti-Semitism did not end with the Allied victory in World War II. Having survived Buchenwald, 15-year-old Ruth returns to Poland, where she and other Jews are treated poorly. She and others make plans to find a new home in Palestine.

Yolen, J. (1995). *Devil's arithmetic.* New York: Puffin.
A unique story-in-a-story structure shows Hannah, who opens the door at a contemporary Passover Seder, transported to a village in Poland in the 1940s. She is taken to a Nazi death camp, sees a friend die, and returns with a new appreciation for her family's Jewish heritage and customs.

REFERENCES

Aarvik, E. (1986). *The Nobel peace prize 1986*. Retrieved November 2, 2005, from http://nobelprize.org/peace/laureates/1986/presentation-speech.html

Drucker, O. L. (1995). *Kindertransport*. New York: Henry Holt.

Elie Wiesel Foundation for Humanity. (2005). Retrieved November 2, 2005, from http://www.eliewieselfoundation.org/default2.htm

Empty Bowls. (2002). Retrieved November 2, 2005, from http://www.emptybowls.net/ImagineRender.htm

For students: Holocaust related art and writing contests. (n.d.). U.S. Holocaust Memorial Museum Art and Writing Contests. Retrieved November 2, 2005, from http://www.ushmm.org/education/forstudents/index.php?content=awcontest/organizations/

Harris, M. J. (Director). (2001). *Into the arms of strangers: Stories of the kindertransport* [Documentary video]. United States: Warner Brothers.

Innocenti, R. (1985). *Rose Blanche*. New York: Harcourt Brace.

Lewis, J. J. (2004). *Indifference quotes*. Retrieved November 2, 2005, from http://www.wisdomquotes.com/cat_indifference.html

Lobel, A. (1998). *No pretty pictures: A child of war*. New York: Greenwillow.

Lowry, L. (1989). *Number the stars*. Boston: Houghton Mifflin.

Ostow, M. (Director). (1994). *America and the holocaust—Deceit and indifference* [Documentary video]. Boston: WGBH Educational Foundation.

Panse, S. (2005). *Elie Wiesel quotations*. Retrieved November 2, 2005, from http:www.buzzle.com/editorials/3-9-2005-66916.asp

Photo Archives. (n.d.). U.S. Holocaust Memorial Museum. Retrieved November 2, 2005, from http://www.ushmm.org/research/collections/

Spielberg, S., & Survivors of the Shoah Visual History Foundation. (1996). *Survivors of the holocaust* [Video]. Atlanta: Turner Home Entertainment.

Sugar, R. (2001). *The kindertransport journey: Memory into history*. Retrieved November 2, 2005, from http://www.kindertransport.org/broch1.html

Wiesel, E. (1960). *Night*. New York: Hill & Wang.

Wiesel, E. (1986). *Nobel prize speech*. The Elie Wiesel Foundation for Humanity. Retrieved February 4, 2006, from http://www.eliewieselfoundation.org/ElieWiesel/speech.html

Wiesel, E. (1996). *Interview: Elie Wiesel*. Academy of Achievement. Retrieved November 2, 2005, from http://www.achievement.org/autodoc/page/wie0int-1

Wiesel, E. (1999). *The perils of indifference*. Retrieved November 2, 2005, from http://www.historyplace.com/speeches/wiesel.htm

Williams, J. (1993). *Schindler's list* [Original motion picture sound track]. United States: MCA.

CHAPTER 5

Deterioration of Family and Culture: The Impact of Japanese Internment (1941–1945)

Yesterday, 7 December 1941—a date which will live in infamy—the United States of America was suddenly and deliberately attacked by naval and air forces of the Empire of Japan. . . . It will be recorded that the distance of Hawaii from Japan makes it obvious that the attack was deliberately planned many days or even weeks ago. During the intervening time the Japanese Government had deliberately sought to deceive the United States by false statements and expressions of hope for continued peace.

The attack . . . has caused severe damage. . . . Very many American lives were lost. In addition American ships have been reported torpedoed on the high seas between San Francisco and Honolulu. . . .

The facts of yesterday speak for themselves. The people of the United States have already formed their opinions and well understand the implications to the very life and safety of our nation. . . . I believe I interpret the will of the Congress and of the people when I assert that we will not only defend ourselves to the uttermost but will make very certain that this form of treachery shall never endanger us again. Hostilities exist. There is no blinking at the fact that our people, our territory, and our interests are in grave danger. . . .

—(Roosevelt, 1941, p. 1)

These lines, excerpted from President Roosevelt's Address to Congress asking for a Declaration of a State of War between the United States and Japan, on December 8, 1941, demonstrate the context of fear in which the decisions were made that resulted in Executive Order 9066. "This act, based on ethnicity, permitted the military to bypass the constitutional safeguards of American citizens in the name of national defense. The order excluded persons of Japanese ancestry then living on the West Coast from residing and working in certain locations" (Lamb & Johnson, 2005, p. 1).

Focused on *Farewell to Manzanar* (1973), Jeanne Wakatsuki Houston's memoir about life in a Japanese Internment Camp, this unit helps students to grasp the devastating impact of the War Relocation Act, Executive Order 9066, on the Japanese people living in the United States during World War II. In particular, Houston's memoir shows how life at the camps eroded the family structures and cultural traditions of the Japanese people.

In addition to educating students about the facts surrounding the Japanese Internment Camps, this chapter offers simulation, role play, and writing activities to engage students in reflection, visualization, and critical thinking about what life in the camps was like. Using a traditional Japanese theater form called Kabuki, students will interpret and perform important aspects of Jeanne's story. Students also will write Japanese poems such as haiku, renga, tanka, dodoitsu, and seddea. Figure 5.1 offers a concise overview of the active learning strategies in this chapter.

HISTORICAL CONTEXT

From 1942–1945 over 110,000 Japanese Americans, two thirds of them having American citizenship, were placed in ten "relocation centers" under control of the newly established War Relocation Authority (WRA). Two of these centers were built in each of the states of Arizona, Arkansas, and

Figure 5.1. Active Learning Strategies in Chapter 5.

Featured Young Adult Novel	Thoughtfulness and Reflection	Simulation and Role Play	Creative and Personal/ Analytical Writing	Active Learning Projects
Farewell to Manzanar	• Meditation #1 • Meditation #2	• Barracks • Bathroom • Mess Hall	• Japanese Poetry • Primary Sources • Reviews • Opinion Essay • Conflicting Opinions • Critical Analysis	• Kabuki Theater • Trifold Display of Research

California, and one each in Colorado, Idaho, Utah, and Wyoming. These centers also have been called relocation camps, internment camps, and concentration camps. This chapter will refer to the centers primarily as Internment Camps, since the term *concentration camp* is heavily reminiscent of the Holocaust of the Jewish people, the focus of Chapter 4 of this book. A brochure distributed as part of *American Concentration Camps: Remembering the Japanese American Experience*, an exhibit at the Ellis Island Immigration Museum from April 3, 1998 to January 5, 1999, included the following information regarding the term *concentration camp*:

- A concentration camp is a place where people are imprisoned not because of any crimes they have committed, but simply because of who they are. Although many groups have been singled out for such persecution throughout history, the term "concentration camp" was first used at the turn of the [20th] century in the Spanish-American and Boer Wars.
- During World War II, America's concentration camps were clearly distinguishable from Nazi Germany's. Nazi camps were places of torture, barbarous medical experiments, and summary executions; some were extermination centers with gas chambers. Six million Jews were slaughtered in the Holocaust. Many others including Gypsies, Poles, homosexuals and political dissidents were also victims of Nazi concentration camps.
- In recent years, concentration camps have existed in the former Soviet Union, Cambodia, and Bosnia.
- Despite all the differences, all had one thing in common: the people in power removed a minority group from the general population and the rest of the society let it happen. (Nelson, n.d., p. 2)

Distress over Evacuation and Relocation

Sharing this information with students can be important, as upon their initial hearing of Japanese concentration camps, some students say things like, "How could we criticize Hitler? We did the same thing to the Japanese." While the internment camps were by no means "like home," they are clearly distinguishable from Nazi death camps, and students need to understand this. The epilogue of this chapter explores the repeal of Executive Order 9066 as well as apologies and issues of redress related to Japanese internment, but initially it may be worth noting that even in the years when these camps were newly formed and operated, there were doubts about whether it was the right thing to do. For example, Milton S. Eisenhower (youngest brother of Dwight D. Eisenhower), who was appointed the first

Director of the WRA, wrote in a letter to President Roosevelt on April 22, 1943:

> My friends in the War Relocation Authority, like Secretary [of the Interior] Ickes, are deeply distressed over the effects of the entire evacuation and relocation program upon the Japanese-Americans, particularly upon the young citizen group. Persons in this group find themselves living in an atmosphere for which their public school and democratic teachings have not prepared them. It is hard for them to escape a conviction that their plight is due more to racial discrimination, economic motivations, and wartime prejudices than to any real necessity from the military point of view for evacuation from the West Coast.
>
> Life in a relocation center cannot possibly be pleasant. The evacuees are surrounded by barbed wire fences under the eyes of armed military police. They have suffered heavily in property losses; they have lost their businesses and their means of support. The State Legislatures, Members of the Congress, and local groups, by their actions and statements bring home to them almost constantly that as a people they are not really welcome anywhere. . . . Under such circumstances it would be amazing if extreme bitterness did not develop.
>
> The director of the Authority is striving to avoid, if possible, creation of a racial minority problem after the war which might result in something akin to Indian reservations. . . . (Weglyn, 1976, n.p.)

Eisenhower ended up resigning his position as Director of the WRA, telling his successor, "I can't sleep and do this job. I had to get out of it" (Weglyn, 1976, n.p.).

Beginning the Evacuation

With the formation of the WRA, roundups began in late March and early April 1942. Notices were posted telling people of Japanese ancestry that they would have 7–10 days to "conclude any business, lock up their homes, and report to a designated location on a specified date with no more baggage than they could carry" (Mackey, n.d., p. 3). In response to this order, the "evacuees," as they were called by the government, typically sold what they could not take with them. "Automobiles were sold for less than half their worth; other belongings often went for ten cents on the dollar; pets were given away or left behind" (p. 3). Some evacuees put things into storage; however, when they returned after the war, many of these items had been stolen or vandalized.

On the designated day, the evacuees boarded trains or buses for what the army called "assembly centers." These centers were established at fairgrounds or horse racing tracks (facilities that already had water and some housing) scattered along the west coast, but predominantly in California. "The housing took the form of exhibit buildings and horse stalls. The horse stalls were whitewashed, as the inmates reported, usually right over the manure, which was splattered on the walls" (Mackey, n.d., p. 4). Japanese Americans resided at the assembly centers until construction of more permanent relocation centers was completed.

Self-Sufficiency of the Relocation Centers

By decision of the WRA, relocation centers were to be self-sufficient; any work that needed to be done was to be done by the internees. The WRA also decided that internees could not be paid more than an army private. As a result, while the United States government paid army privates $21 a month, it paid professional people of Japanese descent working in a relocation center $19 a month. A more striking example comes from Heart Mountain Hospital (in the Wyoming relocation camp), where Dr. Ito, who was in charge of pediatrics, was paid $228 a year, while Caucasian nurses working at the hospital were paid $1,800 a year. The camp's schools also carried this disparity, as internee teachers were paid $228 a year at the same time the base salary for Caucasian teachers was $2,000 a year, with senior teachers earning $2,600 annually (Mackey, n.d.).

FEATURED YOUNG ADULT NOVEL

Farewell to Manzanar

Besides disparity in pay, Jeanne Wakatsuki Houston's personal account, *Farewell to Manzanar* (Houston & Houston, 1973), depicts the gravity of loss in pride, culture, and family that came with life in the camp. Together with her husband and co-author James D. Houston, Jeanne tells her family's story in three parts. Part I begins with the bombing of Pearl Harbor, followed by her father's burning a flag from Hiroshima and several other possessions that might signify any connection to Japan. This attempt at disassociation fails, however, as 2 weeks later he is arrested by the FBI for allegedly delivering oil to offshore Japanese submarines. He is imprisoned in an all-male camp with other aliens. Shortly thereafter, President Roosevelt signs Executive Order 9066, and the family—minus father— is ordered to the internment camp in California called Manzanar. Upon their arrival they experience their first meal from an outdoor "chow line" and then are taken to their new living quarters—a cluster of 15 barracks known as Block 16. The WRA issues the Wakatsukis steel army cots, two brown army blankets, and some mattress covers, and assigns the family of 12 two 16' × 20' units to live in. As months pass, the family grows apart as each member's interests differ. Jeanne is fascinated with the stories of suffering Saints and thus becomes interested in Catholicism. Jeanne's father is released from prison and rejoins the family. Jeanne describes her father as "not a great man. He wasn't even a very successful man. He was a poser, a braggart, and a tyrant. But he held onto his self-respect, he dreamed grand dreams, and he could work well at any task he turned his hand to" (Houston & Houston, 1973, pp. 58–59). He prevents Jeanne from being baptized and begins to drink heavily and isolate himself due to his own unhappiness. Jeanne's father emerges when the men in the camp are asked whether they are willing to sign the government's loyalty oath, serve in the Armed Forces on combat duty, and swear allegiance to the United States, therefore denying any form of allegiance to Japan. Jeanne's brother Woody decides to sign the oath and join the army, and this infuriates his father.

Part II of Jeanne's story unfolds as the family is moved to Block 28, which doubles their living space. Manzanar has become less congested as more loyalty oaths have been signed. The family has more freedom to roam about the camp's surrounding areas, parks and gardens emerge, and the camp takes on the characteristics of a "totally equipped American small town, complete with schools, churches, Boy Scouts, beauty parlors, neighborhood gossip, fire and police departments, glee clubs, softball leagues, Abbott and Costello movies, tennis courts, and traveling shows" (Houston & Houston, 1973, p. 100). In 1944 several Supreme Court rulings lead to the announcement that the internment camps will be closing within a year and internees now have "the right to return to their former homes" (p. 126). This is not, however, received as joyful news by the Wakatsuki family, for they do not have a home to go back to, and wartime propaganda has been brushed with an anti-Japanese sentiment. Jeanne is actually afraid to leave Manzanar and re-integrate into the larger community. The family moves back to Long Beach, this time to a housing project, and Jeanne begins school, where she realizes her fears of physical attack are unfounded, although she still feels like "someone foreign, or someone other than American, or perhaps not seen at all" (p. 158). Jeanne longs for acceptance and is torn between her Japanese and American heritage, between who she wants to be at school and with her Caucasian friend Radine and who her own father wants her to be.

Part III closes the book with a reflection on the way the camp had a lasting impact on Jeanne's life. She describes her return to Manzanar as an adult, accompanied by her husband and children, and ends with a flashback to the day she left the internment camp, signifying her ability to say farewell to Manzanar.

THOUGHTFULNESS AND REFLECTION
THROUGH PRE-READING MEDITATIONS

Rather than beginning a study of Japanese Internment Camps with a presentation of facts, this unit begins with guided meditation to acquaint students with issues and circumstances in *Farewell to Manzanar*. The two meditation scripts that follow place students in the center of several scenarios whereby they reflect on things they value—and may even take for granted—then envision these things being taken away. Teachers may present the meditations on a single class day, making sure to provide ample time for sharing after each, or on different days. Also, either meditation can be further divided by teachers desiring to use the meditations as anticipatory sets, starting points to engage students at the beginning of class. Each meditation begins with an invitation for students to close their eyes and get in touch with their breathing as a way to relax. While the scripts are relatively short, it is vitally important to read them slowly, with plenty of pauses, so that students have ample time to engage their imaginations, visualize, think, and feel.

Meditation #1

Close your eyes. Take deep breaths. Feel the stress in your shoulders work its way down your shoulders, through your arms, and out your fingertips. Relax your body and picture a blank movie screen.

Now think of your home—your kitchen, bathroom, bedroom, and any other living space. What belongs to you? What do you share with others? Is there a place you can go to be alone? Focus on that place, and visualize yourself there. What do you see? Hear? Smell? How do you feel in that place?

Move to meal time—what does that look like for you? Do you have a say in what you eat? Do you make special requests or put items you like on a grocery list? When you eat, where are you? Who is with you? What if you miss a meal—are there leftovers? Can you find a snack in the cupboard or refrigerator?

Now, open your eyes and take out a sheet of paper. List the names of your family and friends. If you have a pet(s), include it (them) on your list. Write down some things you enjoy doing with those on your list. Make sure to include some of the places that you go.

After the visualization and brief written assignment, ask students to share some of the things they visualized about their home, especially revisiting where they go to be alone. Also, revisit meal time and what happens if students miss a meal. Students who have a hard time visualizing may share from the written list of people, pets, and things/places they enjoy doing/going that followed the meditation.

Meditation #2

Close your eyes. Take deep breaths. Feel the stress in your shoulders work its way down your shoulders, through your arms, and out your fingertips. Relax your body, and picture a blank movie screen.

Imagine that you are at home when you hear a knock at the door. A neighbor is there holding a page from the newspaper that lists names of people who are to vacate their homes in 7 days because the government has decided to "relocate" them. That is all that you are told—you do not know where you will be taken, what state, what climate, or any other conditions. What are you thinking? What are you feeling?

All that you are allowed to take with you is what you can carry in two medium-sized suitcases (without wheels). What will you take with you?

Open your eyes and jot down some of the thoughts and feelings you are experiencing, along with a list of things you will take with you as you are "relocated" to an unknown destination.

This time, before asking students to share aloud, continue with the meditation below. The main reason for taking a "time out for writing" here is to make sure that students who have difficulty visualizing still have something to share when the meditation is over. After students have had about 3 minutes to record some things they would take with them in two medium-sized suitcases, continue with the final portion of Meditation #2.

Your bags are packed, and a bus waits to take you to your destination. After a 6-hour bus ride, you arrive at a fairgrounds surrounded by a razor-wire fence. Your family is sent to a whitewashed horse stall and told that this is your new home. Your bed is a cot, an army blanket, and a pillow stuffed with straw.

Engage your senses—what do you see? Smell? Hear? Feel? Taste? What are you thinking and feeling?

Meal time begins promptly at 5:00 p.m. At meal time you stand in line and wait behind 1,000 other people who have been sent to the fairgrounds and given horse stalls to live in; your meal consists of a bowl of rice topped with strawberry jam. What do you think of this?

One day you fall asleep and miss the meal. You feel hungry and will not have a chance to stand in line for a meal again for 14 hours. Imagine what this is like—no refrigerator or cupboard to go to, no choice in what you eat, the feeling of hunger.

What do you miss from home?

After the meditation, again offer students an opportunity to share. Hopefully, as students use their imaginations to put themselves in the situation of the Japanese who were relocated, they will experience vicariously the gravity and personal impact of Executive Order 9066. The point is to move students beyond a mere cognitive understanding of facts and engage their affective domain to dance with emotion and empathy.

SIMULATION AND ROLE PLAY

To help students to visualize and vicariously experience the camp conditions, teachers should ask the class to list some of the scenes that stand out as different and particularly awkward, confining, or difficult from *Farewell to Manzanar*. Once students have brainstormed some scenes, they should work in groups to figure out ways to make these into simulations for the class. Accompanying each scene, students should have a supporting quote(s) from the text and a key question(s) that links or contrasts the students' own living conditions with those depicted in Jeanne Wakatsuki Houston's novel. Having read *Farewell to Manzanar* with a literature circle group of five other students, Stacy Gunsel, a student in my Young Adult Literature class, designed three scenes to give the class a more concrete idea of what life was really like for Jeanne, Jeanne's family, and others who were displaced from their homes and communities. A summary of these simulations, written by Stacy Gunsel, appears in Figure 5.2.

CREATIVE AND PERSONAL/ANALYTICAL WRITING

Japanese Poetry

While the simulation and role plays give students an opportunity to see the effects of relocation on Japanese families, causing the erosion of familial structures and cultural identity, Japanese poetry gives students opportunities to engage with Japanese culture and demonstrate their understanding of various aspects of *Farewell to Manzanar*. There are numerous Japanese

Figure 5.2. Simulations for *Farewell to Manzanar.* Scenes written by student Stacy Gunsel.

Scene 1: The Barracks

Key Question: What do you value about your home or your parents' home?

Description of Simulation: Green paper will create a 16" x 20" border around an open area in the classroom. This will represent the living area typically shared by five to eight people at Manzanar. The rectangular pieces of paper will represent the cots they slept on. Students will arrange the cots keeping in mind that parents, children, newly-weds, and strangers had to share this tiny space. The round piece of paper will represent the oil stove that the camp provided to heat the room.

Supporting Quotes:

"Each barracks was divided into six units, sixteen by twenty feet, about the size of a living room, with one bare bulb hanging from the ceiling and an oil stove for heat. . . . We were issued steel army cots, two brown army blankets each, and some mattress covers, which my brothers stuffed with straw" (21).

"The first task was to divide up what space we had for sleeping. Bill and Woody contributed a blanket each and partitioned off the first room: one side for Bill and Tomi, one side for Woody and Chizu and their baby girl" (21).

Scene 2: The Bathroom

Key Question: How important to you is privacy?

Description of Simulation: Two lines of desks placed back to back will represent the toilet area in the camp. Students sitting there will share their feelings about using an open, completely public bathroom.

Supporting Quote:

"It was an open room, over a concrete slab. The sink was a long metal trough against one wall, with a row of spigots for hot and cold water. Down the center of the room twelve toilet bowls were arranged in six pairs, back to back, with no partitions" (32).

Scene 3: The Mess Hall

Key Question: What kinds of foods do you typically eat together?

Description of Simulation: The table will represent the serving station in a mess hall at Manzanar. Students will wait in line for a long time before receiving their dinner of potato chips drenched in chocolate sauce. This will represent Jeanne's family's experience of being served in the mess hall. Students will share whether they find their dinners appealing or even edible and how that would make them feel if they were very hungry and that was their only choice for dinner.

Supporting Quotes:

"Caucasian servers were thinking that the fruit poured over rice would make a good dessert. Among the Japanese, of course, rice is never eaten with sweet foods, only with salty or savory foods. Few of us could eat such a mixture" (20).

The next day, Jeanne's brother Woody says he's going to find out what the mess hall will be serving for breakfast. "'Probably hotcakes with soy sauce,' Kiyo said, on his hands and knees between the bunks. 'No.' Woody grinned, heading out the door. 'Rice. With Log Cabin syrup and melted butter'" (27).

---

poetic forms that students can experiment with, the most well known being the haiku. All of the forms presented here rely on syllabic counts, as is common in Japanese poetry. The haiku is a three-line poem arranged 5-7-5. The first line has five syllables; the second line has seven syllables, and the third line has five syllables. Building on the haiku, the tanka adds two 7-syllable lines at the end for a sequence of 5-7-5-7-7. A series of tanka linked together become a renga, where each tanka is a stanza of the complete poem. Two additional Japanese poetic forms are the dodoitsu (7-7-7-5) and the sedoka (5-7-5-5-7-7). The concise nature of Japanese poetry requires writers to think carefully about what they want to convey, and often this is more about "creating a moment" or "touching on an experience or feeling" than offering a well-developed description or narration. The Japanese forms epitomize poetry's ability to capture with few words what lengthy works of prose often miss. A sample renga created by Michael Westfall, one of my students in a Young Adult Literature class, follows.

A Threat to Whom
BY MICHAEL WESTFALL

Farewell Manzanar!
Wakatsuki family
either brought to life
much like Jeanne. Or worse, to death!
Like Papa, living but dead.

Internment for Japs!
Must remove them from the coast
but not all a threat,
but all treated just the same.
Treated like savages—why?

Xenophobia!
Ignorant like other hate.
For they are people
just like other immigrants,
trying for a better life.

Personal and Critical/Analytical Responses to *Farewell to Manzanar*

In this section are five prompts (adapted from Meyers & Jones, 1993) followed by excerpts from student-written essays to serve as sample responses. Each question requires students to engage with a text on both personal and critical/analytical levels. Each student may choose or be assigned one question; this is especially effective when students read books in literature circle formats or groups of five, where each student is, in effect, the only one in the class looking into a particular aspect of a particular novel. However, even when the whole class is studying the same book, the questions can be used to illustrate how the same text may be interpreted differently—or at least have varying points of emphasis—because individual readers create distinct "readings." As a guideline, responses to the questions that follow should be two to four pages each.

Prompt #1: Primary Sources. Interview all of your group members about some aspect of the book *Farewell to Manzanar* (it could be what moved them most, what they learned, what startled them, etc.) and record their responses in the form of a brief essay, listing each person's name followed by his/her response (use the words of the interviewee—"I"—to keep things personal and direct). As the final two to three paragraphs of this prompt, the interviewer will address one of the following: (1) What moved you most about the book? What did you understand more deeply or for the first time as a result of reading this book? How were your "eyes opened" by this book? (2) Tell what or how interviewing your group members caused you to "see/perceive" (or see "more" of/about) the text. A sample interview response by one of my students, Maria Apostolou, follows.

> The scene in the novel that moved me the most was the scene where Jeanne's father threatens to beat her mother, and Jeanne's brother Kiyo jumps in to protect their mother (68). It was shocking to see how life in North Dakota changed Papa so much. I couldn't believe that he developed such an addiction to alcohol that he could not even control his actions toward his own family. The violence and fear that the family had to endure were heart-wrenching. I don't know how Jeanne's mother could stand being abused. I don't understand why she did not leave her husband. She seemed to have been doing fine without him while he was gone. However, I thought it was moving that Kiyo risked his own safety to protect his mother. This showed that he had more respect for his mother than his father, and that he valued the idea of "family." While it was difficult to read about the pain the family endured at the hands of Papa, it was nice to see somebody in the family finally take a stand against him.

Prompt #2: Reviews. Do you believe the topic (conflict, time period, characterization, place) was treated fairly and accurately by the author?

Explain your response. A sample response by one of my students, Michael Westfall, follows.

> Because Jeanne Wakatsuki Houston actually had to endure the atrocities in the internment Manzanar, she was able to give a firsthand account of what actually occurred for the 110,000 Japanese placed in internment camps. Although one could argue that she would have a bias against the United States government, through-out *Farewell to Manzanar*, the book she wrote with her husband, James D. Houston, there seems to be an unbiased account of the events. . . . It would have been easy for the authors to vilify many people and even the whole United States government in the convey-ance of the events surrounding the internment camp Manzanar, but this is not the case for this piece. . . . Had the authors decided to take a route which blamed people for the events in the novel, the integ-rity of the whole piece would have been compromised. Although Jeanne and her family actually had to endure the horrible condi-tions, she was able to see it as a turning point for the better for herself.

Prompt #3: Opinion Essay. Have one of the students identify an opin-ion statement from (or strong perspective represented in) the text *Farewell to Manzanar*. The student will trace the evidence, or lack of it, that the au-thor uses to support the opinion or perspective. Following are a sample opinion statement from *Farewell to Manzanar* and a corresponding excerpt from a student-written essay composed by Roxanne Sturm, one of my stu-dents in a Young Adult Literature class.

> *Sample Opinion Statement.* "You might say it would have happened sooner or later anyways, this sliding apart of such a large family, in postwar California. . . . But there is no escaping that our internment accelerated the process, made it happen so suddenly it was almost tangible" (Houston & Houston, 1973, p. 39).

> *Excerpt from Student-Written Opinion Essay.* The first thing that the author and narrator, Jeanne Wakatsuki Houston, did to support this opinion was base the entire novel *Farewell to Manzanar* around the experience of her family as a unit versus focusing solely on her own perspective. In the novel's Foreword, she made sure to point out that in order to write this novel, she was going to have to tell "something about [her] family before the war, and the years that followed the war, and about [her] father's past, as well as [her] own

way of seeing things now." In doing so, Houston was able to paint a portrait of what her family was like before Manzanar so we as readers could see the changes that occurred due to the internment experience. . . .

Prompt #4: Conflicting Opinions. Have one of the students take a point of view from the novel *Farewell to Manzanar* and defend it. In the essay the student should raise challenges, issues, and questions based on conflicting readings/ideas related to the novel. The sample response that follows was written by one of my students, Maria Apostolou.

An obvious point of view from the novel is that Japanese internment camps were forms of cruel and unnecessary punishment for those imprisoned there. Jeanne Wakatsuki Houston makes this opinion clear through her portrayal of life inside Manzanar. She points out several negative aspects of the camp and tells how living in the camp irreversibly changed her family's life. However, it is possible to challenge her opinion and . . . argue that those inside Manzanar led amazingly typical lives. . . .

Prompt #5: Critical Analysis. Have one of the students compose a list of ten (in total) "how" and "why" questions about the book *Farewell to Manzanar* that he or she would like to explore in small-group discussion. The student responding to this prompt should write a response of at least one page for each of the two questions that interest her or him most.

Figure 5.3 consists of two parts—on the left is a list of ten questions written by one of my students, Jeness Duffy, in response to the Critical Analysis Prompt described here, and on the righthand side is her response to the first question, distinguishing how the U.S. government's treatment of Japanese Americans is similar to and different from Nazi concentration camps and the treatment of Jews during World War II and the Holocaust.

ACTIVE LEARNING PROJECTS

Kabuki Theater

Kabuki is a traditional form of Japanese theater that originated in the early 17th century. Traditionally acted out by men, Kabuki is used to tell the stories of great historical events and everyday people. This kind of

Figure 5.3. Critical Analysis Questions. Student-written questions and sample response by Jeness Duffy.

Questions for Reflection Discussion of *Farewell to Manzanar:*

1. How were internment camps and the government's treatment of Japanese-Americans similar to and different from Nazi concentration camps and the treatment of Jews during World War II and the Holocaust?

2. How did imprisonment in Manzanar destroy honor and create shame for some of the characters in the novel?

3. How were characters in the novel torn between Japanese culture and loyalty and American culture and loyalty?

4. Why were Japanese Americans the only race/ethnic group who were relocated? (Why not German Americans, or Italian Americans?)

5. How did people in Manzanar exhibit strength and live by the expression, "Shikata ga nai," or "It cannot be helped"?

6. How did Jeanne's life begin at Manzanar, and how did her father's end in the camps?

7. How did life in Manzanar change family structure/ dynamics and tradition for the Wakatsukis?

8. Why did Jeanne try various hobbies at Manzanar, and how did these attempts and the activities she participated in after Manzanar contribute to her struggle for identity and attention?

9. Why did Jeanne return to Manzanar with her family at the end of the novel, and why did she conclude the book with the memory of her father driving the car?

10. How is Japanese relocation and internment treated/addressed in today's history classes and textbooks?

Having read both *Farewell to Manzanar* and Elie Wiesel's *Night*, Jeness Duffy responded to prompt #1 with the following:

My reading of *Farewell to Manzanar* was affected by my knowledge of concentration camps because I couldn't feel as sympathetic or as appalled by the relocation and internment of Japanese Americans as I always have felt about the Holocaust. In a documentary about the internment camps, *Rabbit in the Moon*, former internees admitted they felt the same way. However, this does not excuse the behavior of our government through Executive Order 9066 or lessen the pain, confusion, and frustration felt by the 110,000 Japanese Americans who were relocated.

What occurred in the Holocaust and in relocation/internment was a stripping of basic human rights, possessions, dignity, and culture, as well as a harsh message that declared, "You are not welcome here because you are different." The fascist leadership of Adolf Hitler and the democratic leadership of Franklin D. Roosevelt convinced their countries that these two ethnic groups posed a threat and needed to be held captive (or exterminated). The movement of Japanese Americans and Jews is similar, as both were uprooted from their homes and moved to designated areas, such as Jewish ghettos and Terminal Island, where the Wakatsukis had to live before moving to Manzanar. The negative stigma of being a "Jap" and being a "Jew" were probably very similar also.

The aerial views of internment camps and concentration camps look similar rows of uniform, shoddy barracks; however, the treatment within the two types of camps could hardly be more different. In the internment camps, though living conditions were uncomfortable, people were allowed to work and live in a manner that preserved a great deal of their lifestyles before camp. Schools, churches, baseball fields, etc., were established within camps such as Manzanar. Families were kept together (for the most part), food was available (though not the best quality), and virtually no torture, murder, or brutality occurred.

However, the concentration camp experience was frighteningly different and marked by starvation, senseless and atrocious cruelty, and genocide. Though the Japanese attack on Pearl Harbor does not justify what the U.S. government did to thousands of innocent Japanese Americans (many of whom were citizens), there is more reasoning behind this movement than there was behind the Nazi persecution of Jews.

performance includes a set, costumes, makeup, props, and music (Manjiro, 1995). While reading *Farewell to Manzanar*, students will work in groups to select scenes from the book that they will transform into Kabuki Theater and perform in front of the class. Kabuki is predominantly pantomime, but may include a voice-over type of script by which a member of the performing group narrates the events being acted out. One of my students, Maria Apostolou, read *Farewell to Manzanar* as part of a literature circle group in my Young Adult Literature class. The group used Kabuki Theater as a way to summarize their book for other students in the class who had read different novels in their literature circle groups. In a summary essay about this active learning project, Maria wrote the following about her group's plan and choice to play traditional Japanese music in the background of their Kabuki Theater performance:

> The music was composed in the 17th century, so it is fitting to be used during a Kabuki performance. In the presentation, one person will act as the narrator, and she will have the primary role in the telling of the story. The other group members will be actors, representing characters in *Farewell to Manzanar*. These actors will use facial expressions, movements, and gestures to portray the events that are being described by the narrator.

Whether studying *Farewell to Manzanar* in literature circles or as a whole class, students can select scenes and use Kabuki Theater as a way to actively engage with storytelling and deciding what parts of the text are most important. Figure 5.4 shows the members of Maria's group dressed for their performance. They painted their faces white, as mimes, with "red cheeks" to represent the female characters and "red lines" to represent the male characters. The narrator is dressed in a white kimono, while the actors have floral kimonos. The kimonos were simply pieces of fabric with no additional stitching. While the makeup and costumes may not be required, they do add a nice touch of authenticity that puts students more in touch with Japanese culture.

Trifold Display of Research

All of the novels featured in this book depict an era of history and conflict over which there is substantial research for students to investigate. While students could compose a traditional essay or research paper to convey these findings, the Trifold Display of Research offers an engaging alternative (or addition). Topics for students to investigate while reading *Farewell to Manzanar* include aspects of daily life such as food and meals,

Figure 5.4. Group Members Dressed for Kabuki Theater. Students from left to right: Roxanne Sturm, Laura Esslinger, Jeness Duffy, Stacy Gunsel, Michael Westfall, Maria Apostolou.

work, factories, socialization, the location of the camps, or the impact on families. Whatever the focus, students should look for pictures that bring the experience to life. One of my students, Jeness Duffy, created a Trifold Display of Research on Japanese Internment Camps (see Figure 5.5) "to convey the power of the novel as well as the humanity and inhumanity of the imprisonment of 110,000 Japanese Americans that our history rarely recognizes" (excerpted from Jeness's essay that accompanied the Trifold).

Jeness's Trifold includes words descriptive of Japanese internment, such as "oppression," "evacuate," and "Manzanar"; she then wrote these in both Japanese and English "to illustrate the dual loyalty/identity that the characters in the novel feel between being Japanese and being American." The Trifold Display of Research gives students an opportunity to blend research and artistic skills; the Trifolds also offer distinctive professional-educational display and presentation features that may be useful for school libraries, media centers, and open houses.

Figure 5.5. Trifold Display of Research Findings About Japanese Internment Camps. Trifold display and accompanying excerpt by Jeness Duffy.

Many of the photos convey the emotion, tension, and humanity of the experience in a more powerful and different way than words can. Most of the photos were taken by the professional and talented photographers Dorothea Lange and Ansel Adams, which shows why so many of the photos capture such striking moments and images. . . . Some of the most shocking photos are of signs that I cannot believe were displayed in our country: "Japs Keep Moving; This is a White Neighborhood," and "Japs Keep Out You Rats.". . . I also included a map of the ten relocation centers to provide a visual depiction of the location of the camps. The [Japanese and American flags represent] the two controversial questions from the 1943 loyalty oath, discussed in Chapter 11 of the novel, show[ing] the "double impulse" (157), as Jeanne phrases it, that many Japanese Americans felt. . . . Finally, the quotation, "When your mother and your father are having a fight, do you want them to kill each other? Or do you just want them to stop fighting?" (64), which Papa says in his interview at Fort Lincoln, North Dakota, simply and poignantly sums up this double loyalty and desire for peace between the two countries many Japanese Americans desired. . . . I feel that this collection of photos represents many aspects of the internment experience that Jeanne includes in her novel as well as the emotion and reality of this piece of history.

EPILOGUE: THE AFTERMATH OF JAPANESE INTERNMENT

In December 1944, the U.S. Supreme Court handed down a decision in *Ex Parte Endo* stating that it was illegal for the government to hold loyal American citizens in concentration camps against their will. One day before the Supreme Court's ruling, President Franklin Roosevelt declared that the war emergency had ended, and internees could return to the west coast in January 1945. While many would look upon Roosevelt's announcement as good news, the transition came with significant hardship for the Japanese who had been interned. Relocation back to the west coast consisted of giving an internee $25 (approximately one month's income) and a train ticket to the destination of the internee's choice (Mackey). Having sold their houses—often at half their value—and given away most of their possessions in the weeks preceding their initial relocation, many internees no longer had homes to return to; this, combined with the anti-Japanese sentiment that had developed during the war years, no doubt made leaving the relocation centers and trying to integrate back into the larger society a daunting and often fearful task. It follows, therefore, that although the WRA encouraged internees to leave the centers at the beginning of January 1945, so the centers could be closed by the end of November 1945, few internees felt ready to leave. Only 2,000 of the 7,000 Japanese interned in the Heart Mountain relocation center had left by June 1945 (Mackey, n.d.).

In the decades following World War II, numerous efforts were made to set right the injustices that accompanied Executive Order 9066. In 1976, America's bicentennial year, President Gerald Ford issued Proclamation 4417, "An American Promise." This proclamation repealed the order, an action that met resistance from many Congressmen and Senators who believed the order might be useful while dealing with tensions of the Cold War (Mackey, n.d.). In the proclamation, Ford (1976) stated:

> We now know what we should have known then—not only was that evacuation wrong, but Japanese-Americans were and are loyal Americans. On the battlefield and at home, Japanese-Americans—names like Hamada, Mitsumori, Marimoto, Noguchi, Yamasaki, Kido, Munemori and Miyamura—have been and continue to be written in our history for the sacrifices and the contributions they have made to the well-being and security of this, our common Nation. . . .
>
> I call upon the American people to affirm with me this American Promise —that we have learned from the tragedy of that long-ago experience forever to treasure liberty and justice for each individual American, and resolve that this kind of action shall never again be repeated. (p. 1)

Four years later, President Jimmy Carter assisted Japanese Americans with the issue of redress by creating the Commission on Wartime Relocation and Internment of Civilians. In 1983, that Commission issued a report that declared that relocation could not be justified as a military necessity and that the relocation "was the result of war hysteria, race prejudice, and a failure of political leadership" (Mackey, n.d.). During their terms in office, Presidents Reagan, Bush, and Clinton issued letters of apology to the camp survivors. While all of these efforts were important measures of redress, the most tangible measure came in 1990, under the leadership of President George H. W. Bush, when the federal government issued checks for $20,000 to each surviving former internee; each check was accompanied by a signed letter of apology from the President.

Although financial compensation and letters of apology are honorable and show a sincere effort on behalf of the U.S. government to atone for the impact of Executive Order 9066, they do not remove the life-changing effect this order had on over 110,000 Japanese individuals, including Jeanne Wakatsuki Houston. While the bombing of Pearl Harbor stunned the nation and found many of its people scattering for ways to protect our homeland, it seems that the first Director of the WRA, Milton Eisenhower, had great foresight in saying:

> The Government may not be excused for not having attempted to distinguish between the loyal and the disloyal in carrying out the evacuation. . . . I feel most deeply that when the war is over . . . we as Americans are going to regret the avoidable injustices that may have been done. (Weglyn, 1976, n.p.)

ANNOTATED BIBLIOGRAPHY

Inada, L. F. (2000). *Only what we could carry: The Japanese American internment experience.* Berkeley, CA: Heydey Books.
Blends poems, news articles, announcements, photos, sketches, cartoons, letters, and narratives to tell the story of Japanese internment.

Mazer, H. (2002). *A boy at war: A novel of Pearl Harbor.* New York: Alladin.
Depicts the bombing of Pearl Harbor and the anti-Japanese sentiment that followed. A close look at friendship between two boys, Caucasian and Japanese American.

Mazer, H. (2004). *A boy no more.* New York: Scholastic.
Adam Pelko's dad dies on the U.S.S. Arizona during the bombing of Pearl Harbor. This complicates his friendship with Davi, a Japanese American whose dad has been taken into custody.

Omori, E. (Director). (1999). *Rabbit in the moon* [Video]. United States: Transit
Media.
Documentary that tells the story of many Japanese Americans who were interned during World War II. The film explores aspects of daily life and hardship in the camps, such as dust storms in the summer; extreme cold in winter;
malnutrition; inadequate school, health care, and housing facilities; and the
destruction of the family.

Salisbury, G. (1995). *Under the blood red sun.* New York: Yearling.
Tomi Nakiji is torn between wanting to respect his grandfather, who puts his
Japanese heritage at the forefront, and being more "American." Shows com-
plications for Japanese Americans that followed the bombing of Pearl Harbor.

Tunnel, M. O., & Chilcoat, G. W. (1996). *The children of Topaz: The story of a Japanese-American internment camp based on a classroom diary.* New York: Holiday
House.
Based on diary entries by third graders over a 6-month period, this book shows
what the Japanese internment experience was like for children.

REFERENCES

Ford, G. H. (1976). *Proclamation 4417, Confirming the termination of executive order
authorizing Japanese-American internment during world war II.* Retrieved July 21,
2005, from http://www.ford.utexas.edu/library/speeches/760111p.htm
Houston, J. W., & Houston, J. D. (1973). *Farewell to Manzanar.* New York: Dell
Laurel-Leaf.
Lamb, A., & Johnson, L. (2005). *Japanese-American internment.* Retrieved July 21,
2005, from http://www.42explore2.com/japanese.htm
Mackey, M. (n.d.). *A brief history of the Heart Mountain relocation center and the Japanese American experience.* Retrieved July 21, 2005, from http://chem.nwc.cc
.wy.us/HMDP/history.htm
Manjiro, I. (1995). *Kabuki for everyone.* Retrieved May 19, 2004, from http://www
.fix.co.jp/kabuki/kabuki.html
Meyers, C., & Jones, T. (1993). *Promoting active learning: Strategies for the college
classroom.* San Francisco: Jossey-Bass.
Nelson, C. (n.d.). *Concentration camps?* Modern American poetry. Retrieved July 21,
2005, from http://www.english.uiuc.edu/maps/poets/g_l/haiku/camps.htm
Roosevelt, F. D. (1941). War message to Congress. Retrieved July 21, 2005, from
http://www.historycentral.com/documents/warmessage.html
Weglyn, M. (1976). *Years of infamy.* New York: Morrow Quill Paperbacks. Retrieved
July 21, 2005, from http:www.geocities.com/Athens/8420/main.html

CHAPTER 6

Korean Perseverance During the Japanese Occupation (1910–1945)

Having lived through this turbulent period of Korean history, I wanted to share my experiences. So little is known about my homeland, its rich culture and its sad history. My love for my native country and for my adopted country [the United States] prompted me to write this book and share some of my experiences and foster greater understanding.

—Sook Nyul Choi

Based on the author's firsthand experience growing up in Korea during the Japanese Occupation that lasted from 1910 to 1945, Sook Nyul Choi's *Year of Impossible Goodbyes* (1991) is the centerpiece of this unit. The unit explores Korean culture, the wickedness of cultural genocide, a loving family practicing different religions, and the importance of upholding strong morals and depending on one another in order to survive and preserve culture, especially in times of foreign occupation or war.

Active learning strategies in this chapter include Socratic Seminars concerning crucial issues of civility and freedom; Lotus Petal Links; Scrapbook for Comparing and Contrasting Students' Lives with Sookan's (the protagonist of *Year of Impossible Goodbyes*); Korean War Survey, Research, and PowerPoint Project; Hangul Name Journal; and Character Portfolio. A summary view of active learning strategies in this chapter appears in Figure 6.1.

HISTORICAL CONTEXT

Having won battles against China (1894–1895) and Russia (1904–1905), Japan, near the turn of the 20th century, had become the most powerful

Figure 6.1. Active Learning Strategies in Chapter 6.

Featured Young Adult Novel	Thoughtfulness and Reflection	Creative and Personal/ Analytical Writing	Active Learning Projects
Year of Impossible Goodbyes	• Socratic Seminar • Lotus Petal Links	• Scrapbook for Comparison and Contrast	• Korean War Survey, Research, PowerPoint, and Self-Reflection • Hangul Name Journal • Character Portfolio

nation in northern Asia (Crystal, 1993). In 1910, Japan annexed Korea. Japan's Imperial forces structured every part of the Korean economy to strengthen the Empire of Japan, which at that time stretched across Manchuria, southeast Asia, the Pacific, and part of China. Japanese officials forced heavy industry on the northern part of Korea and took most of the profits (*Korean War*, n.d.). Under Japanese Occupation, Korean citizens were forced to adopt Japanese names and convert to the Shinto (native Japanese) religion, and were forbidden to use the Korean language in school and business settings (*Life in Korea*, n.d.). The Japanese "corralled people into slave labor gangs to construct factories, mines, buildings, and roads," and the Imperial army drafted Korean men to serve as occupation troops all over Asia (*Korean War*, n.d., p. 1). In addition, more than 200,000 women were forced into sexual slavery for the Japanese troops (Se-moon, 2003).

Korean Resistance

Many Koreans fought against the Japanese Occupation and enslavement of the Korean people. Kim Il Sung aligned himself with the communist party and led a guerrilla resistance movement in the north. Syngman Rhee represented the right-wing resistance groups that protested foreign exploitation by fleeing prison and publicizing Korea's plight before the world (*Korean War*, n.d.). On March 1, 1919, the Koreans launched an Independence Movement. It was, however, brutally repressed by the Japanese, leading to the "killing of thousands, maiming and imprisoning of tens of thousands, and destroying of hundreds of churches, temples, schools, and private homes" (*Life in Korea*, n.d., p. 1). Throughout World War II, Japan forced Koreans to serve in the imperial army and fed its war machine through Korean labor and resources. When World War II came to an end with Japan's surrender on August 15, 1945, Korea came under the divided rule of Russian Occupation north of the 38th parallel and American Occupation of the southern section. Under the direction of the United Nations, the Republic of Korea (South Korea) established a democratic government in 1948 with its capital in Seoul. The Communists formed the Democratic People's Republic of Korea (North Korea) with its capital in P'yongyang.

The Cold War Era

With the end of World War II and the division of Korea, hostilities emerged between the communist and capitalist forms of government embodied by the USSR and the USA. During this Cold War era (1946–1989), the superpowers (USSR and USA) built up stockpiles of nuclear weapons and formed alliances with nations they could use for their strategic advantage. It was in this Cold War climate that North Korea invaded South Korea on June 25, 1950. The United Nations and the United States helped the South, while Communist Chinese volunteers sided with the North in this war, which lasted 3 years. Sook Nyul Choi's novel, *Year of Impossible Goodbyes*, spans 1945–1950 and encompasses both the end of the Japanese Occupation and the beginning of the Russian Occupation of North Korea. While not going into much detail about America's involvement in the Korean War, Choi, writing from her personal experiences, clearly shows her family's fear of Communist rule. This novel, therefore, is useful as a springboard to help students understand both the Korean War and the Cold War era at large.

FEATURED YOUNG ADULT NOVEL

Year of Impossible Goodbyes

Sook Nyul Choi's honest—sometimes heart-wrenching—account, *Year of Impossible Goodbyes* (1991), reveals the atrocities and cruelties endured by Koreans throughout the Japanese Occupation of their country from 1910 to 1945. While the narrator, Sookan, must wear a uniform and attend a Japanese school, her brothers have been sent away to labor camps. Sookan's mother is forced to oversee a sock factory, and her father is required to serve in the military in Manchuria. Sookan's grandfather, once a respected Buddhist scholar, is forbidden to practice his art of using oxtail brushes to script the Korean language of Hangul and forced to suppress his strong religious beliefs. Likewise, Sookan's mother, a devout Catholic, is driven to hide her religious convictions. When World War II ends, and the Japanese are defeated, Korea is its own again for a time. However, Communist Russia soon takes control of North Korea, leaving Sookan's family oppressed once again. Sookan's mother has a plan for the family to escape to the freedoms of South Korea, but she is detained en route by the Russians, leaving Sookan, and her little brother, Inchun, abandoned and having to fend for their own safety. In the book's climax, Sookan and Inchun, both with bleeding feet, literally run for the border, dodging searchlights, dogs, soldiers, and barbed wire. Initially sheltered by the Red Cross center at the 38th parallel, Sookan and Inchun are soon reunited with their parents and brother who also made it safely to the South. Sookan enjoys her new life and school, but says, "Our freedom and happiness did not last long. In June 1950, war broke out. North Korean and Communist soldiers filled the streets of Seoul, and were soon joined by Chinese Communist troops. Russian tanks came barreling through" (Choi, 1991, p. 168). Choi's novel ends with the beginning of the Korean War.

THOUGHTFULNESS AND REFLECTION

Addressing Crucial Issues of Civility and Freedom

Through the experiences of Sookan and her family, *Year of Impossible Goodbyes* explores a number of serious issues that provide the basis for rich and potentially thoughtful and sensitive Socratic Seminars and/or class discussions. The issues of Forced Military and Factory Work; Punishment, Abuse, and Political Execution; and Humiliation and Brainwashing at School are outlined in the section that follows. The section concludes with a model Socratic Seminar and Lotus Petal Links, a strategy to help students identify, sort out, and visually arrange important themes in the book.

Forced Military and Factory Work. Sookan's father and three older brothers, like many Korean men during the Japanese Occupation, were forced to fight in the military. Her mother, Aunt Tiger, and cousin Kisa ran an ill-equipped factory that knitted socks for the Japanese military. Many able-bodied Korean girls and women from the region worked from dawn to dusk under harsh conditions that provided no breaks, food, or water. In deplorable conditions and under the watchful eye of Captain Narita, the overseer of the town and factory, these workers were forced to produce seemingly unattainable quantities of socks.

Punishment, Abuse, and Political Execution. The overbearing Captain Narita also ordered the pine tree at Sookan's house to be chopped down by the Japanese police as punishment for the family's having a birthday party for Haiwon, one of the young girls who toiled daily at the factory. When the tree, having been a special place of private prayer for Sookan's grandfather, was "hacked to pieces" (Choi, 1991, p. 29), his health deteriorated, as though his very spirit had been under the axe. Nearing his death, Sookan's grandfather revealed that he had been captured and tortured by the Japanese for his involvement in the establishment of a Hangul newspaper. Before his death, however, he whispered, "Do not feel bitter about what happened. I am not angry anymore. I know that better times will soon come to you." His final parting left Sookan's mother and Aunt Tiger in despair and angry over the unfair rule of the Japanese. Shortly after the grandfather's death, Captain Narita dealt another blow to Sookan's mother as he announced:

> Your sock girls did not do good work this week. We Imperial soldiers can put them to better use. Our victorious Imperial soldiers need to be rewarded for their heroic achievements on the battlefields. Our great Heavenly Emperor will be pleased to know that your girls volunteered to help our soldiers fight better. Your girls will be honored to bring glory to the Emperor. (p. 52)

Despite Sookan's mother's efforts to increase production at the sock factory and protect the girls, Captain Narita burst in with two soldiers who "herd[ed] the girls toward the truck. Some screamed and fell to the muddy ground, but were jabbed with guns and forced onto the truck" (p. 59). Euphemized by the Japanese as "spirit girls" for "giv[ing] the soldiers the special spirit to fight harder against the White Devils" (p. 59), these young Korean women were kidnapped, raped, and sometimes murdered. Aunt Tiger, envisioning the horrors to come for these girls, reported hearing that "half of them killed themselves by jumping off the speeding trucks rather than be locked in those latrines and used by the soldiers" (p. 56).

In the book's epilogue, the reader learns that Sookan's cousin Kisa and Aunt Tiger were found by the Town Reds and named "traitors" for having helped people escape from North to South Korea. "They were shot with machine guns, and then hanged in the town square to serve as a lesson to others" (p. 169).

Humiliation and Brainwashing at School. Chapter 5 of Choi's novel focuses on Sookan's experience attending a Japanese school where her teacher, Narita Sensei, looked on her with disdain. Sookan was no longer called by her Korean name and, along with many of the other children, was degraded. In addition to having to sing the Japanese national anthem (and deny her own), Sookan had to recite a daily pledge of her "undying loy-alty and good wishes and prosperity and good health of the Heavenly Emperor," and "wish for the victory of the heavenly Japanese soldier and the defeat of the White Devils" (Choi, 1991, pp. 71–72). Sookan had to sit on the floor and was driven to tears when Narita Sensei banged a ruler on her desk, sending a pencil flying that hit Sookan in the eye (p. 73). Sookan was baffled as she saw the students repeat "ridiculous slogans" of propa-ganda against the White Devils, but she realized that to do differently could result in her family's starvation (p. 74). She, and all of the other girls at the school, were to spend their days sharpening "small pieces of glass and rock to throw at the White Devils . . . the boys made spearheads, which they fastened to the end of long bamboo poles. The smaller boys were filling bags with sand" (p. 79). Sookan saw students humiliated as they wet their pants, unable to use the restroom. "She [Narita Sensei] made us all feel very worthless and ashamed of ourselves" (p. 75). Even sharing was forbidden, a lesson Sookan learned when she gave part of her lunch to a girl with little food, only to have a monitor come and take the "beautiful lunch box that Grandfather had made" (p. 76).

Socratic Seminar

The Socratic Seminar that follows is built on some of the key issues in *Year of Impossible Goodbyes*. This is presented as a model and can be ex-panded to include other questions, especially ones that arise out of student sharing in response to Question 5 in the list of Opening Questions.

Opening Questions. The teacher/facilitator should read all of the Open-ing Questions and ask students to choose one to respond to. The Opening Question of the Socratic Seminar is the only one students are required to answer—every student must share something. Questions 1–3 are of a more personal nature, and questions 4 and 5 are more general/impersonal. This variety of questions is aimed at addressing comfort levels of different types of students.

1. Tell of a time when you made a decision that had a negative impact on someone around you (friend, family member, classmate, etc.).
2. Tell of a time you (or someone you know) felt out of place or were treated in a derogatory fashion because of your race, gender, na-tionality, or religious or cultural background.
3. Tell of a time you or a friend or family member lost something you valued greatly. Or tell of a time when you had to say goodbye to someone you cared about.

4. Share an example of where and for what purposes you have seen the use of propaganda.
5. *Year of Impossible Goodbyes* is really about . . . (complete the phrase).

Core Questions. Once all students have responded to one of the Opening Questions, the teacher/facilitator should use the following questions to develop the bulk of the seminar. The teacher/facilitator's role should be limited so that students rely on one another in developing a dialogue. Ideally, each Core Question will involve at least 10 minutes of student dialogue.

1. How would you define "power" as it is represented in *Year of Impossible Goodbyes*? Who has power and who does not? What shifts of power do you see? Where do you see power used appropriately and inappropriately?
2. How do symbols play into the story? What about euphemisms? How did these elements work to build up or tear down the culture and identity of the Korean people under the Japanese Occupation?
3. What character or conflict most captured your attention and why? (It could be because you liked and admired the character or because you found the character despicable in some way.)
4. Despite all of the terrible things that happen to Sookan's family, how is this story one of hope and faith? How do faith, prayer, and religious freedom (or lack thereof under Communism) play into *Year of Impossible Goodbyes*?
5. Where do you see propaganda and discrimination in the book? How are the two linked?

Closing Questions. The Closing Questions are designed to extend the discussion of the book to students' own lives and current learning. They also provide an opportunity to bring closure to the seminar. Ideally, 5–10 minutes would be devoted to these questions. The teacher can list all of the questions (as with the Opening Questions), then have volunteers respond to whatever question most appeals to them, or simply can go down the list or choose one question if time is running out.

1. If you could give advice to any character in the book, who would it be? What advice would you give and why?
2. What questions remain unresolved for you having read this book? What would you like to learn more about as a result of having read this book?
3. Having read *Year of Impossible Goodbyes*, how important do you think it is to know your family's genealogical history and cultural traditions?

4. I leave *Year of Impossible Goodbyes* with . . . (complete the statement. It could be with a particular emotion, a better understanding of the history and conflict, etc.).
5. A good alternative title for this book would be _____ because _____ . . . (complete the statement).

Lotus Petal Links

Having touched upon some of the major themes and hardships depicted in Choi's novel through the Socratic Seminar, students now apply their creative and analytical skill to explore the book and Korean culture in greater depth. For example, the lotus blossom is a symbol for the "causality of the spiritual life" (Johnson, 2001, p. 1). Without going deep into spiritual/religious teachings drawn from the Buddhist Sutra, the teacher can impart the more secular, universal concept of the inseparability of cause and effect, and this can be represented in the Lotus Petal Links activity. As a way of examining the themes present in *Year of Impossible Goodbyes*, students are to draw a lotus blossom (pictures can easily be found by searching askjeeves.com) and fill the petals with concepts from the book, especially showing how big ideas stem to (or can be supported by) smaller ones. Students might think of this as a Concept Web whereby themes are linked with supporting words, phrases, characters, and examples from the text. The teacher-created model in Figure 6.2 has four subcategories, all representations of the central petal labeled Survival in Times of War: Family, Culture, Freedom, and Spirit. As a variation of this activity, students also could fill the petals or lotus pads with quotes, symbols, and pictures representing the book and aspects of Korean culture.

In addition to drawing or filling out a premade lotus blossom to link themes and supporting ideas from the book, students should write about—or at least verbally explain—their choices. Figure 6.2 illustrates a teacher-created written explanation of the Lotus Petal Links.

CREATIVE AND PERSONAL/ANALYTICAL WRITING

Scrapbook for Comparison and Contrast

While the Lotus Petal Links strategy helps students to identify major themes in *Year of Impossible Goodbyes*, the writing-intensive Scrapbook described here helps students better understand Sookan, the main character of Choi's novel. The Scrapbook includes the following components to facilitate students' creative and personal/analytical writing:

Figure 6.2. Example of Lotus Petal Links. Teacher-created model and corresponding written explanation by Linda Rice.

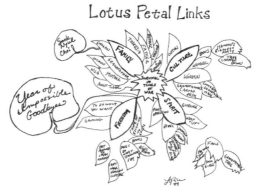

Lotus Petal Links

Family: The family members' names surround the key word Family. The names listed below the main Family petal are those who remained in P'yongyang during the Japanese Occupation, while the names listed above the Family petal are those who were out of town or even out of the country. Theresa was at a convent as a nun, Father was in Manchuria with the military, and Sookan's brothers had all been ordered to labor camps.

Culture: Among the supporting petals surrounding Culture are Hangul, the Korean script Grandfather so loved to write; some handcrafts; clothes; and books. Separated from the Culture petal are "Haiwon's birthday party" and "tree chopped down." As Sookan's family punishment for having the party, Captain Narita ordered Japanese soldiers to chop down the tree that had been a private, favorite spot of prayer for Grandfather. When the tree was chopped down, Grandfather's health began to decline, and soon thereafter he died; part of the family's culture was forever lost as a result.

Freedom: The Freedom petal demonstrates almost equal representations of having and losing freedom. While the hope of escaping to the South is linked with Freedom, what the family endures in the interim during Japanese and Russian Occupations of their country is a loss of freedom. Sookan is not allowed to wear Korean clothes or speak her native language at school, and citizens become parrots of what the Japanese say about the White Devils. Then, under Russian Occupation, the Koreans feign themselves to be Communist supporters to avoid being called and discriminated against for being "capitalists" and "traitors." Rather than being true Communists (Reds), they refer privately to themselves as Pinks or Phony Reds.

Spirit: The Spirit petal is divided between positive examples and failures that resulted from the constant oppression the Koreans experienced at the hands of people like Captain Narita who ordered the sock girls be taken as "spirit girls"—who would serve as sex slaves for the "victorious Imperial soldiers [who] need to be rewarded for their heroic achievements on the battlefields" (Choi, 1991, p. 52). Sookan and her friend Unhi had a private rebellion to keep up their spirits and endure through the Japanese Occupation when they were forced to make weaponry to defeat the White Devils. Sookan yearned for the Japanese to be defeated and removed from her country, so when her teacher Narita Sensei "told us how to make pieces extra sharp, Unhi and I looked at each other, smiled, and nodded our heads in silent agreement. We bent our heads over our work and revealed our secret. We rubbed the little pieces of glass and rock against the bricks and made them smooth and round" (p. 79).

- Pictures of Korea, its culture, and the war
- Exploration of family relationships and experiences
- Explanation of Scrapbook
- Original poem and personal reflection

The challenges faced by Sookan and her family, living in Occupied Korea, provide a great means of contrast for students to examine their own lives and challenges living in the United States. The Scrapbook combines writing with pictures to show comparisons. In their search for pictures of Korea and its culture, students should look for symbols, traditions, and conflicts that help them visualize Sookan's hometown of P'yongyang, the factories, homes, police, soldiers, trees, and other elements integral to Choi's novel. This section presents the Scrapbook for Comparison and Contrast by explaining various components and useful resources, then highlighting each with examples created by one of my students, Dillon McGuiness. Dillon is a preservice teacher who made his Scrapbook in one of my teaching methods classes.

Pictures of Korea, Its Culture, and the War. Pictures are an effective way to broaden students' vision of a foreign country, culture, or conflict. To begin their Scrapbook of Comparison and Contrast, students should look at pictures from the period surrounding the Korean War. Teachers should note that due to Japanese-imposed restrictions, very few photos exist that show daily life during the period of Japanese Occupation (1910–1945). One book that has been particularly effective in depicting some of the tragedies of war and the attempted genocide of the Korean culture is Arthur Wilson's *Korean Vignettes: Faces of War* (1996). The book focuses on the period of war that followed Sookan's escape to South Korea. Some of the pictures are graphic, in a manner appropriate to the subject, and move students to see, as the title implies, "faces of war"—real people, real human suffering. Dillon McGuiness wrote about his search for pictures this way:

> I saw a picture of a dead North Korean soldier, his face shot almost entirely off. The picture struck me initially with its violence, but it had a second impact on me when I considered that this soldier could very well have been a Korean citizen who had no desire to fight in the war. Maybe he had wanted to cross the 38th parallel south, but had been unable to make it or had not had the courage for the journey that Sookan did.

With the help of pictures, students are able to visually contextualize aspects of Choi's novel like victimization, conflicts between two countries, and what happened to Sookan's homeland after her escape to South Korea.

Exploration of Family Relationships and Experiences. After reading *Year of Impossible Goodbyes* and perusing pictures of Korea, students should begin to make some comparisons between their lives and/or family experiences and those of Sookan. In consideration of students who may have negative home and family experiences, teachers should offer an alternative approach to this assignment by asking students to compare either their "ideal family life," "the American dream," or American democracy with what Sookan experienced in Japanese-occupied Korea. Dillon McGuiness chose the first approach and looked through photo albums to compare his life and family with that of Sookan. Dillon explained his process for this part of the project as follows:

> Sookan and her little brother went through hell in the end of the novel. So I [looked] for photographs of my cousin Max (I have no siblings and only one first cousin) and me going through a rough time in our lives. . . . [Sookan] lived more in the course of a few years than I had lived in 16. The most difficult hell that Max and I ever went through was when we would get into a petty argument. . . . Looking at [my] pictures, the obvious fact fell down upon me that each picture is a happy one. . . . Many, if not all of them, are indicative of a typical life for a son of a suburban American family. I have had a good, simple life. I have always had food and clothing and freedom in abundance. . . . I have not experienced the trials and tribulations of the people I read about in Choi's novel. How dare I pretend that I had not learned something from her novel or that it was all old news to me.

Explanation of Scrapbook. Once students have made some comparisons and contrasts between their life and family experiences and Sookan's, they begin putting the actual Scrapbook together. The Scrapbook should include photos or illustrations with captions and an introduction to how it is set up and what it conveys. Figure 6.3 shows a sample page from Dillon McGuiness's Comparative Scrapbook.

Original Poem and Personal Reflection. The final two required Scrapbook components are an original poem and personal reflection. Students can write any kind of poem they want, so long as it demonstrates comparison or contrast of their life (or American culture) and something from *Year of Impossible Goodbyes.* The self-reflection paper is a place for students

Figure 6.3. Sample Page from Scrapbook for Comparison and Contrast. Student-created scrapbook and excerpt by Dillon McGuiness.

Left:
- Black and white pictures paralleled this quote from *Year of Impossible Goodbyes*: "Aunt Tiger took my hand, and we walked through the streets in our colorful silk hanbok, speaking freely in Korean. Many Koreans were out in their hanbok, talking, laughing, and crying. Korean flags were proudly flying in front of almost every home" (92).
- Dillon contrasted this with his own photo captioned this way: "The Disneyworld Toy Story parade is the closest I have come to being a part of a victory parade."

Right:
- Black and white photos of hungry Korean children linked to this quote from Choi's book: "My shoes were wet and my feet were frozen. My stomach growled with hunger. Little Inchun was still crying. I stopped to comfort him and picked him up to carry him on my back. His tears fell on my neck" (135).
- Dillon contrasted this with a picture of him and his cousin captioned, "This is probably the hardest of times Max and I ever went through. I am trying to read a comic book, and he is interrupting me."

to report what they learned in completing the Scrapbook. Upon studying Sookan's perspective as a girl growing up in Japanese-controlled Korea, student Dillon McGuiness found himself "obsessed with the theme of contrast . . . and obsessed with [his] ignorance of other people" (excerpted from Dillon's essay accompanying the Scrapbook). This intense focus on contrasting the student's life with that of the book's main character, Sookan, and the desire to know more, is reflected in a poem, and the explanation that follows it, that Dillon included with his Scrapbook. "Simple, Lovely Ways" (see Figure 6.4) contrasts the student's life with that of Sookan.

Figure 6.5 offers the student's reflection on and explanation of "Simple, Lovely Ways." It is worth noting how personal the tone of the essay is in terms of serious reflection and being critical of oneself for taking the relative ease of life for granted. This reflection helps to affirm the importance of teaching and studying great young adult novels with important life themes that offer real-world relevance. Also, this attests to the value of studying historical fiction as a way to help students learn about the past and expand their understanding of the world in which they live and the conflicts individual people, nations, and cultures have endured.

ACTIVE LEARNING PROJECTS

Korean War Survey, Research, PowerPoint, and Self-Reflection

As *Year of Impossible Goodbyes* paints a picture of the Japanese and Russian Occupations of Korea and the events leading up to the Korean War, it will be helpful for students studying the book to conduct an inventory of what they know and become acquainted with some of the significant events, people, and terms associated with the war. This project begins with students, working in pairs, forming a hypothesis about their assigned topic and creating a survey to check its validity. The hypothesis should concern some aspect of the Korean War (see Figure 6.6 for a list of topics).

Survey on the Korean War. After forming the hypothesis, students should derive three to five questions for a survey that will inform their hypothesis; see Figure 6.7 for an example.

Students can decide who the primary audience is for their survey questions (peers, relatives who remember the Korean War, veterans, etc.) and administer their survey to that group to check their hypothesis. After administering the survey to at least ten people, students should create some

Figure 6.4. Poem for Comparison and Contrast by Dillon McGuiness.

Simple, Lovely Ways

Her young fingers held the scattered fragments
Of her grandfather's dead tree.
(Fragments of dreams, traditions, and a humble life.)

My young fingers hold a stainless steel spoon,
Hovering over my cereal bowl
As I watch morning American television.
(The news of the day concerns professional baseball.)

At nights she might have whispered a prayer
Or two, if she dared.
The devil was not white and to the east,
But much more real.
And prayer was defiance.

At night I say the Lord's Own Prayer,
And the words comfort my tired head
With their empty familiarity.
(As a child I looked forward
To the snack table after Sunday sermons,
Donuts, cookies, and tea.)

Her tears held the memories of her family
And an easier life from so long ago.
She said goodbye to birthday parties, tasty salted meats,
And watching her mother brush her hair at night.
My daily complaints are the evidence
Of a life where even love can be taken for granted.
"Things are always the same and never change."
I have had the love of my parents;
That was the way things were.
I have had friends who would die for me;
That was the way things were.
The way things were is a bland thought,
And I devour new experiences and sensations.

She said an impossible goodbye
To the simple, lovely way things were.

Figure 6.5. Personal Reflection on Poem for Comparison and Contrast by Student Dillon McGuiness.

Explanation of "Simple, Lovely Ways" (see Figure 6.4)

I find I am obsessed with this theme of contrast. I am obsessed with my ignorance of other people.

I am being hard on myself. This is very true. However, it feels necessary and right. I am not wallowing in sadness over my own happiness. It would be a disrespectful waste of my life to be broken-hearted over what I have been blessed with.

I am being constructive with these thoughts, especially in this poem. I do not wish to demean my happy childhood or wonderful friends by shunning their existence. However, I do wish to remind myself of what I have.

Sookan's life got worse as the novel went on. She once had a happy family as I do now, but it was taken from her. If I remind myself of this, of what the Korean people of this time period lived through, then I will not take for granted, for example, the time I have with my loving, unharmed family.

This poem says, in the fewest words I could use, all of what I had in my head upon finishing Choi's novel. *Year of Impossible Goodbyes* made me look at my morning breakfast cereal differently, and I wanted to relate that.

---

type of table or graph (pie chart, line graph, bar graph, etc.) to represent the results; see Figure 6.8 for an example.

Having represented their survey results in graphic form, students answer a series of questions to reflect upon what the survey revealed. Figure 6.9 shows the questions, along with responses by one of my students, Andrea Hannon.

Figure 6.6. Research Topics for Investigating the Korean War.

Significant Events	People	Terms and Places
NK invades South Korea	Joseph Stalin	The Forgotten War
Task Force Kean	Mao Zedong	ROK
Massacre of Prisoners at Hill 303	Harry Truman	Manchuria
Inchon Landings	Syngman Rhee	38th Parallel
Battle of Bloody Ridge	General MacArthur	MASH
Battle of Heartbreak Ridge	Maxwell Taylor	Pattons, Pershings, and Shermans
Stalemate on the MLR; Talks at Panmunjom	Georgi Malenkov	
	Kim Il Sung	P'yongyang
POW Olympics at Camp 5, Pyuktong		Cease Fires
		Old Baldry, T-Bone, Eerie, and Pork Chop
Truce Talks (1953)		Chuch'e

Figure 6.7. Sample Hypothesis and Survey Questions. Student-created example by Wendy Frantz and Andrea Hannon.

Term: The Forgotten War

Hypothesis: The Korean War is easily confused with the Vietnam War and thus left out of history classes.

Survey Questions:

1. Have you heard of the Korean War prior to reading *Year of Impossible Goodbyes*?
2. What countries fought in the Korean War?
3. Have you ever been given the opportunity to read about the Korean War or Vietnam War in school before reading Choi's book? (If you only know about one please list which one.)

Note. Adapted from Glasgow (2002).

Researching the Korean War. Moving from the survey where they formed a hypothesis to see what their peers knew about some aspect of the Korean War, students now research their assigned event, person, term, or place in preparation for writing a 2- to 4-page paper about it. Following are the focus questions/prompts to guide students' research investigation:

- *Significant Event(s):* Explain what the event was and why/how it was significant. Explain how it affected the Korean War as a whole. Explain how it affected the Korean people or others.

Figure 6.8. Sample Pie Chart Depicting Student Response to Survey Question 3. Teacher-created model by Linda Rice.

Which war have you been given an opportunity to read about in school?

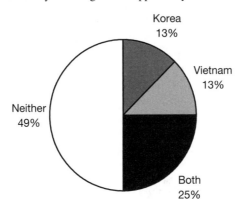

Figure 6.9. Sample Reflection on Survey. Student-written questions and excerpts of responses by Andrea Hannon.

1. What was your assigned event, person, or term?

    Our assigned topic was "The Forgotten War." Rachel and I think that it means that the Korean War is also known as the forgotten war. We think that it means this because . . .

2. Were the responses to your survey what you expected? Explain.

    Rachel and I were not surprised by the results of our survey because we thought that even though we are now studying the Korean War that most students had not heard of it before. We also think that it is not studied or people know very little about it because . . .

3. What surprised you about the responses?

    The thing that surprised us the most about our results was the fact that a few people had heard of both the Korean and the Vietnam Wars back in 7th grade. We did not think that many students had heard about either war before now . . .

4. What would you change about your survey if you tried it again?

    If Rachel and I were to conduct this survey again we might have changed the questions so that we could get more detailed information. Some of the additional things we would want to know from the respondents are . . .

5. What about your survey worked well?

    We think the thing that worked out best for our survey was the fact that we got so many responses back since we were able to have the students in the history classes respond to our survey. This allowed us to see . . .

- *Person(s)*: Explain who the person is/was, including what country the person is from, why it is important to know about the person, and what the person's job/title was during the war. Explain any decisions or actions the individual made or took during the Korean War that had a significant impact on the war. Also, explain how this person interacted with other important people during the war.
- *Term(s) and Place(s)*: Explain and define the term/place. Explain why the term/place was significant to the Korean War. For terms, tell how they came about (i.e., What are the origins of this term? Who began saying this and why?). Explain whether the term was used in an honoring or a derogatory fashion in relation to the war.

PowerPoint Presentation. After writing a brief paper about their topic, students are to create a PowerPoint presentation that illustrates or explains it to the rest of the class and/or classroom visitors. The PowerPoint should consist of at least six slides, including a cover slide with students' names (working in pairs) and project title, explanation of research findings, significance of topic to the Korean War era, and what they found to be particularly interesting in the process or content of the research. Students should make sure to document all research research findings, pictures, graphics, and symbols in the PowerPoint. Figure 6.10 offers seven slides adapted from a project by one of my students in a teaching methods class, Andrea Hannon.

Self-Reflection Paper. The final component of the research endeavor is for students to write a self-reflection paper. Each student should respond independently (not in pairs) to the four questions listed below.

1. What did you know about your topic prior to your research?
2. What did you learn about your topic that you did not know?
3. During your research, what was the most interesting thing that you learned?
4. After conducting your own research on a topic and listening to everyone else's PowerPoint presentations, what questions are still unanswered about the Korean War? Is there anything that you need more information about?

Hangul Name Journal

While the Korean War Research Project focuses students' attention on a large-scale conflict in which the United States intervened, hoping to stop the spread of Communism and restore independence to South Korea, the Hangul Name Journal focuses students' attention on a much smaller, but deeply significant aspect of Korean culture: names. In *Year of Impossible Goodbyes*, Sookan's grandfather, once a respected Buddhist scholar, was forbidden to practice his art of using oxtail brushes to script the Korean language of Hangul. Names written in Hangul were considered to be very special; this is evidenced in the book when, for Haiwon's birthday, Grandfather wrote her name as a gift. Also, Choi's novel explains that Sookan and her brothers have the name "chun" because it represents spring, and that was very important to their grandfather as a season of hope.

Since Hangul is adapted from Chinese, students will research their own names and those of their family members to see what they mean in Chinese. Students should interview their parents about why they chose to name their child(ren) what they did and what their parents' names mean as well. Visiting the "Get Your Own Chinese Name" website (www.mandarintools .com/ chinesename.html), students will then figure out what their family members' names look like and mean in Chinese. Students are to record this

Figure 6.10. Sample PowerPoint. Teacher-created model by Linda Rice, adapted from student project by Andrea Hannon

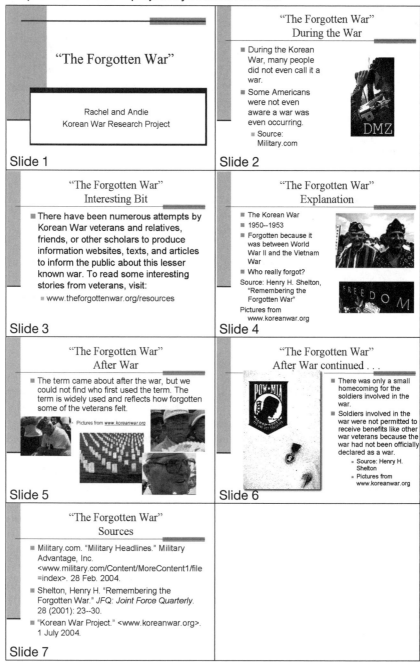

information, along with what they learned from their parents about family names. Finally, students are to compile their information in a Hangul Name Journal. The journal should have a page for each member of the student's family and include the following: English name of the person; name in Chinese characters; Chinese name in writing; a paragraph (or more) describing the person and the origin and/or meaning of his/her name; and whether the Chinese name the website gave describes the person accurately. Figure 6.11 gives an example of the Hangul Name Journal created by James Schurrer, one of my students in a teaching methods class. The top portion of the figure shows several pages laid out, along with the cover, which includes a family photo; the bottom portion includes an actual page from the journal, including the Chinese name and explanation.

Character Portfolio

As the Hangul Name Journal prompts students to take inventory of what they know about themselves and their family members, the Character Portfolio prompts students to take inventory of what they know about characters in the novel and creatively represent this understanding. Adapted from Glasgow (2002), the Character Portfolio, as described here with student samples, includes four distinct parts: Resume, Collage, Connection, and Poem. Students should focus all four parts on a single character of their choosing from *Year of Impossible Goodbyes*.

Resume. After selecting a character from the book, students begin by taking inventory of what they know about him/her by completing a Character Resume. The Character Resume also can prompt a review of various elements of plot and conflict. Wendy Frantz, a student in my teaching methods class, made a Character Resume for Aunt Tiger, Sookan's aunt in *Year of Impossible Goodbyes*. Aunt Tiger's resume (see Figure 6.12) alludes to the death of her father, her missing husband, factory work, and fear of being controlled by the Japanese and Russians. The circumstances surrounding each of these aspects also would provide solid grounds for class discussion.

Collage. Students can draw on the information from the Character Resume to make a Collage about the character. After choosing pictures, words, drawings, clipart, symbols, and/or artifacts that represent the character, students should write a paragraph describing the Collage. Wendy Frantz wrote the following about the Collage she made to accompany the Character Resume of Aunt Tiger:

Figure 6.11. Sample Hangul Name Journal. Family photo and view of multiple pages of the Schurrer Family's Hangul Name Journal by student James Schurrer, followed by James's Page (name in Chinese followed by explanation).

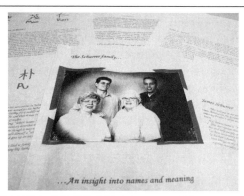

James Schurrer

After talking to my parents, I realized that my name was given to me because of the famous Apostles in the Gospels. James and John were supposedly Jesus's two favorite Apostles. Because my brother's name was already John, my parents were really excited to be able to name me James.

My Chinese name is "Xun Jiaomeng," and it means a teacher, a dreamer, a visionary, and wishful. This description describes my personality almost completely. I have always wanted to be a teacher and help people, and many times, my parents tell me that I "dream big." I was impressed at how accurately this website described my character.

Like Sookan's family, there are many things that are very important to me. One of the most important things in my life is music. I love music and playing the guitar. It is something that keeps me going every day, and I can't imagine myself without it.

Figure 6.12. Character Resume.

Name Aunt Tiger   Location (if known) Kirimni, Pyongyang

Physical Description:
Height 5'0 Weight 135 Hair color black   Eye color dark brown Age 35-40
Other features (glasses, scars, acne, etc) dry, chapped fingers with needle marks; stocky and
round

Family:
Married / Single / Divorced / Widow (circle one)
Children   none
Siblings   Hyunsuk (Sookan's mother)
Relatives   Sookan (niece), Inchun (nephew), Grandfather
Pets   none
Friends   Kisa

Demographics
Education   n/a   Religion   Buddha and Catholicism
Employment sock factory and Party   Hobbies/Interests telling animal fables,
member   gardening
Ethnicity   Korean

Personality
Personality (shy,outgoing,etc) pessimistic   Attitude toward Life   bitter, sad, pensive
Fears   never seeing husband again, never
being free from Japanese or Russian control Attitude toward Death does not seem to
Problems/Hardships keeping secrets from   care
the Party, hunger, hard work in the factory, Favorite Foods white rice cakes
losing father   Favorite Color yellow
Dreams for the Future helping Koreans   Favorite Animal tiger
escape to South Korea
Favorite Season spring

Philosophy of Life (in a phrase) "I now have many people. I've found new purpose in life. This
simple woman is going to do some good (The Year of Impossible Goodbyes, p.123)."

The tiger symbolizes Tiger's name and personality. The "Once Upon a Time" and storytelling pictures indicate that Aunt Tiger enjoys telling wild animal fables to Sookan and Inchun. The socks signify that Aunt Tiger works in the sock factory with the girls, Kisa, and her sister. The man in the suit represents Tiger's husband who was taken away by Japanese soldiers.

Connection. While the Collage gives students an opportunity to think visually and symbolically about the character's life, the next component of the Character Portfolio, the Connection, encourages students to compare and contrast the character in the book with a real person in the student's own life. Instructions are as follows: Characters in novels often remind us of people we know in real life. Identify the family member, friend, or acquaintance that the character you are choosing to investigate reminds you of. Describe the

similarities and differences between the two. This assignment could be ex-
panded by asking students to choose a scene from the novel that reflects the
likeness of the character to the family member, friend, or acquaintance they
have chosen for comparison. Figure 6.13 shows a Character Connection created by Wendy Frantz. The Connection compares her Aunt Alberta with
Sookan's Aunt Tiger in *Year of Impossible Goodbyes*.

Poem. The final component of the four-part Character Portfolio is the
Character Poem. For this task, students draw on the information they have
gathered and compose a poem about their focus character from Choi's
novel. Wendy Frantz wrote the following poem about Aunt Tiger:

Finding Her Way
BY WENDY FRANTZ

Full of love
Sincere with affection
Seeking answers from above
Never knowing of protection

Wild and free she lives
But bitterness makes her sad
To her family her heart she gives
Japanese gone makes her glad

Finding a purpose, a call
Willing to stand brave
She plans to survive through it all
Doing good, her life she gave

Aspects of the student's Character Resume, Collage, and Connection merge
in this poem—the Resume revealed Aunt Tiger's bitterness and sadness,
the Collage showed her love of family, and the Connection conveyed her
willingness to make sacrifices for the benefit of others. In the end of Choi's
novel, the reader learns that Aunt Tiger was put to death for helping her
sister's family escape to South Korea, thus the final line of Wendy's poem,
"Doing good, her life she gave."

EPILOGUE: UNDERSTANDING PERSEVERANCE

In reviewing the significance of Choi's book and students' investigation of its themes and characters through the variety of active learning

Figure 6.13. Character Connection.

Characters in novels often remind of us of people that you we know in real life. Identify the family or a close friend that the character that you have chosen reminds you of. Describe the similarities and differences. Compare and contrast them. Describe a scene in the novel that truly reflects the likeness of the character with the likeness of your family member or close friend.

Character name___Aunt Tiger_____

Person_____Aunt Alberta_____

     My aunt Alberta is similar to Aunt Tiger, because they both love to tell stories. My aunt Alberta is nicknamed Tinkie and that is what I call her – Aunt Tinkie. Aunt Tiger is a nickname, also. My aunt Tinkie, however, is not married. I think Aunt Tiger and Aunt Tinkie have the same body shape. My aunt is short and round. Both women value family and have sacrificed much for them. On more than one occasion my aunt has told me that she is willing to die for me.

     I think the most similar thing about Aunt Tiger and Aunt Tinkie is there relationship with their sister. My mom and Aunt Tinkie have a unique and strong bond. They are very close and share everything with one another. My aunt Tinkie at times depends on my mom, but in the past few years she has come into her and has found things that she does for herself.

---

strategies detailed in this chapter, the reflections of one of my students (Dillon McGuiness) again come to the forefront. As Dillon's comments indicate, the impact of this unit, centered around *Year of Impossible Goodbyes*, both expands students' understanding of the world around them and personalizes human conflicts in history to help students more deeply understand the human spirit of perseverance.

> Neither Aunt Tiger nor Sookan's mother were the passive easterners I had expected them to be. Not only was Aunt Tiger decidedly unspiritual, but she had a vehement, vocalized hatred for the Japanese that was slightly surprising given my unfounded perception of serene Korean woman. Sookan's mother was not a serene Korean housewife either, but a strong woman and a strong Catholic who would fight for those she cared about. . . . Sookan's grandfather was initially the stereotypically philosophical, humble Korean, but I found that Choi imbued his soft-spoken nature with a genuine moral strength beyond any of the other, more aggressive characters of the novel. His love for the humble traditions of Korea's past was so strong that they were at the forefront of his thoughts even while he was on his deathbed. . . .

Reading *Year of Impossible Goodbyes* made me realize there were real families and real people who endured this time in history. A man just like my father was made to endure what might as well have been severe physical torture when the symbol of his entire belief system was cut down before his eyes. Women that could have been class-mates of mine were shipped off to be raped by Japanese soldiers. Sookan's sister, a Catholic nun, could have served in a New York City church. Sookan's mother could have been my own. . . . Choi did not ignore the hard facts she wished to confront and present, or even pull back from them enough to keep these facts blurred and far off. She pulled in close on her subject, and treated her readers with respect. (Excerpt from student essay by Dillon McGuiness)

ANNOTATED BIBLIOGRAPHY

Choi, S. N. (1993). *Echoes of the white giraffe*. New York: Yearling.
Book two in the autobiographical trilogy that began with *Year of Impossible Goodbyes*. Sookan, now a refugee in South Korea, deals with missing her fa-ther and older brothers, school pressures, and forbidden love.

Choi, S. N. (1994). *Gathering of pearls*. New York: Houghton Mifflin.
Book three in the trilogy that began with *Year of Impossible Goodbyes*. Sookan has survived the Korean War and immigrated to the United States, where she enters college. Deals with the pressures of living in a new place, making friends, and adapting to a new culture.

Jiang, J. (1997). *Red scarf girl: A memoir of the cultural revolution*. New York: HarperCollins.
Autobiographical account of a teenager's life experience during the Cultural Revolution in China. Shows many abuses of power, such as brainwashing, beating, and murder. While this book is not about Korea, it shares the theme of hardship and transition from a young adult perspective in a similar way to books written about the Japanese Occupation of Korea.

Park, L. S. (2002). *When my name was Keoko*. New York: Dell Yearling.
Autobiographical account of the author's family experience trying to main-tain cultural identity while living in South Korea during the Japanese Occu-pation before World War II.

REFERENCES

Choi, S. N. (1991). *Year of impossible goodbyes*. New York: Bantam Doubleday Dell.
Crystal, D. (Ed.). (1993). *The Cambridge factfinder*. New York: Cambridge Univer-sity Press.

Glasgow, J. (Ed.). (2002). *Standards-based activities with scoring rubrics: Middle and high school English: Vol. 1. Performance-based portfolios.* Larchmont, NY: Eye on Education.

Johnson, P. (2001). *The lotus blossom.* Retrieved June 28, 2004, from http://www.tientai.net/teachings/Pundarika/renge.htm

Korean War Veterans Memorial. (n.d.). National Park Service. Retrieved October 12, 2005, from http://www.nps.gov/kwvm/war/originsprint.htm

Life in Korea. (n.d.). Retrieved October 12, 2005, from http:ww.lifeinkorea.com/Information/history2.cfm

Se-moon, C. (2003). Comfort women and forced labor. *The Korean Times.* Retrieved October 12, 2005, from http://times.hankooki.com/1page/opinion/200306/kt2003060616141211310.htm

Wilson, A. W. (1996). *Korean vignettes: Faces of war.* Portland, OR: Artwork Publications.

CHAPTER 7

Literature of the Civil Rights Movement (1950s–1960s): Snapshots, Speeches, and Travels That Challenged Young Adults and Changed Them Forever

> *Being an African American woman, reading* [Spite Fences] *brought forth many emotions due to the honest portrayal of violence within the Civil Rights era. I have sat in numerous discussions where Caucasian students do not know of the unspeakable injustices faced by those living in 1954 and the implications of the* Brown v. Board of Education *decision. . . . Reading this novel has reinforced to me the importance of teaching diverse attitudes and combating the negative stereotypes and ignorance. . . . I have not personally lived through the Civil Rights Movement to speak as an authority, but I have reaped the benefits of the blood, sweat, and tears of those working toward liberation within the United States for people of color.*
>
> —Tiffany Thomas, Ohio University student

This chapter features three novels set in the Civil Rights Movement of the 1950s and 1960s: *Spite Fences* (Krisher, 1994), *Just Like Martin* (Davis, 1992), and *The Watsons Go to Birmingham—1963* (Curtis, 1995). These novels, as well as those that appear in the annotated bibliography at the end of the chapter, illuminate the struggle for racial equality in America in ways that readers can experience deeply and personally. These texts invite their readers to feel what it is like to be oppressed and abused, to long to speak and travel freely, but know that each word and each mile must be weighed carefully due to the turbulent—often violent—climate that existed in some neighborhoods and cities.

Active learning strategies in this chapter to help students explore crucial issues and conflicts related to the Civil Rights Movement include a variety of three-dimensional creations, a scrapbook, and several speech- and poetry-writing exercises. The unit closes with a Futuristic Script in which students imagine themselves as characters from one of the featured young adult novels. In the character's shoes, students project into the future, years after the Civil Rights Movement, and examine how the era influenced their views. A summary of specific strategies used in this chapter appears in Figure 7.1.

HISTORICAL CONTEXT

In thinking about the Civil Rights era of the 1950s and 1960s as a movement, we need to think about what a movement is. The word *movement* may make us think of the kinds of energy and forward motion that were characteristic of the Civil Rights era. By definition in the Merriam-Webster dictionary, a movement is a series of organized activities working toward

Figure 7.1. Active Learning Strategies in Chapter 7.

Featured Young Adult Novels	Active Learning Projects	Creative Writing	Simulation and Role Play
The Watsons Go To Birmingham—1963	• Showing the Setting 3-D Style • Singing with Symbolism • Layering the Life of a Character • Scrapbooking the Story		
Spite Fences		• Speech Writing • Grammatical Music	
Just Like Martin			• Futuristic Script
General, Applicable to Any Novel		• Acrostic Poem	

an objective. Often, the Civil Rights Movement is framed by the 1954 Supreme Court ruling in *Brown v. Board of Education of Topeka, Kansas*, unanimously agreeing that segregation in public schools is unconstitutional, and Congress's passage of the Voting Rights Act of 1965, making it easier for southern Blacks to register and vote. But what provides impetus for a movement? An understanding of the answer to this question adds relevance to the study of the Civil Rights era of the 1950s and 1960s because it establishes why change was essential for America's social and moral growth.

From Slavery to the Civil War

The history that led up to the Civil Rights Movement can be envisioned as hundreds of years in the making (how I wish this book could be long enough to include chapters on Slavery in America and the Civil War). From the beginnings of slavery in North America in 1619 when a Dutch ship brought 20 enslaved Africans to the Virginia colony at Jamestown, nearly 240 years passed until the Thirteenth Amendment to the U.S. Constitution officially ended slavery in 1865 (Davis, 2005b). From that first ship until 1808, the year the United States put an official end to the importation of enslaved Africans by European traders, 500,000 slaves came to this country (Davis, 2005b). Over those 12 generations, the descendents of Africans enslaved in the southern states grew to 4 million (Davis, 2005b). The Emancipation Proclamation issued by President Abraham Lincoln on January 1, 1863 (2 years into the Civil War), turned the war into a revolutionary moral battle. What began primarily as a war to preserve the union (after the secession of 11 states that formed the Confederacy), became a war over the abolition of slavery. Although the war ended and the Thirteenth Amendment was added to the U.S. Constitution in 1865, equality was far from the daily lives of African Americans, as evidenced by what became known as Jim Crow laws.

Jim Crow Laws and Legalized Segregation

The term *Jim Crow* originated around 1830 when a White minstrel show performer blackened his face and danced a ridiculous jig while singing the lyrics to the song "Jump Jim Crow" (Davis, 2005a). This character became a standard part of minstrel shows in America, and the term held throughout the 19th century, even after the Civil War ended. The Jim Crow era refers to the period after the Civil War when southern states began "systematically to codify (or strengthen) in law and state constitutional provisions the subordinate position of African Americans in society" (Davis, 2005a, p. 1). Jim Crow laws imposed racial segregation in transportation, health care, and public facilities—including schools and parks. Segregation laws were further supported by brutal attacks and ritualized mob violence against southern Blacks (Davis, 2005a). From 1889 to 1930, over 3,700 men and women were reported victims of lynchings in the United States, and that number does not include hundreds of other lynchings that occurred but went unreported (Davis, 2005a).

A further blow to the cause of equality came in 1896 when the U.S. Supreme Court upheld the lower court's ruling in *Plessy* v. *Ferguson*, which began the "separate but equal" doctrine (Cozzens, 1995, p. 1). More than 50 years passed until that doctrine was overturned with the U.S. Supreme Court's ruling in *Brown* v. *Board of Education* in 1954, which effectively concluded that separate is "inherently unequal" (King, 1999, p. 5).

The Impetus for the Civil Rights Movement

The landmark desegregation ruling in *Brown* v. *Board of Education*, along with the arrest of Rosa Parks and the murder of 14-year-old Emmett Till in 1955, became the impetus for the Civil Rights Movement of the 1950s and 1960s. Rosa Parks was arrested for refusing to give up her seat to a White person on a segregated city bus in Montgomery, Alabama. Emmett Till was a 14-year-old African American boy from Chicago who was visiting relatives in Money, Mississippi. Hanging out on the front porch of Bryant's Grocery and Meat Market, Emmett showed off some photographs and joked that a White girl in one of the pictures was his girlfriend. Then, one of the boys dared Emmett to go into the store and get a date with the "pretty little White woman" standing at the counter. Having no experience with the severe penalties inflicted on Blacks who broke the Jim Crow laws of the South, Emmett walked in as the other kids gathered near the window to see what would happen. Witnesses reported that when he left the store a few minutes later, Emmett said, "'Bye, baby,' and whistled the two-note 'wolf whistle' at the white woman who worked behind the counter" (Crowe, n.d., p. 1). Three days later, when the woman's husband, Roy Bryant, returned from out of town, he and his half-brother, J. W. Milam, decided to "teach the boy a lesson" (p. 2). The two broke into the home where Emmett was staying, yanked him out of bed at 2:30 a.m., and took him away in their car. Three days later, Emmett's naked, battered body was found in the Tallahatchie River. While Bryant and Milam were charged with murder, they were found innocent by an all-White jury that deliberated less than an hour (p. 2). A tide of outrage over the acquittal swept across the nation, and people mobilized a movement for change. The Civil Rights Movement had begun.

Key Figures and the Cause

In addition to Rosa Parks and Emmett Till, a great number of other people devoted their lives to the cause of desegregation and equal rights. Organizations such at the National Association for the Advancement of Colored People (NAACP), the Southern Christian Leadership Conference, Montgomery Improvement Association, the Congress of Racial Equality, and the Student Nonviolent Coordinating Committee worked tirelessly to arrange creative, nonviolent avenues to promote change. "Freedom riders" rode buses to test the implementation of new laws prohibiting segregation in interstate travel facilities, while other activists participated in marches, bus boycotts, and lunch counter sit-ins. At times, nonviolent demonstrations to promote change turned violent, as was the case on March 7, 1965, when Blacks marching from Selma to Montgomery in support of voting rights were stopped on Pettus Bridge by a police blockade. Fifty marchers were hospitalized in the incident known as "Bloody Sunday," in which police used tear gas, whips, and clubs against the marchers (Haney & Brunner, 2000, p. 4). Other significant tragedies that occurred in this era include the assassination of 39-year-old Reverend Martin Luther King, Jr., and the murder of 37-year-old Medgar Evers, who was Mississippi's NAACP field secretary. Four young girls attending Sunday school also were killed when a bomb exploded at the Sixteenth Street Baptist Church in Birmingham, Alabama. While the historical context provided here is by no means exhaustive, sharing it with students—or having them engage in research that they may share with one another—is important to framing this unit and establishing why, at times in human history, change is the only answer.

FEATURED YOUNG ADULT NOVELS

In the first decade of the 21st century, many years after the Civil Rights Movement of the 1950s and 1960s, it may be easy for some young adults to look back on that period of history and "know," or at least firmly believe, that they would have "done the right thing," standing up for racial equality, even if it meant facing personal risk. Books like Trudy Krisher's *Spite Fences* (1994), Ossie Davis's *Just Like Martin* (1992), and Christopher Paul Curtis's *The Watsons Go to Birmingham—1963* (1995) complicate this assumption, however, by the way they poignantly portray the abuses heaped on Black citizens as well as Whites who supported desegregation. For those who have not pondered seriously the plight of the "other," or seen or experienced abuse firsthand, these books plunge readers into situations whereby they come to understand why, at times, the necessity of change becomes so urgent. These books prompt readers to consider the power of speeches and nonviolent protest to effect change; they also demonstrate how the legal system can be a constructive vehicle for delivering justice. Each of the novels inspires readers by showcasing a protagonist who, in light of observed tragedy and/or personal danger, faces and overcomes fears.

The Watsons Go to Birmingham—1963

Although all three novels relate at least one serious episode of violence in the movement to obtain equal rights, *The Watsons Go to Birmingham—1963* is the most lighthearted novel, overall, as much of its story focuses on sibling rivalry and humorous events that depict a strong, loving family through Curtis's carefully crafted characters, Daniel and Wilona Watson and their children Byron, Kenneth (Kenny), and Joetta (Joey). The family travels from Flint, Michigan, to Birmingham, Alabama, to see Grandma Sands and leaves Byron with her for the summer in the hopes that she can improve his behavior. The family's visit, however, coincides with the bombing of the Sixteenth Avenue Baptist Church on September 15, 1963, in which four young teenage girls—Addie Mae Collins, Denise McNair, Carole Robertson, and Cynthia Wesley—were killed during Sunday school (Curtis, 1995). This event sends Kenny into a spiral of guilt, grief, and confusion; he has brushed against the face of human cruelty and realizes he is no longer a child. With the support of his family, in particular Byron, the brother who used to tease, taunt, and bully him, Kenny finds healing, acceptance, and the ability to resume daily life (he had spent a period of weeks hiding behind a couch in denial). Byron affirms the importance of Kenny's life, of his being there for his sister Joey, who, otherwise, also might have died in the church arson.

Spite Fences

In contrast to the strong, supportive Watson family in Curtis's book, Krisher's *Spite Fences* presents neighboring families—the Pughs and the Boggs—wrought with dysfunction and contempt. Maggie Pugh (the honorable protagonist) is beaten by her mother on several occasions. Her parents argue constantly and favor Maggie's younger sister, Gardenia, whom they believe will bring pride to the family by winning beauty pageants. Virgil Boggs is a contemptuous racist who willingly terrorizes anyone who shows kindness toward African Americans. He dismembers Gardenia's doll; cuts Gardenia's blonde curls, making it almost impossible for her to win a beauty pageant; and attempts to rape Maggie. Betty Boggs destroys Maggie's most prized possession, a camera given to her by her friend Zeke, and the whole Boggs clan spray paint graffiti on the Pugh's new fence. The most heinous act of the story occurs when Zeke, after being arrested for using a White man's restroom, is taken to the Negro park by Virgil Boggs and his gang. They tie Zeke's hands behind his back, strip him naked, beat him unconscious, and urinate on him. As his final act before his awe-struck cronies, Virgil ejaculates on Zeke's naked body; the gang members laugh, pat each other on the back, and disperse. What they don't know is that Maggie was in the horse chestnut tree above the park watching the whole incident unfold. Working with Zeke's friend George Hardy, a civil rights lawyer, Maggie agrees to testify in court to help the cause of desegregation.

Just Like Martin

Desegregation was, of course, the primary aim of the Reverend Dr. Martin Luther King, Jr.'s mission during the Civil Rights Movement. The title of Ossie Davis's book refers to the 14-year-old protagonist, Isaac Stone, who desires to be *Just Like Martin*. But as much as Isaac Stone desires to embrace King's nonviolent activism, his father, Ike Stone, a bitter Korean War veteran, does not believe in the nonviolent approach, considering it to be "the same as cowardice." Isaac's father forbids him to attend the March on Washington (April 28, 1963) with fellow members of the Holy Oak Baptist Church. From his home, Isaac watches the D.C. Freedom March on television and listens intently to King's "I Have a Dream" speech. The speech resonates deeply in Isaac, who takes a personal vow of nonviolence and works with Reverend Cable to plan a series of workshops on the subject. After the first workshop, Isaac gets into a fight with his friend Pee Wee, thus breaking his own vow of nonviolence. When Isaac is in Reverend Cable's office being reprimanded, a bomb goes off in the Young People's Sunday School class; two of Isaac's friends die and another is seriously wounded. While this tragedy has Isaac's father thinking of moving to California, Isaac and Reverend Cable begin planning a Children's March. Isaac's father allows him to participate in the Children's March and plans to accompany him. The night before the march, Isaac has a dream in which his dead mother tells him to take the pistol out of his father's truck; he does this. Isaac's father gets in a fight and is badly beaten at the rally. He is imprisoned, but Reverend Cable gets him out of jail and takes him to the church where Doc Wheeler cares for his injuries. Again, Isaac's father has the opportunity to hear Martin Luther King speak, and this time he tells Isaac he liked listening to Dr. King. In his reconsideration of violence, Ike

Stone drops his gun into the lake, decides to support his son's vision of nonviolence, and help to rebuild the church.

Whether students read one or a combination of these novels, they will have the opportunity to investigate the human tragedies that were part of the Civil Rights Movement, how they affected young people, and ways that young adults became advocates of social change, working for equality and justice. While all of the active learning strategies presented in this chapter are applicable to any of the three novels—and certainly adaptable to other literature as well—one novel will be the focus for each of the major strategies presented here. Supported by student examples, the active learning projects portion of this chapter will focus on *The Watsons Go to Birmingham—1963*; the creative writing portion will focus on *Spite Fences*, and the Futuristic Script simulation/role play will focus on *Just Like Martin*.

ACTIVE LEARNING PROJECTS

The active learning projects in this chapter are designed to engage students in personal and critical reflection about young adult novels set in the Civil Rights era. As indicated by their names, these projects focus on textual elements such as character and plot development, setting, symbolism, and theme. The projects are: Showing the Setting 3-D Style, Singing with Symbolism, Layering the Life of a Character, and Scrapbooking the Story.

Showing the Setting and Plot 3-D Style

To assist students with their exploration of setting and plot development, this project option asks them to think of a way to establish setting and convey major plot points in a three-dimensional (3-D) format. Some students may opt to create a mobile or string together connecting events depicted with pictures, quotes, and captions; others may design a fancy timeline—the kind that departs from a simple, linear listing and instead integrates three-dimensional artifacts and revolves around an important symbol from the text, such as the road, a record, or the church. If the timeline were to be designed around a record, the events could be arranged as concentric circles; if the timeline was designed around the church, the events could begin at the cornerstone and build upward toward the steeple. Being creative and "thinking outside the box" are crucial to making this active learning strategy a success. Students should begin by simply listing events they believe are pivotal in the text, then brainstorm ways to represent these in a three-dimensional form.

Two of my students in a Young Adult Literature class, Courtney Baxter and Sara Roberts, made the "Brown Bomber" (see Figure 7.2) as a creative way to show aspects of setting and plot in *The Watsons Go to Birmingham—1963*. The "Brown Bomber" is the name of the car in which the Watson family traveled from Flint, Michigan, to Birmingham, Alabama; it is therefore an apt emblem to represent the story as a whole. In their essay accompanying this project, Courtney and Sara used quotes

Figure 7.2. Example of Showing the Setting 3-D Style. Student project by Courtney Baxter and Sara Roberts.

This student project by Courtney Baxter and Sara Roberts shows the "Brown Bomber," the family car in *The Watsons Go to Birmingham—1963*. In the car are elements to depict the story such as Wilona Watson's journal and Daniel Watson's Ultra-Glide and "Yakety Yak" record. The project also demonstrates setting, as the "Brown Bomber" is positioned on Interstate 75 alongside the states the family traveled through en route from Flint, Michigan, to Birmingham, Alabama, to visit Grandma Sands. The students used white and green felt to depict the change in climate from the snows of Flint to the warmth of Birmingham.

from the text to show the family's journey "into foreign territory" (Curtis, 1995, p. 146). They also stated that this 3-D project emphasized the way the "Brown Bomber" served as a catalyst for change in Curtis's story and was therefore a fitting centerpiece in representing setting and plot. The car "safely carried [the Watsons] to their destination where they experienced life-changing and character-building events. It kept the family together through their toughest times and then returned them safely back to Flint."

Singing with Symbolism

This project option asks students to consider what symbols are used in the literature and/or how they can use symbols to represent elements of the story. Because specific songs are mentioned in both *The Watsons Go to Birmingham—1963* and *Just Like Martin*, teachers can encourage students to search for songs from the era that relate to each of the main characters. If finding songs from the era is a problem, an alternative is to have students link the characters or events with contemporary songs. Students could even create a sound track to go along with the book; however, it is advisable to have students limit any one song segment to 15 seconds so that they can really zone in on the essential/relevant lyrics. This time limitation also makes it possible to share the sound tracks in class (specifying that lyrics are appropriate, not profane) or for the teacher to listen to them without consuming more time than is needed to establish the literary link.

In an exemplary project, one of my Young Adult Literature students, Jim Schurrer, used an old record player as the medium to represent the importance of the TT AB-700 Ultra Glider purchased by Daniel Watson (the father in Curtis's book) for the family's road trip. On the inside of the record player, Jim included a road map from Flint to Birmingham and other symbols and pictures important in the story, including a book of matches, the "Wool Pooh," and a photo of the actual church that was bombed. In keeping with the "musical theme" of his project, Jim used 45-rpm records decorated with symbols for important characters and events from Curtis's novel on the front side and a song to describe each on the back side. Figure 7.3 shows a visual of this project, along with an excerpt from the essay that accompanied it.

Layering the Life of a Character

This project option requires students to think of events that change or influence a character's thinking, actions, sensitivity, or state of mind, and

Figure 7.3. Example of Singing with Symbolism. Student project by Jim Schurrer. Jim made a record for each major character from *The Watsons Go To Birmingham — 1963*. Byron and Joetta (mentioned in Jim's essay below) are two of the Watson children in the story. Jim added a record for Dr. Martin Luther King, Jr., since he was such an integral leader in the Civil Rights Movement.

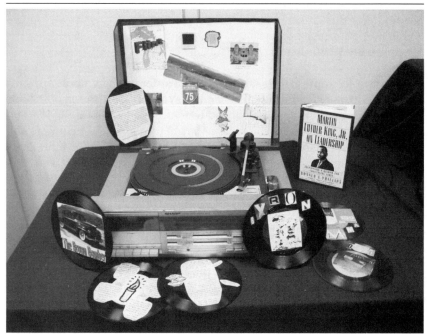

On Byron's record, on the front I put a picture of a bully in action to represent how he was a troublemaker at home and at school. On the back, I put the lyrics to the spiritual "We Shall Overcome." I picked this song for two reasons. First, I chose this because this song was an extremely important song during the Civil Rights Movement, and second because I think that Byron personifies this song because he overcame his immaturity and developed into a good, experienced child.

Joetta's record has pictures of black shoes on the front because that was the image Kenny focused on during the bombing. On the back, I used the lyrics from "This Little Light of Mine," the classic Sunday school song. I chose this song because when I think of Joetta, I think of a young innocent girl in a Sunday school dress.

Also, on one record, I put a picture of Dr. King on the front because he was a very important figure in this time period. On the back, I put part of his eulogy from the funerals of the four girls who died in the bombing.

then to represent these in a layered fashion, as if dressing the character. To begin, students should list the pivotal relationships and situations that influenced a character of their choosing. Next, students should create a cutout of the character. This becomes the first layer, the place where students use quotes from the text, pictures, and their own prose to reveal various traits of the character. When approaching the second layer, students should consider where they can apply symbolism. For instance, for a character with a burned hand (like Billie Jo from *Out of the Dust*; see Chapter 2), the second layer could be a bandage. Or for a character who joined the army (as Richie did in *Fallen Angels*; see Chapter 8), the second layer could be a boot or piece of camouflage clothing. The main point is that as students add layers to their cutout, they are to reveal how the characters change as a result of the people and situations they encounter. Each piece added should be labeled with a quote and/or picture and a brief explanation of the change. One of my students in a Young Adult Literature class, Joe Perkins, used this layering strategy to explore the character of Kenny Watson in *The Watsons Go to Birmingham—1963*. Joe named his project "Bundled up" to parallel the cold winters of Flint, Michigan, from which the Watson family disembarked for their journey. A picture of the student's project plus an excerpt from the accompanying essay appear in Figure 7.4.

Scrapbooking the Story

As a way to show character development, illuminate some of the influential events of the text, and expose the effects of racial violence, students can create a scrapbook of the story. The scrapbook should be designed to feature the characters and events by combining pictures, words, and symbols. The scrapbook should be accompanied by either a lengthy diary entry in which the student assumes the role of a character (the imagined creator of the scrapbook) or a letter that presents the scrapbook as a gift from one character to another in the story. The diary entry or letter should provide information about what each page recalls or perceives about the text; it should convey a sense of deep understanding or empathy for the tragedy that occurred. Figure 7.5 shows three pages from a scrapbook and excerpts from the corresponding letter that were compiled by two of my Young Adult Literature students, Erin Mesek and Anastasia Parc. These two students imagined themselves as the Watson children, Byron, Kenny, and Joetta, from *The Watsons Go to Birmingham—1963*, making a scrapbook to send to Grandma Sands after their visit in Alabama, where they witnessed the bombing of the Sixteenth Avenue

Figure 7.4. Example of Layering the Life of a Character. Student project by Joe Perkins, with excerpts from his essay.

This project is a composite of the main character Kenny all bundled up in his winter clothes, ready to face the cold winters in Flint, Michigan. Though Kenny hates wearing all of those layers, momma makes sure he has enough clothing on to protect him from the nasty weather. Kenny meets or introduces many characters to the reader throughout the novel. Some are protectors, others are aggressors, in Kenny's eyes. It is the combination of these characters though, both good and bad, that shapes Kenny's thoughts and ideas. Without all of the situations and characters Kenny encountered, he would not be the complete bundle the reader leaves him as at the end of the novel.

Each piece of clothing was specifically chosen for the character or event. For instance, Kenny's younger sister Joey is present on the boots because Kenny used to struggle to pull her boots off at school in the morning. Kenny is left clean to represent a blank slate to learn on. He is an open book, and it is these people and events, plus many, many more, that will slowly mold Kenny throughout his life.

My hopes in this project are to fully convey the atmosphere that Kenny lived in, from his family, to his imagination, to tragic events. I also hope to capture the simple innocence of Kenny through the clothing pieces and colors.

Baptist Church on September 15, 1963, which resulted in the deaths of four young teenage girls. While much of the letter reflects the fun-loving family depicted in Curtis's novel, the paragraph about Kenny Watson reveals the character's need to cope privately after the tragedy, and the closing paragraph shows the students' empathy for those who died as well as a renewed appreciation for family.

Figure 7.5. Sample Scrapbook and Letter. Student-created scrapbook pages and letter by Erin Mesek and Anastasia Parc.

Dear Grandma Sands,

We had such a memorable time while visiting you in Birmingham. When we came back to Flint, Momma had the idea that we should send you a little something to remind you of all of us, so we decided to put together a scrapbook full of poetry, photographs, and mementos of our family.

The first page shows a map of our state and yours to symbolize our journey to the South. We also included a lovely photograph of you. And on the second page, you will find a picture of the five of us so you will remember our faces, although I doubt you could forget us!

Dad is on the next page.

On Momma's page, we included the notebook she kept during our road trip, and the shopping list she gave Kenny and Byron when they suspected we were on a welfare list. And since Momma's specialty is her "throat-choking" peanut butter sandwiches, we added a label from one of the peanut butter jars.

The next page is all about By and his "Latest Fantastic Adventures," as Momma and Dad call them. We nicknamed him the "Lipless Wonder" after he got his lips frozen to the car door mirror. Also included is a bag of Swedish Crème cookies and a picture of the poor bird he killed... .

Kenny's page... [shows how]... he thought he could make things better by sitting behind the couch in the World-Famous Watson's Pet Hospital.

Joey is next, ...

Last but not least are pictures of the four little girls that were killed at the church where Joey was at Sunday school. We wanted to remember them and their families because we know how important family is and we don't know what we would have done if we had lost Joey on that tragic day. The whole experience has made us even more grateful that we have such a loving family. By sending you this scrapbook we are hoping to keep in better touch with you, because we want you to know that we love you and are thankful for you, too.

We miss you and we hope to come back to Alabama next summer.

Love,
Byron, Kenny, and Joetta

CREATIVE WRITING

Speech Writing to Reveal Multiple Perspectives

In addition to the creative writing that flowed from the project options already described in this chapter, this active learning strategy requires students to write scripts from different characters' perspectives as a way to examine an issue or scene in a novel from multiple points of view. Where authors have used dialect to anchor distinct character voices, students should aim to recreate the dialect in their own script(s). After writing the scripts, students may elect to tape record the speeches to dramatize the content and delivery. Alternatively, students may recruit other class members to dress up as the various characters and read the speeches in front of the class, or create a visual depiction of each character to serve as a backdrop to the speeches. With or without the tape recording, costuming, or visual representation, the thoughtful analysis students must apply to write the speeches representing multiple perspectives on a single issue or scene, is demanding and engaging. This active learning strategy is one of the best in terms of helping students "become" the characters, identify and distinguish differing points of view, and feel empathy or other types of emotion. In addition to the actual speeches, students should write an essay in which they reflect on the cognitive processes that went into their decision making, such as how they envisioned each character and what they wanted to emphasize about each.

An outstanding example of Speech Writing to Reveal Multiple Perspectives was created by one of my students, Kirsten Lutz. Kirsten wrote three speeches that depict the struggle for racial equality in Trudy Krisher's *Spite Fences*. Each of Kirsten's speeches carries a distinct dialect consistent with Krisher's portrayal of the individual characters: Virgil, Maggie, and Zeke. Making her project truly exceptional, Kirsten accompanied each of her speeches with a 3-D head, showing how she envisioned the characters to look. Excerpts from Kirsten's speeches and the three character heads appear in Figure 7.6.

While the speeches written by Kirsten convey her deep understanding of three distinct characters (Virgil, Maggie, and Zeke) from *Spite Fences*, her accompanying essay (excerpts follow) reveals her evaluation of the characters. The reflective essay is, therefore, a vital component that ensures students take time to distinguish right from wrong, or at least identify bigotry—as applies to the character Virgil Boggs, for instance—when they see it. Kirsten wrote the following to reveal her evaluation of characters from *Spite Fences*:

This is a story of civil rights for Zeke and all Black people, but it is also the story of Maggie's coming-of-age journey. . . . Maggie's journey of discovery leads both to personal freedom from her mother's simmering, explosive rage and to a spiritual freedom as she encounters—and finally embraces—the humanity of all men, regardless of color or faith. . . .

Clearly representing the skewed views of white supremacists, Virgil becomes the symbol of all prejudiced people. His attitude toward Black people resounded with the rhetoric of the Ku Klux Klan. . . . In the monologue I created for him, I presented his cocksure nature as well as his miniature mind at work.

Zeke is a quiet man of immense dignity and courage. He could not physically rise up against his tormentors, but they could not defeat his spirit. He could have chosen to slink away as Virgil's monologue states, but Zeke's soul only grew stronger. . . . His faith in himself, his people, and their cause threw off the White men's blows and scorn. Zeke rose like a phoenix and his inner power shone like the sun.

Grammatical Music: Using Rhythm and Repetition

In addition to dialect, as just seen in the speeches of Virgil, Maggie, and Zeke, good literature often is embedded with repetition and lyrical qualities that emphasize a point or simply make the writing more engaging. For this writing strategy, students begin by examining *Spite Fences* for passages that demonstrate repetition. For example:

Do you call it "independence" when there's a law that says a black man can't even sit down and play *checkers* with a white man? . . . Do you call it "independence" when a black man buys a bus ticket same as a white man and isn't allowed to take any seat that he wants? . . . Do you call it "independence" when you have to take the balcony seats at the movie theatre, face an all-white jury, and answer stupid questions like "How many bubbles in a bar of soap?" when you line up to register to vote? . . . Do you call it "independence" when a black man can't sit down at a lunch counter in the middle of Kinship when he pays his bill same as white? . . . And do you call it "independence" when they did what they did to Zeke Freeman, our brother here, arresting him, jailing him, beating him to a pulp. . . . We don't call that "independence," . . . [pp. 181–182] we call that *injustice*. We know words like *shame, ignorance, injustice*. . . . But we're not going to study those words anymore, are we? We're going to study words that are fit to read. Words like *equality, mercy, justice*. (Krisher, 1994, pp. 181–182, p. 188)

Figure 7.6. Character Heads and Speeches. Student-created character heads and speeches by Kirsten Lutz.

Maggie's Speech

Mama says we're not white trash like that Virgil Boggs and his kind. She's right. We don't go 'round beatin' up coloreds, terrorizing little girls, or trying to rape someone like me. Yet, my friend Zeke says blacks and whites sweat alike under one sun so why do we drink from separate water fountains, not eat at the same table—why? We even have separate bathrooms!

Trouble sure rained down on Zeke beginning that day at Byer's Drugs. . . . I'd been up in the big tree restin' and thinkin'. When the truck pulled up and spewed forth Virgil and his boys, I sat quiet. When they beat on Zeke until he seemed nigh upon dead, I sat frozen to my bones. Then they peed and did something else all over Zeke. . . .

Zeke quit coming uptown much after that night, so I just set myself to finding him. I'd seen news stories about bus station sit-ins and church kneel-ins and even on a black man who KO'd a white man in boxing. I wanted to see how Zeke was and to ask him why coloreds seemed to be so fired up to pushing whites. I kept hearing Zeke's words that night under the Ghost Tree. He held his head proud-like and said, "Just wantin' my rights, is all. My rights and my people's."

What is civil rights, anyway?

Virgil's Speech

Whoo-ee! What a night! Me and the boys have set that old nigger, Zeke, straight! He'll be tuckin' tail and runnin' scared from now on. Guess he and that fancy lawyer thought a change was a-comin'. Gawd!

Our venerable KKK Grand Wizard says coloreds are the mongrels of the world. . . . We don't let no canine dogs eat at our tables and drink from our glasses, so why would we let nigger-dogs do it? Why, those colored folk should be glad we whites let them have their own public bathrooms, and we cleared out the back of the buses for them so they can get somewhere. Where in 'tarnation do they think they're going anyways? They're not fit for any work but what we give them.

Well, one thangs for sure, Zeke got our message tonight. He ain't gonna see, hear, or speak no evil against whites no more. That's one terrified nigger. He'll keep . . . out of whites' bathrooms and he'll sure 'nuf keep his gorilla trap shut. Yes, boys, we have struck a blow for our cause tonight.

Figure 7.6. (cont'd)

Student Kirsten Lutz with character heads she made from Styrofoam face mannequins. Kirsten arranged the character heads on a lazy susan and turned each toward the class while playing a tape recording of the corresponding character speech.

Zeke's Speech

"Never be afraid of the truth," that's what I said to young Maggie that day she wanted to buy her daddy a birthday present with two nickels that weren't hers. Now, I'm fighting for my own brand of truth. It seems, most ways, I've been fighting for truth all my life. Sure, I'm afraid. Equal rights for my people is gonna be a hard road to travel. There will be worse things than beatings between now and the victory-time. It's wrong to treat any man different 'cause his skin is not the same color as another man's.

That Virgil Boggs and his white supremacy buddies believe they have silenced me. Their taunts and name-callings are kindling and their pummeling fists, stomp-kicking feet, and acrid urine all provide fuel to keep the desire for freedom burning within my soul. They have made this desire even stronger. No, Sirree! It's Virgil and his kind who are wrong, and I am more determined than ever to follow Dr. King's vision. Yes, we shall be free.

After examining some examples of repetition from professional writers, students are to apply this technique by assuming the role of a character from the text and writing an interior monologue reflecting that character's perspective. Examples from *Spite Fences* include Maggie asking her mother to stop her abuse, Zeke explaining why he wants to sit and eat, George asking the jury to convict Virgil of his crime(s), and so forth. In their writing, students should capture and convey the emotion of the character and use repetition to add emphasis and build intensity.

One of my students, Shannon Wensyel, assumed the character role of Magnolia from *Spite Fences* and used repetition to develop a scene entitled "Mama, Please" (see Figure 7.7).

Acrostic Poetry

A relatively simple creative writing assignment (in contrast to those already presented in this chapter), the Acrostic Poem can serve as a vehicle for students to define a term (or theme) related to the literature of the Civil Rights Movement. For this writing strategy, the teacher can provide

Figure 7.7. Example of Grammatical Music. Student-written example by Shannon Wensyel. Shannon assumed the role of character, Magnolia, from *Spite Fences* when composing this extended scene using rhythm and repetition.

Mama, Please

Mama, I see the way you look at me, and I know it's not the way a mother should look at her daughter. I know it's not the way other mothers do, and I know that if I ever have a daughter, I won't look at her this way. I see how angry you get when I let you down, when I make you ashamed, or when I am just in the way. But I don't understand, Mama. I don't understand why you get so angry. I don't understand why you act as if you hate me, as if I'm the worst of the worst.

I am tired of trying to understand you. That's why I am leaving—because I'm just plain tired. I don't want to have to be afraid to come home anymore. I don't want to have to lie about my marks and welts and bruises. I don't want to have to flinch when you raise your hand. I'm tired of being afraid of my own mama.

Mama, please—just love me. It makes me sick that I have to ask you—that I have to ask my own mama to care about me and not do me wrong. Doesn't it make *you* sick, too? Doesn't it make you sick that your daughter fears you, that your own daughter can't bear to be in the same house as you anymore? Well it makes *me* mighty sick, Mama.

I can't really believe I've stayed *this* long. Despite your beatings and abuse, despite the fact that my hard work went without notice or thanks, despite the pain of always being the "other" child—the lesser child—and even despite the fact that I was blamed for bringing shame to this family when the most shameful thing of all is your anger and ugliness, I stayed. Maybe I was waiting for things to change—for *you* to change. But it's all gotten to be too much, Mama; and if you can't love me, if you can't promise me here and now that you'll never say another word to hurt me or lay another hand on me, I am leaving. I will leave, and I will not look back. Mama? Mama, please.

---

a list of terms from which students choose, or the teacher can assign all students the same term, thus revealing how many different ways a term can be interpreted. Possible terms that reflect major themes in the novels featured in this chapter include *desegregation, discrimination, justice, nonviolent protest, prejudice,* and *racism.* If students write their Acrostic Poems before reading the literature of the Civil Right Movement featured in this chapter, they may revisit the poems after reading to evaluate the definitions and build on the knowledge acquired while reading the novels. Following is a poem written by one of my students, Tiffany Thomas. Tiffany used the Acrostic Poem to define racism.

> **R** Red streams of blood flowing from the battered heads of peaceful demonstrators.
>
> **A** Achieving ideas of separate but equal, something that in no way is right.

C Creating a scary place to live in, unsure if someone will hurt you because of the color of your skin.

I Increasing feelings of hatred in those who think they are better than others.

S Separation of the same places, using different bathrooms and fountains.

M Murder, violence, and fear, what a world this is.

FUTURISTIC SCRIPT SIMULATION/ROLE PLAY

Along with *The Watsons Go to Birmingham—1963* and *Spite Fences*, *Just Like Martin* immerses readers into the Civil Rights Movement. This novel, in particular, emphasizes the influential role that children and young adults played in the movement, embracing nonviolence, education, and an unyielding faith in God as tools for change. The Futuristic Script strategy requires students to use their understanding of the characters as well as their own imaginations to project into the future (beyond the book) and envision a dialogue between characters. This prediction strategy is applicable to any novel where characters seem to be growing/changing in their attitudes toward a particular issue. Students will determine what a character's attitude is toward a particular issue in the novel, take inventory of what has influenced that attitude, and then imagine how time and/or circumstances may change the attitude. At a minimum, students will enact the script as a talk-show style interview; more "action-oriented" approaches will involve memorizing lines, dressing up as the characters, and dramatizing the performance.

In response to *Just Like Martin*, two of my students in a Young Adult Literature class collaborated to write a script "to show how important the idea of nonviolence was in the novel and that it applies to everyday situations, not just . . . the Civil Rights Movement" (excerpted from student-written essay by Leah Alexander and Wendy Frantz). For their script, students Leah and Wendy imagined that the protagonist of *Just Like Martin*, Isaac Stone, has grown up and now has a son of his own, nicknamed Tre. Even though Isaac has tried to teach Tre about nonviolence, Tre gets into a fight at school with Hookie, Jr., the son of Isaac's childhood tormentor. Isaac's father, Grandpa Ike, joins in to teach Tre that violence is not the answer. Ike brings up the fact that he too originally thought violence was the answer, but learned that nonviolence is a better way to handle disputes. In discussing Grandpa Ike's move toward nonviolence, students will likely consider that if Isaac had not hidden his dad's gun on the day of the Children's March, someone might have been killed when fighting broke out at the rally. In the script shown in Figure 7.8, Tre realizes that

Figure 7.8. Sample Futuristic Script. Student-written script by Leah Alexander and Wendy Frantz.

A Peek into the Future for *Just Like Martin*

CAST:

Isaac "Ike" Stone: Father of Stone and Grandfather of Tre

Isaac "Stone" Stone, Jr.: Son of Ike and father of Tre

Isaac "Tre" Stone, III: Son of Stone and grandson of Ike

Stone and his 8-year-old old son, Tre, enter stage in an argument.

STONE: I had to leave an important meeting at work to come pick you up at school. And for what? Hitting Hookie, Jr.?

TRE: But it ain't-isn't-my fault, he was saying I was a cry baby and I had to prove to him I wasn't.

STONE: I've told you again and again violence isn't the answer!

Ike enters.

IKE: What's all the commotion about? What is going on?

STONE: Tre here got in a fight in school even though he knows better than to use violence to prove a point.

TRE: But I had to stand up for myself.

IKE: Ah, your father and I used to get in the same argument when he was a boy, but he taught me better and I'll teach you. Sit down and let me tell you a story. Back when your father was a boy he participated in one of the most important eras of history- the Civil Rights Movement.

TRE: Aww Grandpa, I've heard this story before.

IKE: Well I'm sure you've heard that your father headed the Children's March and was a friend of Martin Luther King, Jr.'s. But, you haven't heard how he convinced me to participate in the nonviolence movement, because I certainly didn't want to.

STONE: Oh Dad, you don't have to go into this.

IKE: No, it's about time the boy heard the truth about how I was too stubborn and too afraid to believe nonviolence could actually be beneficial to the cause.

TRE: What are you talking about? I thought you were always on Daddy's side.

IKE: Not at first. At first I was too stubborn. After fighting in the Korean War I had seen too many terrible things and I didn't know how it was possible to accomplish anything without using my fists and guns. But your Daddy and some other friends showed me the way and it saved my life. I owned my own pistol and I was more than willing to use it if I needed to. I was willing to use it to protect your Daddy, even if it meant spending time in prison.

STONE: That's right, I remember you kept that pistol locked in the glove compartment of your truck and I had to sneak out and steal it so that you didn't use it.

Figure 7.8. (cont'd)

IKE: That's right, I was so angry at you. Especially after the police beat me and jailed me for being at the Children's March to honor your classmates. I said something to you that day, something I have regretted all my life. *(Looks down and shakes his head)* I told you that you were the worst thing that ever happened to me. The minute it came out of my mouth I knew it was the worst lie I had ever told. You are actually the best thing that ever happened to me, you showed me how to be nonviolent.

TRE: Oh grandpa, if you had had your pistol you could have killed those men that bombed the church, killing those little girls and killed the policemen that beat you up.

IKE: That's exactly what they would have wanted, Tre, but just think if I had done that. I would be in jail and no one would have been there to protect your Daddy or watch him grow up and see him attend Morehouse College. If I had used my pistol I would have been going against the movement itself and going against my people and what they were trying to accomplish. If I had used my pistol what kind of example would that have set for your father? You might not even be here today if I had used that pistol.

STONE: That's right, your Grandpa was so angry he wanted to pack up and head to California after that happened.

TRE: Well, how come you didn't?

IKE: Because I realized something, I realized I wasn't angry at your Dad or nonviolence itself. I was angry at myself because I had let my past and the war eat me up inside. I had let your Grandmother's death affect me so much that I couldn't even see what was in front of my eyes.

TRE: What was right in front of your eyes?

IKE: My son, your Daddy, was there the whole way being patient and trying to teach me about Martin Luther King, Jr., Jesus, and all the good men who fought for what was right without using violence. Every time you use your fists to prove a point that is just a step back from everything we worked for during the Civil Rights Movement.

STONE: Do you understand now, Tre, why it is so important to not use violence? Why you should find alternative ways to deal with your problems? You can always, always turn the other cheek and if that doesn't work you can come to me first and we'll talk about it and figure something out. I will always be here for you. If you find it really hard to resist using your fists, remember the phrase "just like Martin."

TRE: You're right. I'll apologize to Hookie, Jr. tomorrow and we will work something out. Thanks, Grandpa, for showing me the way.

---

violence may not be the way to deal with difficult situations and agrees to explore alternatives to using his fists. Beyond a study of the Civil Rights Movement, this script can be used in conjunction with any novel designed to present alternative ways of dealing with peers at home or at school.

In addition to the numerous elements of plot woven into the script, is an intergenerational message that reiterates the importance of knowing our nation's history, learning from its mistakes, and expanding its wisdom and virtue.

EPILOGUE: THE POWER OF LITERATURE

The books discussed in this chapter have affected the lives of students by offering them a window into the Civil Rights Movement and highlighting universal aspects of life and struggle they find themselves dealing with. The reflections of one of my students in a Young Adult Literature class, Alyssa Manley, exemplify this. She wrote:

> Trying to go to bed after I finished reading *The Watsons Go to Birmingham—1963* was a hopeless cause. . . . The book moved me to thinking about all kinds of different things, [including] the four girls [who died in the fire]. I was especially moved during the time that Kenny thought Joetta was dead and the Wool Pooh was only bringing her around to see her family one last time. . . . After losing my mom 3 years ago, themes like family loss can keep me awake and thinking about all sorts of themes of life and death for hours.

Whether teachers utilize a single book in the chapter or all three, and whether they adapt one active learning strategy from this chapter or use the gamut of strategies in a comprehensive unit, they should remember that literature has the power to educate, touch, and transform. Literature can open doors that help us to explore and understand the past, while simultaneously speaking to our hearts, letting us know we are not alone. What a unique opportunity, indeed what a privilege, teachers have been given to nurture young minds by sharing stories and history, by learning and growing together.

ANNOTATED BIBLIOGRAPHY

Hesse, K. (2003). *Witness*. New York: Scholastic.
    Victimized by the Ku Klux Klan, the families of a 12-year-old African American girl and a 6-year-old Jewish girl living in a small Vermont town are the

focus of this novel told in poetic format. Eleven narrative voices tell of actual events in 1924. Although not about the Civil Rights era per se, this book conveys similar aspects of cruelty and injustice.

Holiday, L. (2000). *Dreaming in color, living in black and white: Our own stories of growing up black in America*. New York: Archway Paperbacks.
Spanning 50 years, the accounts of racism experienced by the writers of this book bear witness to the injustices that propelled the Civil Rights Movement. Entries are accompanied by brief biographies, and an annotated civil rights chronology appears at the end of the book.

Lee, H. (1960). *To kill a mockingbird*. New York: Warner Books.
The classic tale of racial injustice in a small town in Alabama told from the perspective of 8-year-old Scout Finch. Scout's father Atticus defends an African American man wrongly accused of raping a White woman. Although the book takes place in the Depression era, it shares qualities of abuse depicted in books about the Civil Rights Movement.

Levine, E. (1993). *Freedom's children: Young civil rights activists tell their own stories*. New York: Avon Flare.
Desegregation of schools, Freedom Riders, and lunch counter sit-ins are among the historical references that will inform readers about the Civil Rights Movement. Based on true accounts of brave, faith-filled teens who lived during the era.

REFERENCES

Cozzens, L. (1995). *Plessy* v. *Ferguson*. Retrieved October 21, 2005, from http://www.watson.org/~lisa/blackhistory/post-civilwar/plessy.html

Crowe, C. (n.d.). *The lynching of Emmett Till*. Retrieved November 2, 2005, from http://www.jimcrowhistory.org/resources/lessonplans/hs_es_emmett_till.htm

Curtis, C. P. (1995). *The Watsons go to Birmingham—1963*. New York: Bantam Doubleday Dell.

Davis, O. (1992). *Just like Martin*. New York: Puffin.

Davis, R. L. F. (2005a). *Creating Jim Crow: In-depth essay*. Retrieved October 21, 2005, from http://www.slaveryinamerica.org/history/hs_es_overview.htm

Davis, R. L. F. (2005b). *Slavery in America: Historical overview*. Retrieved October 21, 2005, from http://www.jimcrowhistory.org/history/creating2.htm

Haney, E., & Brunner, B. (2000). *Civil rights timeline*. Retrieved November 1, 2005, from http://www.infoplease.com/spot/civilrightstimeline1.html

King, W. (1999). *"Inherently unequal": The access and right to basic education in the United States*. Retrieved October 21, 2005, from http://www.connectforkids.org/node/146/print

Krisher, T. (1994). *Spite fences*. New York: Bantam.

CHAPTER 8

The Plight of the American Soldier and Children Left Behind in Vietnam (1959–1975)

After reading the book, my eyes were definitely opened to the mental and physical damages that war causes. I could not imagine having to watch friends die in front of me. While reading, you could really see the internal suffering that Perry was going through. When you hear stories or see movies regarding those that never could get over the war they served in, you begin to understand why after reading Fallen Angels. *I think it would be impossible to erase the images that Vietnam forever embedded into the heads of the soldiers.*
—Molly Dubinsky, Ohio University student

This chapter features three novels that highlight different aspects of the Vietnam Conflict and its aftermath. *Fallen Angels* (Myers, 1988) and *Dear America: Letters Home from Vietnam* (Edelman, 1985) emphasize the plight of the American soldier through fictional storytelling and actual letters that reveal the hardship and toll of warfare. *Song of the Buffalo Boy* (Garland, 1992) tells the story of children fathered (and abandoned) by American soldiers and born to Vietnamese mothers. These children found themselves unable to fit in, victims of discrimination, and often treated like second-class citizens in their own country.

This unit opens with a small-scale research investigation of Vietnamese words to help students think about and reflect on the similarities of and differences between the cultures of the United States and Vietnam. Then, a variety of simulation, role-play, creative writing, and research strategies follow. These active learning strategies are designed to help students try on different perspectives, including those of the American soldier serving in the jungle and the Amerasian children who remained in Vietnamese villages at the war's end. A summary of the active learning strategies in this chapter appears in Figure 8.1.

Figure 8.1. Active Learning Strategies in Chapter 8.

Featured Young Adult Novels	Thoughtfulness and Reflection	Simulation and Role Play	Active Learning Projects	Creative Writing
Fallen Angels		• Minefield Simulation	• Venn Diagram	• Tracing Character Transformation • Poetic Linking of Personal Experience to the Text
Dear America: Letters Home from Vietnam		• Negotiating Survival	• Thematic Artifact	• Imagined Last Letter
Song of the Buffalo Boy	• Vietnamese Vocabulary		• The Shoes Tell the Story	
General, Applicable to any Novel				• Emotional Word Poem

HISTORICAL CONTEXT

To many students, the Vietnam War seems as far removed as World Wars I and II, yet the impact that the war had on our nation, our military, and our faith in political leaders makes it an important war to understand. During the 2004 presidential elections and throughout the war in Iraq, politicians and the greater citizenry have alluded to America's historical involvement in Vietnam, not wanting to repeat the mistakes of the past. Of course, there are many things that distinguish the Vietnam War from others in which the United States has fought, but two of the most significant are that we withdrew our troops without a clear victory—even the idea of "the enemy" did not always seem clear—and that when our troops did come home, they were not universally treated as heroes. Unlike their fathers and grandfathers who had served in Korea, in the Eastern and European Theaters of World War II, and in the Great War, veterans of Vietnam returned home to a divided nation of hawks and doves. While many citizens supported the war's aim of halting the spread of Communism, others vehemently protested the war. And while a majority of antiwar actions were nonviolent and respectful of soldiers, others left a dark spot on the nation's treatment of military personnel. Some protests erupted into violence and caused deep rifts between soldiers who believed they had served their country honorably and protestors who spit on them and called them murderers and baby killers.

The Human Cost of War

America's involvement in the Vietnam Conflict (the official term since Congress never declared war against Vietnam) lasted from 1959 to 1975. In that time both Vietnam and the United States suffered significant casualties. The number of Vietnamese military and civilian casualties is unclear, partly because the Vietnamese Communists may have falsified casualty figures to keep from demoralizing the population during the war (Smith, 2000). Without clear records to draw from, Vietnamese military casualties have been estimated at as high as 1.1 million and civilian casualties at as high as 4 million (Smith, 2000). Numerical reports of U.S. military casualties are much more concrete. There were 47,378 hostile deaths, 10,824 nonhostile deaths, and 153,329 personnel who incurred injuries requiring hospitalization (Smith, 2000). Agent Orange, the herbicide and defoliant used by the military to clear vast areas of the Vietnamese jungles, further escalated the injury and death toll, as the effects of its toxic dioxin contaminants and carcinogenic properties affected soldiers even years after the conflict officially ended (Weisman, 1986). Agent Orange caused serious health problems and birth defects for both the Vietnamese population and U.S. war veterans.

The American Soldier

According to the Vietnam Veterans of America *Speakers Bureau Handbook*, of the 2,594,000 personnel who served within the borders of South Vietnam between 1965 and 1973, 88.4% were Caucasian, 10.6% were Black, and 1% were of other races. Of those who perished in the war, 86.3% were Caucasian (includes Hispanics), 12.5% were Black, and 1.2% were of other races. One hundred and seventy thousand Hispanics served in Vietnam, and of that total, 3,070 died there (Thomas, 1988).

Vietnam has been called the "young man's war" and the "poor man's war," for whereas the average age of soldiers serving during World War II was 26, the average age of soldiers in Vietnam was 19; and although 79% of draftees during the Vietnam War did have high school or higher educations, 76% of them were from lower-middle- /working-class families (Thomas, 1988). Often, more-affluent potential draftees went to college to avoid going to war. A further statistical comparison of interest reveals that only 25% of the total U.S. forces serving in Vietnam were draftees, as compared with 66% during World War II (Thomas, 1988). Despite harrowing atrocities such as the My Lai Massacre, in which Lieutenant William L. Calley was accused, court-martialed, and convicted of the "premeditated murder of 109 Oriental human beings" (*Pacific*, 1969, n.p.), approximately 97% of Vietnam veterans were honorably discharged, and 87% of the general public now hold Vietnam veterans in high esteem (Thomas, 1988).

A Time of Change

The Vietnam Conflict spanned both Democratic and Republican administrations, including those of Eisenhower, Kennedy, Johnson, and Nixon. The Conflict overlapped with other events in history, including the building of the Berlin Wall, the Cuban Missile Crisis, the assassination of John F. Kennedy, the Women's Liberation Movement, the Civil Rights Act of 1964, the Cultural Revolution in China, the assassination of Martin Luther King, Jr., Neil Armstrong's moon landing, the outbreak of troubles in Northern Ireland, and the Fourth Arab–Israeli War (Crystal, 1993). In the context of 20th-century history, America's involvement in the Vietnam Conflict has turned out to be one of the most perplexing, debated, and regretted actions. For many, the Vietnam Conflict ushered in an era of distrust in government that continues to plague the American psyche. Naturally, we should be diligent to obtain information, ask vital questions, and analyze complex situations so as to make sound, critical decisions about our present and future, rather than act on emotion or uninformed assumptions that we treat as fact. For this reason and for the sake of deepening students' sociohistorical understanding and human compassion, there is value in studying the Vietnam Conflict and its aftermath. By combining the young adult novels featured in this chapter and research about the era, we can help students to identify with those who have been hurt and to distinguish the Vietnam Conflict from other conflicts so that they do not become jaded and skeptical of America's ability to engage positively in world affairs.

FEATURED YOUNG ADULT NOVELS

Fallen Angels

With this context of history, discerning the uniqueness of the Vietnam Conflict as compared with other wars in which the United States has been involved, this unit unfolds with three novels at its core. *Fallen Angels* (1988) by Walter Dean Myers paints the picture of Richie Perry, a 16-year-old from Harlem who envisions going to war in Vietnam as a good alternative when his dream of attending college disintegrates. The book plunges the reader into several graphic descriptions of warfare and death, while simultaneously conveying heartfelt emotional turmoil in the characters and the need for interdependence, sound leadership, and racial equality.

Dear America: Letters Home from Vietnam

Edited by Bernard Edelman, *Dear America: Letters Home from Vietnam* (1985) is a compilation of letters from more than 100 men and women who were stationed in Vietnam. In his endorsement of Edelman's book, Sydney Schanberg states, "What makes this book special is its honesty. The letters are real; there is no embellishment. You keep turning pages because you're finding out—for the first time—who our Vietnam soldiers were and are." Arranged in chronological order, the letters show a progression of emotion from the patriotic, optimistic arrival "in country" to defeat the Communists, believing the war would soon be over, to layers of combat experiences where friends and fellow soldiers die or are wounded, the war seeming to have no end, causing the soldiers' fears and depression to intensify. Some of the letters are to moms and dads, some to lovers and friends, others to children of the soldiers. Each letter is followed by a brief note about what happened to its writer. Paired with *Fallen Angels*, Edelman's nonfiction expands the study of the warfront from one platoon in depth to a wide variety of perspectives and relationships, including personal poetry, photographs at the beginning of each chapter, and an Epilogue about the Vietnam Veterans Memorial, more commonly called "the Wall."

Song of the Buffalo Boy

The third book explored in this unit looks at the aftermath of war, not as it affects American soldiers, but as it left the *"con lai,"* or *"*half-breed," children fathered (and abandoned) by American soldiers and born to Vietnamese mothers. Sherry Garland's *Song of the Buffalo Boy* (1992) abounds with details of village and city life as well as Vietnamese culture. The book includes a four-page dictionary of Vietnamese words that are used throughout the text in a way that immerses the reader into the life and struggles of protagonist Loi. The Vietnamese community ostracizes Loi for being *con lai,* and her mother and the Vietnamese matchmakers seek to arrange a marriage for her to Officer Hiep, a man whom Loi finds repulsive. Interwoven in Loi's story is her attraction to Khai, a young friend who carves water buffalo for extra money and respects her as no other. Loi's desire to escape the arranged marriage and find the American soldier whom she knows to be her father, after finding a picture of him and discussing the matter with her mother, causes her to leave the village and go to Saigon. Loi's journey includes numerous elements of great danger, including attempted rape. With the help of Raymond Smith, an investigative reporter who is researching stories of American Vietnamese or Amerasian children fathered during the war, Loi has the opportunity to be reunited with her father in the United States. On her journey, Loi meets a Vietnamese orphan who calls himself Joe and longs for nothing more than to go to America. In the book's gripping conclusion, Loi asks Khai to go with her to America because her father is willing to take two children. Khai replies:

> No. I can't, Loi. That's why I had to find you—to tell you that I can't live in America, or in a big city. I've wrestled with this ever since you left. I'll always love you, but my home is here in Vietnam. . . . Stay in Vietnam with me, Loi. Be the wife of a simple farmer and the mother of happy children. (Garland, 1992, pp. 258–259)

Loi accepts Khai's offer and sends Joe to America in her place. Despite this idealized ending, there is no absence of realistic hardship; the characters must be bold and crafty, face prejudices, and overcome significant obstacles to improve their lot in life.

THOUGHTFULNESS AND REFLECTION

Discussing Vietnamese Vocabulary

Vietnamese culture is rich with history and tradition that make it unique. Events such as the Vietnam Conflict and traditions such as the Moon Festival have shaped the culture into what it is today. As a distinct culture, Vietnam also has its own vocabulary—important words that can be used for more than just memorizing definitions. Over 30 Vietnamese words are embedded in Garland's *Song of the Buffalo Boy*. Interspersed with English, the Vietnamese words help to immerse the reader into the culture by revealing connotations and tones that otherwise would not be fully felt or understood. One way to assist students in thinking and reflecting about

how Garland wrote the novel in a way that embeds cultural elements is to
ask them to discuss the following questions:

- What effect did the embedded Vietnamese words have on your reading of *Song of the Buffalo Boy*?
- What words carry different connotations in Vietnamese (as compared with their English counterparts)?
- Are any of the words immediately interchangeable with English
  words? Explain.
- How did the embedded Vietnamese words affect your understanding of the characters or Vietnamese culture?

The Vietnamese words interspersed throughout *Song of the Buffalo Boy* are
defined in a four-page glossary at the end of Garland's novel; however,
the definitions are short and leave room for students' further exploration.
After a class discussion on the way the words affected students' reading
and understanding, students can investigate the Vietnamese words and
traditions in more depth to determine their meanings and significance.

Researching Vietnamese Vocabulary

To engage students with Vietnamese culture on a deeper level, the
teacher should assign each student (or pair of students) a term from the
glossary that accompanies Garland's *Song of the Buffalo Boy*. Students are
to research their term and create a visual representation of it to share with
the class. Students should begin by locating their assigned word in the text.
After writing out the sentence to show the word in context, students should
examine the context clues and propose their own definition of the term.
From here, students move to the library or media center where a more formal research investigation unfolds to reveal a more contextual or "true"
definition of the term. One of my students, Katie Hall, used this strategy
to develop a deeper understanding of the term *Ao Dai*; Katie's research
appears in Figure 8.2.

After students find the word in the text, use context clues to create their
own definition, and go to the library or media center to research and come
to a true understanding of the term, they make a visual aid to represent
the term and write a descriptive paragraph about it. The visual aids and
descriptive paragraphs become the basis of students' teaching the terms
to one another. These can be posted on a bulletin board or compiled in a
class book for reference while reading *Song of the Buffalo Boy*. A sample
visual aid and descriptive paragraph for the term *Ao Dai*, created by Katie
Hall, appears in Figure 8.3.

Figure 8.2. Sample Student Research for *Ao Dai.* Example by student Katie Hall.

Vocabulary Word: Ao Dai

Sentence word appears in and context clues:

Sentence: (page 2) The child's mother crosses the room wearing a blue <u>ao dai</u> with a golden phoenix embroidered on the front panel

Important Context Clues: wearing—it must be an article of clothing "a"—it must be like a dress because "a" means it's all she's wearing

Proposed Definition: A Vietnamese traditional dress

True Definition: Tight-fitting, long tunic that is open on the sides and is worn over billowy pants

Research:

- Seen as a symbol of beauty, very flattering because every *ao dai* is custom made
- Body-hugging top that flows over trousers
- Splits in gown extend well above waist (this adds comfort; can show bear midriff, sexuality)
- Practical uniform for daily wear
- Generally for women, but men wear *ao dai* in special ceremonies such as weddings and funerals
- Color is indicative of girls' age and status (young girls wear pure white which symbolizes purity; as they grow older but are still unmarried, they move to soft pastel shades; married women wear gowns in strong, rich colors)
- The *ao dai* is rapidly becoming the national costume for ladies—yet relatively young in the country's history
- Dates back as early as 1774, but not popularized until the 1950s
- Always been more prevalent in south than north
- Popularity is spreading; variations in colors are no longer so rigid

SIMULATION AND ROLE PLAY

Take Only What You Need: Negotiating Survival Activity

When members of America's armed services are deployed overseas in times of war, they must live without many of the conveniences we consider part of being "home." Soldiers in the jungles of Vietnam were often on patrol for hours and days at a time, away from the base camp, and relegated to survive with the things they could carry. Wearing full military

Figure 8.3. Sample Visual Aid and Descriptive Paragraph for *Ao Dai*.
Student-created visual aid and corresponding paragraph by Katie Hall.

Pure White Ao Dai
Young Girl

DEFINITION

A tight- fitting long tunic open on the sides and worn over billowy pants

Pastel Ao Dai
Unmarried Woman

Rich colored Ao Dai
Married Woman

Descriptive Paragraph: The *ao dai* is a traditional, tight-fitting Vietnamese dress. It is open on the sides with long slits and is worn usually over black flowing pants. The splits in the gown add comfort and can be seen as provocative. The *ao dai* is traditionally worn by women.

The *ao dai* comes in many different colors, all of which indicate the girl's age and status. Younger girls wear pure white *ao dais* which symbolize purity. Older girls, who are still unmarried, wear pastel colored *ao dais*. Lastly, married women wear *ao dais* that have strong, rich colors. Recently, the gown colors have become less strict. Furthermore, because the popularity has grown, a wide array of styles and colors have been produced.

Lastly, the *ao dai* is seen as a sign of beauty because it is very flattering. This is because each gown is custom made for the individual. With beauty, the *ao dai* is also very practical for a daily uniform. It is a versatile symbol of Vietnamese culture that will undoubtedly last the test of time.

uniforms and helmets and carrying heavy backpacks and weapons, American soldiers serving in Vietnam endured the heat and humidity of the jungle while being on the lookout for the "enemy." Adapted from a lesson plan written by one of my students, Tiffany Thomas, this active learning strategy begins as the teacher reads aloud the following paragraph. Students should close their eyes as the teacher reads slowly, giving plenty of time for visualization.

> *Imagine this:* You are trudging through a swamp with water up to your waist, pained by hunger and worried about the enemy's bullets. You have walked miles upon miles in this damp unfamiliar place, and your feet ache. Every step you take brings the threat of a landmine and the potential fatal shot from an enemy unseen. Your only protection, other than the soldier on your left and the soldier on your right, are the items in your backpack. Space is limited, and you have been told by your commanding officer to lighten your pack and take only what you need to survive.

As the "Imagine this" opening indicates, what soldiers would carry with them became of utmost importance; the very decisions they made could make the difference between life and death, comfort or misery. Considering this aspect of the warfront, students, working in groups of 3 to 5, will go through their "backpack" (envelope or baggie with slips of paper identifying the items) and determine which items are most important. Given 17 items (see Figure 8.4), students work in teams to negotiate which eight are the most essential; they must leave the other nine behind.

Having received their "backpacks," each group will appoint a recorder to note the rationale for keeping (and discarding, if desired) each of the items. After all groups have had time to choose what eight items they will keep, class discussion may resume based on the following prompts:

- Are there any items that were more for your emotional survival (such as keepsakes) than physical survival? Explain.
- Were there any items that were particularly hard to choose? Explain.
- Which do you deem more important, emotional or physical survival? Why?

This discussion is designed to engage students on an emotional level and help them consider the plight of American soldiers in Vietnam, having to make hard choices about what to take with them on the warfront and what to leave behind.

Figure 8.4. Items in the Backpack.

1. Rifle with ammo	10. Lucky baseball
2. Socks	11. Cigarettes
3. Canteen	12. Lighter
4. Bible	13. Camera
5. Letter from your mother	14. Extra set of dry clothing
6. Pencil and paper	15. Magazine
7. Photo of your significant other	16. Tin of homemade cookies
8. C-rations	17. Map
9. Grenades	

Note: If students are unfamiliar with any of the items, the teacher can either have reference materials for students to look them up or simply explain them briefly. For example, "C rations" were commercially prepared meals used in the field when hot meals were not available. Students also might imagine the "Lucky baseball" as one they brought from home to bring them good luck.

Student-Created Simulation/Role Play for Aspects of the Vietnam Conflict

Often we teachers think of simulation and role play as something we create for our students to experience or enact; however, to encourage students to think carefully about the text, use their imagination, and personally engage with an aspect of conflict present in literature, we may require students to be the creators. Working in small groups, students are to think of a way to bring the class closer to an aspect of the text by creating a simulation or role play. Some options for this active learning strategy are: creating a guided imagery exercise that requires participants to close their eyes and imagine a scene of the book, writing a script and calling on volunteers to act out the parts, or setting up experiential learning centers that model conflicts. While teachers will want to rely on students' own ideas and hope for creativity to abound, it is wise to have a list of specific ideas for students whose brainstorming may grind quickly to a halt. Teachers also may need to emphasize that students approach the activity with due seriousness and maturity in keeping with the grave nature of the Vietnam Conflict, struggles faced by soldiers, and discrimination endured by Amerasian children like Loi in *Song of the Buffalo Boy*.

Minefield Simulation. A group of students in my Young Adult Literature class created a Minefield Simulation in response to *Fallen Angels*. This simulation would apply equally well to *Dear America: Letters Home from*

Vietnam as a way to help students imagine themselves as soldiers. Lindsey Widener, one of the students in the group that created the Minefield Simulation, wrote an essay about what her group set out to accomplish. Lindsey described the group's simulation as one designed "to create an environment like that of the jungle . . . to have the class experience the heat, the struggle, and the responsibility [soldiers had for one another] . . . comparable to the intensity of the battleground." This group divided the class into four "platoons" and began with "boot camp" in the hallway outside the classroom. Each platoon had to appoint a captain, point person, and rear person and decide in what order the "soldiers" would enter "the minefield" that lay waiting in the classroom. At boot camp, each soldier was issued a heavy backpack that he/she would have to carry throughout the simulation. Each platoon completed marching and crawling drills to prepare them to navigate through the minefield. Lindsey wrote that the boot camp portion of the role play was also to help the class "understand the fear that a soldier faces not knowing what is behind the door, or mission. We attempted to physically and mentally prepare [each platoon] so they would be able to go in, complete the mission, and come out safe in the end."

As each platoon left boot camp, the members entered the minefield of the classroom with the following instructions written by Dave Dakolios, one of the students in the group:

> The 20th Explosives Brigade has been assigned an extremely important, but very dangerous, mission. You will be sent out into the jungle of Binh Hoa near Long Thanh on a reconnaissance mission. This jungle is known to be an intricately lined minefield, as well as a Vietcong stronghold. Your training in finding and disarming these North Vietnamese mines is crucial to the U.S. takeover of this jungle. You will be given 4 days worth of rations, enough for you to complete the mission. In your brigade you will have to select someone to be the captain, point person, and rear person. The captain will give orders; the point person will lead through the minefield; and the rear person will make sure no Vietcong are advancing behind your brigade. If any are wounded or die on your mission, you must take them with you—no one will be left behind in the 20th Explosives Brigade.

With these instructions, the minefield simulation began. Imagine lights off, jungle CD on, space heater on high, narrow pathways of desks blocked by stacks of pillows and covered with blankets to make a tunnel, and one member of the simulation group lying on the ground "dead." Lindsey described the minefield simulation this way:

As the students entered the classroom, they were forced to crawl to make it through the mission. . . . We used water bottles and [wadded up] paper to simulate the mines and grenades that the soldiers were threatened with. As Vietcong soldiers, we stayed on the floor and threw grenades at the [platoon] in order to scare [them,] and at this point we killed one soldier. After this, [a platoon member] was forced to carry the dead [soldier] through the rest of the minefield which created a more intense environment as well as more responsibilities for the rest of the soldiers.

Follow-up Reflections. Following the simulation, the group members who planned it should reflect in class discussion or writing on their individual roles, how the activity affected their thinking and understanding of the Vietnam Conflict, what worked well, and what could be improved. This time for reflection emphasizes the active learning that takes place in simulation/role play and demonstrates how being a planner in creating the simulation/role play can be as valuable as participating in one created by someone else.

ACTIVE LEARNING PROJECTS

Venn Diagrams

Having read one or more of the novels about the Vietnam Conflict and completed a simulation/role play to envision the plight of the American soldier, students are ready to make a Venn Diagram. Venn Diagrams offer a way to visually represent similarities and differences and are therefore an excellent tool for students' analysis of literature. This graphic format can be used to analyze characters, cultures, settings, or purposes of different organizations. In relation to this chapter's focus on the Vietnam War, students will utilize a Venn Diagram, consisting of two overlapping circles, to examine similarities and differences between the American soldiers and the Vietcong. In the area of overlap, students will identify the similarities. In the remaining portion of each circle, students will note what is distinct about the American and Vietnamese soldiers. This type of graphic representation appeals to visual and logical/mathematical learners and helps students to see how, even in the midst of war, opposing groups can share aspects of life and loss. A sample Venn Diagram based on one created by a student of mine, Lindsey Widener, appears in Figure 8.5. Note that "other similarities" are listed in a column beside the actual diagram—this is rec-

Figure 8.5. Sample Venn Diagram. This Venn Diagram was created originally with pen and markers by a student, Lindsey Widener. It has been recreated here for improved legibility.

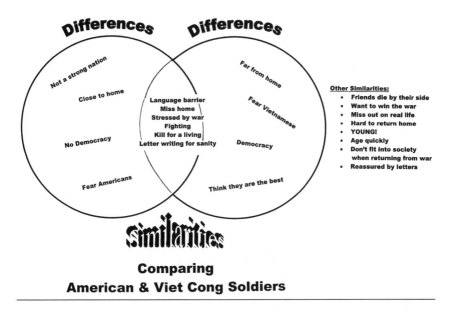

What's the Same?

Differences   **Differences**

Not a strong nation

Close to home

Far from home

Fear Vietnamese

Language barrier
Miss home
Stressed by war
Fighting
Kill for a living
Letter writing for sanity

No Democracy

Democracy

Fear Americans

Think they are the best

Other Similarities:
- Friends die by their side
- Want to win the war
- Miss out on real life
- Hard to return home
- YOUNG!
- Age quickly
- Don't fit into society when returning from war
- Reassured by letters

Similarities

Comparing
American & Viet Cong Soldiers

ommended when so many comparisons emerge that they do not all fit in the small overlapping part of the circles.

Thematic Artifact

For this active learning project, students identify and visually represent a theme in the book(s) they have been reading, and then think of a three-dimensional artifact that represents the theme. Students show how the theme is developed throughout the text by choosing symbols to accompany the artifact. An example of the Thematic Artifact is a helmet created by one of my students, Lindsey, in response to *Dear America: Letters Home from Vietnam*. Lindsey chose a helmet as the central artifact in exploring the theme she identified as "soldiers are more than tanks and guns." To demonstrate this idea, she decorated a helmet (actually a metal bowl with a satin strap) on the outside and the inside. A picture and explanation of this Thematic Artifact appear in Figure 8.6.

The Shoes Tell the Story

This active learning project is similar to the Thematic Artifact, but it focuses on shoes that represent characters from *Song of the Buffalo Boy*. To begin "The Shoes Tell the Story," students participate in a discussion of the following questions:

- Why do we say, "never judge others until you walk in their shoes"?
- Do you agree with the saying? Why or why not?
- What examples can you think of where this idea is important?
- Have you ever been judged unfairly because someone didn't know you or your circumstances?

Figure 8.6. Theme Helmet. Photo and explanation of student project by Lindsey Widener.

Outside of Helmet   Inside of Helmet

Outside of the helmet: Camouflage and small GI men represent the killing side of the soldiers. The American flag is a symbol of what kept the soldiers going through hard times.

Key words and phrases: "M-16," "kill the enemy," and "die for you country" show how aggressive the army expected men to be.

Inside of the helmet: The words are lighter in terms of their color, and there are bandages and cotton balls instead of camouflage and tanks to represent how the soldiers were hurt, afraid, and homesick during the war.

Project Summary: I wanted the helmet to represent the issues that were not discussed directly in the novel, but could be implied if the reader felt emotionally attached to the soldiers... I learned that what is really important to understand is that soldiers have feelings, frustrations, and fears, and that they are not only concerned with killing the enemy.

- How does this adage apply to *Song of the Buffalo Boy* (or any other book you choose to focus on when using this strategy)?

This kind of discussion is particularly useful when studying literature that is from or about another place, time, or culture, such as those in this chapter surrounding the Vietnam Conflict and its aftermath. From this point, students need to bring in a pair of shoes (sandals or boots are fine also) that they believe represent a character in a book they have read. For students who do not have extra shoes, teachers may bring some extras from home or a thrift shop. Another option is simply to make construction paper available so that students can cut out a pair of shoes for the assignment. Next, students need to find symbols from the story that convey the unique journey of the character. Who and what has shaped the character's life? What is important to the character? Where has the character been physically and emotionally? Students can either draw pictures or find them in magazines, on the Internet, through clip art, and so forth. Key words also may be used. In essence, the students create a collage on the shoes, which could be done on a standard, flat sheet of paper, but the idea of actually putting the symbols on the shoes, especially for students who carefully choose the shoes to begin with, helps to emphasize the common theme. The symbols also serve as a review of the plot, setting, conflict, and character relationships, making this a multifaceted project in terms of usefulness in exploring literature. One of my students, Jessica Gresh, chose a pair of sandals, with one sandal representing Loi and the other sandal representing Khai, the main characters in *Song of the Buffalo Boy*. Jessica's project and written explanation appear in Figure 8.7.

CREATIVE WRITING

Tracing Character Transformation Through Poetry

Just as simulations and role plays can actively engage students in exploring conflicts, and visual representations can help them to identify and portray symbols and themes pertinent to literature, creative writing can serve as a doorway to enter characters' thoughts and emotions, particularly as they change throughout the development of a story. As students approach this writing assignment, they need to think of a character who demonstrates significant change during various parts of the novel. The change may be physical, emotional, or spiritual; it may come about as a result of how the character was treated, an incident of success or failure, moving, or even an accident. Whatever the case, students should begin by

Figure 8.7. The Sandals Tell the Story. Photo and explanation of student project by Jessica Gresh.

I chose sandals which offer minimal foot coverage because Loi comes to the city with no shoes on her feet, and because of this she is scrutinized. She also gets a deep cut on her foot from a piece of glass that she stepped on and this wound is persistent throughout the novel. . . .

The items I put on the shoes vary in their significance. First, I put on names of some of the main characters and I also put on words that signify the main themes in this novel.

The photos on the right shoe are a map of Vietnam, a picture of a buffalo (signifying the carving Loi carries around from Khai), a picture of an American with two Vietnamese women (this reminded me of the American in the novel, Raymond Smith), the Vietnamese flag and a photo of a Vietnamese woman harvesting her crops.

The photos on the left shoe are faces of American soldiers who fought in Vietnam, an American flag (signifying Loi and Joe's dream of going to America), Joe Cool (this reminds me of the character Joe), and other pictures of Vietnam.

---

listing noticeable changes in the character's thoughts, emotions, actions, and attitudes. Once students have completed this brainstorming process, which also serves as a review of the story and character development, they are to write a poem in which each stanza shows a distinct part of the character's life. The stanzas should flow naturally, one to the next, to parallel the character's transformation. It may be worth emphasizing to students that "transformation," like real life, comes with ups and downs; therefore, a character does not necessarily begin as a hopeful optimist and gradually decline into a forlorn pessimist—or vice versa. Students should be on the lookout for "growth points"—pivotal events and/or relationships that precipitate change in the character. Such events can seem like a roller-coaster ride, wrought with adventure, a little bit of fear, and the promise of volatility.

One of my students in a Young Adult Literature class, Kimberly Franks, wrote a poem called "Young Harlem Boy" (see Figure 8.8) to show the transformation of Richie Perry, the main character in Walter Dean Myers's novel *Fallen Angels*. The reader first encounters Richie Perry as a bright, capable teenager who considers joining the army because his family does not have the money for him to go to college. As the book progresses, Richie goes to

Figure 8.8. Sample Tracing Character Transformation Poem by Kimberly Franks.

Young Harlem Boy

A young Harlem boy with promising potential
Whose destiny seemed unclear
His mother and brother he left behind
To face a life of unexpected fear.

He is sure he is not going to fight like the rest
Because of his medical report
So he doesn't worry and hopes for the best
For he knows that for him, battle is the last resort.

But the men in the unit don't care about his knee
He is sent out with his men and watches one die
The vision will plague him for eternity
As he struggles to keep the tears from his eyes.

His comrades attempt to keep him strong
He struggles to write to his young brother
He wants to tell him he'll be home before too long
Though he knows that men here are dying one after another.

The more brutality he witnesses in this terrible war
Makes him question its morality
The line between good and bad becomes a blur
As he participates in civilian mortality.

He regrets signing up to be a part of such a mess
But he wanted to leave his hard Harlem life
And come home as a military success
But it seems he'll forever be filled with strife.

Vietnam and is transformed by the horrors of the front line of battle. While Kimberly's poem reveals Richie as a soldier with comrades helping him to focus on his duties, it also reveals his conflicted spirit that questions and struggles to know whether the war is even worth fighting.

Imagined Last Letter from Vietnam

As its name suggests, *Dear America: Letters Home from Vietnam* is a compilation of letters written by soldiers "in country" to friends and family members back home. The letters spotlight the diverse range of emotions experienced on the warfront. At the beginning of the anthology's eighth and final chapter, entitled "Last Letters," students read these words by the book's editor, Bernard Edelman: "The letters which follow are, in many respects, unremarkable—except for the fact that they are the last letters written by GIs who within days would become statistics in the body count." Over 58,000 American soldiers died in Vietnam; letters from 11 of them appear in the final chapter of Edelman's book. As students reflect on what they have read and imagine themselves in the place of the soldiers, they are to write a letter to someone they care about, drawing on the examples in the book. Figure 8.9 provides a sample last letter written by one of my students, Dave Dakolios. Of particular note in Dave's letter is the sense of eagerness to return home; mingled with this are other major themes that emerge in the letters—courage, questions about the war, environmental factors, and attempts to calm the people back home.

Poetic Linking of Personal Experiences to the Text

Building on the events and/or relationships present in any of the three novels discussed in this chapter, students are to write a poem relating some aspect of their own experience to a similar aspect of the text. Students responding to *Song of the Buffalo Boy* might relate a time they were separated from a friend, as Loi was from Khai; or they might relate a time that they were pressured by a parent or authority figure to make different choices, as Loi was by her mother and Officer Hiep. Students responding to *Fallen Angels* might relate a time they had to work as a team in order to accomplish as task, as Richie, Lobel, Johnson, Brunner, and Peewee did. A moving example of this assignment created by one of my students, Stephanie Nally, appears in Figure 8.10. Stephanie's poem, "The Two Best Friends," was written in response to *Dear America: Letters Home from Vietnam* and draws on the student's real-life, tragic loss of her best friend in a car accident. The inspiration for Stephanie's poem came from a line written by Lieutenant Timothy Schlink: "I must go on" (Edelman, 1985, p. 209).

Figure 8.9. Sample Last Letter from Vietnam Written by Dave Dakolios.

Dear Father,

    Only one more month here in this unforgiving jungle. I cannot wait until I make it back home and get to see you, Mother, sis, and Amy as well as the beautiful landscape I have grown so much to love since coming over here and not being able to experience it every day. If I make it out of here alive I will always appreciate beautiful America because of being away from it for so long, and seeing some of the things I have seen here. I have told you about most of the things I have seen, but a few more gruesome events I have left out so as not to worry you all. It will be wonderful to actually eat a home-cooked meal again after living off the rations we have to eat here in the jungle. They're not so bad after you have been eating them for long enough, but once I leave here I know for sure I will never have a longing for one of them ever again. It has been relatively quiet for my battalion as of late. Quiet, that is, compared to the last couple weeks. I didn't have to watch any of my friends be KIA or WIA this week, so that is a bit of a victory for the group's morale. But, the word is that we are going to be sent back out to a pretty hot area in not too long. While we were at base camp I was extremely jealous of the soldiers who got to do their tours there. The chance of them getting injured or killed is a lot less likely than it is for us. I don't see the fairness of us being put in harm's way the entire time, while they remain fairly safe most of the time. It seems like we share the easy and bad details equally. But, what is my complaining going to do—probably nothing. Hopefully this letter gets to you before I do. Pray for me and all of the troops over here. Tell all I miss and love them, and make sure that Mother doesn't worry about me.

Love,
Dave

Emotional Word Poem

This creative writing option requires students to find an outside text resource related to the Vietnam Conflict and turn it into poetry. Students can choose additional novels or picture books with captions; children's books also would work—anything with writing. Once students have selected their outside resource, they need to look for single words that can be woven together in poetic form to convey a story, especially tracing the emotional development of a real or imagined character. One of my students, Caitlin Zimmerman, wrote an Emotional Word Poem (see Figure 8.11) for Carl, the main character in her outside resource, *Carl Melcher Goes to Vietnam* (Clayton, 2002). In her written explanation of what she aimed to accomplish with her poem, Caitlin explains that Clayton's book portrays the life of a young American male (Carl) and his personal transformation from a popular high school senior to a weary Vietnam infantry soldier. It is

Figure 8.10. Poem Linking Personal Experience to *Dear America: Letters Home from Vietnam* by Stephanie Nally.

The Two Best Friends

They fought side by side for six long months, and
We were best friends for five long years,
But we both saw the look of death in their eyes,
Why them and not us.

He lost his friend in a war, to a landmine.
I lost my friend in a car, to a drunk driver.
Very different situations, but the same emotion,
Why them and not us.

He talked and laughed as time went by,
She and I did the same.
None of us thought we'd be the ones to die,
Why them and not us.

His friend left a wife behind to cry,
Mine left a grieving mother alone in life.
They're dead, they're dead,
Why them and not us.

As he says, "We must go on."

---

evident that Caitlin's Emotional Word Poem encapsulated Carl's story. The reader vicariously experiences the transformation of Carl's attitude from optimistic to scared, scarred, and deeply hurting.

Caitlin also reflected on what she gained from this outside resource in terms of deepening her understanding of the Vietnam Conflict. She writes:

> This fiction novel . . . drives home the point that the soldiers fighting the war were kids—kids not unlike ourselves. Because Carl is a positive, likeable character, the novel stimulates the reader to ask, "Did the war ruin the men of that generation? Was it fair that the soldiers were not only asked to surrender their lives, but also (if they survived) their future happiness?" This novel creates a realistic understanding of the soldiers as real people, not just faceless warriors.

Such a response emphasizes the value of sending students on a search for additional texts. Having the class share their poems and resources with one

Figure 8.11. Sample Emotional Word Poem by Caitlin Zimmerman.

Excited!
Optimistic Hot girls
Football Friday nights Prom . . . Homecoming . . . Sadie Hawkins
Fast cars Letterman jackets Graduation Day! Ready for college Oh no . . . my
draft number

Patriotic
Strong Fighting for my nation . . . for my freedoms
Because our flag was still there Sore Lonely Yet ready to protect
"The Home of the Free and the Brave" Big planes, big guns
Goodbye, America Hello Vietnam

Far from home
Hot . . . sweaty Mosquitoes Mosquitoes Mosquitoes
Fire Death Tears Fire Emptiness Hollow Why me? Why him? Fire Pain
Help me I want to go home Good bye, Vietnam

Hello America
Honey, I'm home Baby-killer Nightmares
Still hot Why me? Beer Whisky Beer Sex
Nightmares Divorce Fights Rage I'm sorry

I

Just

Want

My

Life

Back

another is a simple way to expand the curriculum and recommend where interested students might go for further reading.

EPILOGUE: WHAT WE LEARN FROM WAR

The student work showcased in this chapter demonstrates that all three books discussed here have had a significant impact on students' consideration of the Vietnam Conflict and its aftermath. Balancing historical research with fiction and nonfiction that depict grave aspects of war and discrimination toward the *con lai*, this unit is both informative and personally engaging. Stepping into others' shoes in terms of examining the Vietnam War era will help today's students better understand their parents' and grandparents' generations, as well as the reason the emphatic declaration, "We don't want another Vietnam," periodically circulates in the media when we debate and make decisions about why, where, and for how long America will deploy troops to various parts of the world. Predominantly, America is a conscientious nation, a people who want to apply the hard lessons of the past to ensure a better present and future. Above all, the texts featured in this chapter put a human face on the American soldier and the Amerasian child whose stories of sacrifice intermingle defeat and triumph, despair and hope, loss and purpose.

ANNOTATED BIBLIOGRAPHY

Butler, R. O. (1992). *Good scent from a strange mountain*. New York: Henry Holt.
    This work blends Vietnamese folklore and American life to show the transition of Vietnamese expatriates who moved to the United States.

Cao, L. (1997). *Monkey bridge*. New York: Viking.
    Rich with Vietnamese folklore, this story depicts the Vietnamese American immigrant experience of Mai Nguyen, who was airlifted from Saigon in 1975, and explores the family's dark past.

Deneberg, B. (1995). *Voices of Vietnam*. New York: Scholastic.
    Drawn from actual words of people who were involved in various aspects of the Vietnam Conflict, including people like President Johnson, antiwar activist Jane Fonda, and journalist Walter Cronkite, this book has a serious focus on coping strategies used by soldiers who feared death.

Hahn, M. D. (1991). *December stillness*. New York: Clarion.
    Kelly, age 14, befriends a homeless Vietnam War veteran who spends his days outside the library.

O'Brien, T. (1990). *The things they carried*. New York: Houghton Mifflin.
    Through 22 short stories depicting one fictional platoon, readers see the many experiences and emotions of service personnel in the Vietnam Conflict.

Paterson, K. (1988). *Park's quest*. New York: Puffin.
    Because his mother will not answer his questions, Park knows little about his father except that he died in Vietnam. Given the opportunity to visit his father's family in Virginia, Park learns many family secrets, including that he has a Vietnamese half sister.

REFERENCES

Clayton, P. (2002). *Carl Melcher goes to Vietnam*. New York: St. Martin's Press.

Crystal, D. (Ed.). (1993). *The Cambridge factfinder*. New York: Cambridge University Press.

Edelman, B. (Ed.). (1985). *Dear America: Letters home from Vietnam*. New York: Pocket Books.

Garland, S. (1992). *Song of the buffalo boy*. San Diego: Harcourt.

Myers, W. D. (1988). *Fallen angels*. New York: Scholastic.

Pacific stars and stripes. (1969, November 26). Retrieved July 21, 2005, from http://25thaviation.org/id298.htm

Smith, R. (2000). *Casualties–US vs NVA/VC*. Retrieved November 2, 2005, from http://www.rjsmith.com/kia_tbl.html

Thomas G. (1988). *Vietnam war statistics & exclusive photos*. Retrieved February 4, 2006, from http://www.veteranshour.com/vietnam_war_statistics.htm

Weisman, J. M. (1986). *The effects of exposure to agent orange on the intellectual functioning, academic achievement, visual motor skill, and activity level of the offspring of Vietnam veterans*. Unpublished doctoral dissertation, Hofstra University, Hempstead, NY.

Index

SUBJECTS

About the Author

Linda J. Rice, Ph.D., is an Assistant Professor in the Department of English at Ohio University where she teaches Integrated Language Arts methods courses (Teaching Language and Composition and Teaching Literature), Young Adult Literature, and a variety of other courses such as Women and Writing, Writing and Research in English Studies, and Critical Approaches to Fiction. Beyond the classroom, she enjoys working with students as the faculty advisor of OU NCTE, the Ohio University student affiliate of the National Council of Teachers of English. She has worked on special projects with the Ohio Department of Education and regularly presents at state and national conferences. Linda serves on two executive boards, the College English Association of Ohio and the Ohio Council of Teachers of English Language Arts (OCTELA). She also has written chapters for books edited by contributing author Jacqueline N. Glasgow as well as several articles.

Before coming to Ohio University, Linda taught middle and high school English for 10 years in rural and suburban schools in Pennsylvania and Ohio. She is a National Board Certified Teacher and was named Outstanding High School English Language Arts Educator by the OCTELA in 1998. Linda also received the University Professor Award from the Center for Teaching Excellence at Ohio University for 2006–2007.

Beyond young adult literature and teaching methods, Linda's research and professional interests include African literature, literary theory for high school teachers, recruiting and retaining high-quality teachers, and promoting teacher creativity, confidence, and efficacy to combat anxiety related to standards and assessment.

When not teaching and writing, Linda can be found gardening, golfing, antiquing, helping out at her church, horseback riding, fishing, or enjoying time with family and friends.

ABOUT THE CONTRIBUTING AUTHOR

Jacqueline N. Glasgow, Ph.D., taught high school English and French for 18 years, earned her doctorate in Curriculum and Instruction in Literacy, and now is a Professor in the Department of English at Ohio University.

She received the Education Press Association of America's Award for Excellence in Educational Journalism in 1994 and was named Outstanding College English Professor by the Ohio Council of Teachers of English Language Arts (OCTELA) in 1998. She is a former OCTELA president and a frequent presenter at OCTELA and National Council of Teachers of English conferences, as well as at the Summer Institute of Reading Intervention sponsored by the Ohio Department of Education. Jacqueline is the author of numerous articles in state and national journals and the editor of four books.